T0208310

"Dr. Brenda Hunter is a brave woman. She dares to tell a culture intoxicated with self that maybe our children really do need us. She boldly challenges the notion that just about anybody can care for and nurture our children. She winsomely asks us to reexamine our priorities. But most importantly, she gently reminds us that we really do have a choice—a choice to discover the magnificence of motherhood. Be prepared. Reading *Home By Choice* just might change the lives of your children—and you!"

JANET PARSHALL, NATIONALLY SYNDICATED TALK SHOW HOST

"Dr. Brenda Hunter's scholarly yet sensitive work encourages and educates women about the extreme value and impact of a mother's love, influence, and presence in the lives of her children. Dr. Hunter's vulnerability in sharing from her life and her understanding of the causes of youth violence make this book a 'must read.'"

JOANNE KEMP, MOTHER OF FOUR, GRANDMOTHER OF TWELVE, AND WIFE OF
JACK KEMP, FORMER CONGRESSMAN AND PRESIDENTIAL CABINET MEMBER

"I highly recommend this thought-provoking, well-researched book to every couple faced with the difficult choice of 'mother at home or mother at work.'"

SENATOR DAN COATS (RET.), FORMER CHAIRMAN OF THE SENATE
SUBCOMMITTEE ON CHILDREN AND FAMILIES

"Dr. Hunter offers much-needed support for those mothers who have made, or are making, the decision to stay at home to provide their children with the care that only a mother can give. I recommend this book to every young mom to read."

BEVERLY LAHAYE, FOUNDER AND CHAIRMAN,
CONCERNED WOMEN FOR AMERICA

"Congratulations to Dr. Brenda Hunter for expanding and updating this classic book. *Home By Choice* is a book for and about strong mothers who are without apologies or excuses, who are serious about building a home and protecting their children, and who do not intend to be pushed around anymore by those who claim that full-time mothering is a misuse of a woman's time and energy. It's a book for mothers who know—or want to know—what motherhood is and just how much it matters."

DAVID BLANKENHORN, PRESIDENT OF THE INSTITUTE FOR AMERICAN
VALUES AND AUTHOR OF *FATHERLESS AMERICA*

When I read Dr. Hunter's book ten years ago, it changed my life. Her incredible research, carefully intertwined with her own experience, made a great impact. This second edition takes the research a step further, addressing the concerns all families are facing and exploring the basic emotional needs of a child. Motherhood is the most important job in the world, and *Home By Choice* shows us why."

JILL SAVAGE, NATIONAL DIRECTOR, HEARTS AT HOME

"A rare and wonderful combination of practical, scientific, and personal information on the most important decision any parent will ever make. It shows how to create a happy life for—and with—one's children."

KARL ZINSMEISTER, MANAGING EDITOR, *AMERICAN ENTERPRISE* MAGAZINE

"Most women discover that mothering is both the hardest and most worthwhile work of their lives—yet they are rarely told this in a meaningful way. Dr. Hunter's wisdom and warmth come through the pages of *Home By Choice* to mother and mentor us. With updated research information, this classic book is now an even more powerful tool to educate mothers about their role and to teach others the vocation of motherhood."

HEIDI BRENNAN, PUBLIC POLICY DIRECTOR, MOTHERS AT HOME

"If you want to stay at home and need encouragement; if you are alarmed by kids and violence; if you want proof that a mother impacts society, then this book is a **must** read for you."

SUSAN ALEXANDER YATES, AUTHOR OF *HOW TO LIKE THE ONES YOU LOVE: BUILDING FAMILY FRIENDSHIP FOR LIFE*

HOME *by* CHOICE

*Rearing Emotionally Secure Children
in An Insecure World*

Brenda Hunter, Ph.D.

Multnomah®Publishers *Sisters, Oregon*

HOME BY CHOICE
published by Multnomah Publishers, Inc.

© 1991, 2000 by Brenda Hunter, Ph.D
International Standard Book Number: 9781590528105

Cover photo by Ariel Skelly/The Stock Market Photo Agency

Multnomah is a trademark of Multnomah Publishers, Inc.
and is registered in the U.S. Patent and Trademark Office.
The colophon is a trademark of Multnomah Publishers, Inc.

For information:
MULTNOMAH PUBLISHERS, INC.
POST OFFICE BOX 1720
SISTERS, OREGON 97759

00 01 02 03 04 1466510862 11 10 9 8 7 6

*This book is dedicated to mothers everywhere
who have chosen, at no little personal sacrifice,
to be home with their children.*

*I applaud you for your courage
in a culture that is hostile to your choice.
I support you in your willingness to put
your children's well-being ahead of
any career advancement.
And I uphold your conviction that you
are the best person to raise your child.*

You are the unsung heroines of this century.

I have written this book for you.

ACKNOWLEDGMENTS

I am a fortunate woman. Not only do I have a talented, multiskilled family, but my husband and daughters have been my encouragers and my cheerleaders through a long, arduous doctoral program, and, of late, through the writing of this book.

Additionally, Don and Holly edited the manuscript before my editor at Multnomah, Liz Heaney, ever saw it. Don worked with me on ideas and logic; Holly, on word choice and writing style. As the deadline approached, the three of us were up early and late, working as a team.

I also wish to thank Liz Heaney for her substantial contributions to this book. After Liz saw the initial draft, she asked thoughtful, hard questions that sent me back to the library for a deeper, broader look. Because this book makes strong statements, it needed a strong, intelligent editor who captured the author's vision. I found that in Liz, and I am grateful. When this book was revised, Nancy Thompson did a first-rate job helping me update the book and make it culturally relevant. Thanks, Nancy.

I also want to thank the mothers at Mothers at Home, Inc. for their help with some of the book's statistics. Mothers at Home, Inc., in McLean, Virginia, is an organization that every mother at home needs to contact. Their magazine, *Welcome Home,* is written by and for mothers on the home front. The women who run this organization are smart, savvy, and generous with their ideas and time.

Finally, I wish to thank the individuals who have allowed me to share their deeply personal stories. Some appear in the book under their own names; others simply gave me permission to share their pain, but anonymously. It was their hope—and mine—that by honestly sharing their struggles, they could help others find healing.

CONTENTS

FOREWORD

Being a mother to my children is without question the highest honor of my life. It is a role both noble and mundane. As females, our bodies can cooperate with God in the miraculous creation of new life, which culminates in the birth of a new child. But giving birth is only the beginning. Mothering is for life.

When Dr. Hunter's book was first published, I read, underlined, and starred it. And then for years, I quoted from it. The words of her book were a meaningful encouragement to me in times when stay-at-home moms were thought to be wasting their potential supervising on playgrounds and wiping runny noses. Her well-documented research bolstered my confidence that I was doing what was right by investing my life daily in the rearing of our six children.

Even though I chose my role as a full-time mom, I still remember feeling embarrassed at times when asked what career I was pursuing by another obviously career-minded mother at our school's PTA, or by some stranger seated next to me on an airplane. I wanted to be home with my children and had no desire to work outside our home, but the cultural climate was less than friendly to those of us devoted to the cause of mothering our children.

Thankfully, the pressure on women to "do it all" in marriage, career, and family has lessened. However, and I can't say this strongly enough, the deception is still there. It used to be believed that mothers were unnecessary and could be replaced. More independent children would be the result, we were told. Now the deception is that we mothers aren't essential as our children get older. As long as we are around most of the time and give them as many advantages as possible, even if we have to work part time or full time to do it, it is currently believed they will turn out all right. I am convinced that this deception works its way out in parents who attend their child's plays, recitals, ballgames, and performances, but are increasingly disconnected. Dr. Hunter's updated book on the significance of a mother throughout her child's life gives the answer to this modern dilemma.

In the early '90s this book was an important statement on behalf of motherhood. Today it is desperately needed by a generation of mothers who have never seen real mothering modeled. May Dr. Hunter's insights encourage you as they did me.

BARBARA RAINEY

JUNE 2000

It's not often that I read a book that prompts a torrent of emotion. *Home by Choice* made me both weep and want to pound the table.

I first read Dr. Hunter's book on an airplane. As the truth on the pages sank in, I felt conspicuous. I wished I could transform my aisle seat into one next to the window so I could turn away from other passengers. There I was—a grown man reading a book on motherhood—tears streaming down both cheeks.

I was profoundly moved. Page after page I was gripped with the power of a mother.

I was also gripped with grief—sadness at the lack of value our nation places on the office of motherhood. I was grieved for the next generation that is being duped by a culture that tends to value career advancement over a child's nurture. And

I grieved for future generations that will suffer because motherhood is a disappearing art.

On that plane ride I recall thinking, *This book is a book for our times. This ought to be required reading for every woman and man about to become parents.* I still believe that—now more than ever.

Maybe Dr. Hunter's book touched me so deeply because for fifty-two years I have known the love of a devoted mother. Even now that she is eighty-seven, when I visit I never question that she loves me and believes in me. Mom has poured her life into me, and her value to me is unfathomable.

It wasn't until some time after my plane ride that I met Dr. Hunter, and after several hours of interviewing her for *FamilyLife Today* radio broadcast, I was not disappointed. She has become a good friend and a kindred spirit to both Barbara and me. To us she is a heroine, a champion for the worth and dignity of motherhood. She is genuine, tender, and gentle—yet powerful—a person you want to know and be around.

I believe in the message of this book. It is one of those rare, clear statements of truth that people need today in order to find their way or stay on the right path. Every chapter brims with encouragement.

Our sons and daughters need to read this book, not merely for their families, but to appreciate the gift given to them—a mother who nurtured them, invested her life in them, and gave up much so that they might enjoy success in life.

You're going to enjoy reading this book and experiencing Dr. Brenda Hunter's heart. But let me warn you—don't read it sitting in the aisle seat of an airplane.

DENNIS RAINEY

EXECUTIVE DIRECTOR, FAMILYLIFE

JUNE 2000

AUTHOR'S NOTE

AUTHOR'S NOTE

The year was 1991, and I was fulfilling a personal dream, so why did I feel so queasy as I talked to my publicist? As the author of a brand-new book, *Home by Choice*, I was about to embark on a nationwide book tour. Little did I know what lay ahead. Within days of the launch of my tour, I flew to Secaucus, New Jersey, to debate five other women on WWOR TV, including an editor for *Working Mother* magazine. The women were manageable, but I had a sixth sparring partner in the host, who suggested that I was trying to make working mothers feel guilty (not true) and that the infant day care research I quoted was inconclusive (also not true).

Near the end of that show the tide turned. A teacher called in from Brooklyn to say he had worked with the "victims" of parental neglect and absence.

"Then you agree with Dr. Hunter?" asked the interviewer.

"Yes," said the teacher. "These kids have nowhere to go after school. Nobody's home."

Later the show did a call-in poll, asking viewers: "Are young children harmed when mother works full time?" Fifty-nine percent said yes.

During a station break I had a telling conversation with the camerawoman, who appeared to be bored.

"You must have heard this a hundred times," I said to her.

"Yes, too many times," she replied. Reflectively she continued, "I've worked for twenty years, and my only child, a daughter, is nineteen years old. What we've missed is simply having time to relax and enjoy each other."

I left the studio pondering her words. *Time to relax and enjoy a child's company*—that's a lot for any mother (or father) to miss.

After that media experience, I was off and running. Other shows and debates followed. Ah, *controversy*. That was just what my publicist had hoped for. I must admit that sometimes I felt elated, other times just plain scared. But God was with me, and I was aware that He was orchestrating the media blitz.

That was nine years ago. And oh, what a time I had! I appeared on *CBS's This Morning*, along with Pat Ireland, president of the National Organization of Women, and Beverly LaHaye, president of Concerned Women for America. I also addressed the issue of teen violence on CNN's *Crier and Company* and debated a nationally known psychologist on CNN's *Sonya Live*.

When I appeared on CNN's *Larry King Live*, the subject was nanny care. With persistence and compassion, I insisted that mother care was best. At one point, Larry King, clad in his trademark suspenders, leaned forward and asked, "Does it really make a difference which arms hold the baby, Brenda?" This was before his current wife had a baby.

"Yes, Larry, it does. You see, *babies are born programmed to fall in love with their mothers, not nannies or baby-sitters.*"

I believe this more strongly today than when I wrote this book. In the intervening years we have witnessed a new cultural phenomenon as kids have begun to maim and kill their peers, parents, and teachers. From Springfield, Oregon, to Pearl, Mississippi, to Jonesboro, Arkansas, to Littleton, Colorado, young white males, all seventeen years of age and under, have taken this country to a new level of teen violence. Whence this rage and darkness in their minds and hearts? I believe the desire to kill and be killed is rooted in a child's failure to forge the most basic human attachments to his parents. And when a child fails to develop loving parental bonds, he also fails to develop a conscience, as well as any feelings of remorse or empathy. The sad truth is that we are rearing a generation of children in this country who are emotionally deprived and neglected. And some have learned to "cry bullets."

Many parents, in their pursuit of materialism and the good life, have forgotten to meet their young children's most basic emotional needs, with the sad result that hundreds of thousands of children complain of depression and emptiness inside. And while we would, in our guilt, like to blame the media, video games, violent movies, and drugs, the truth is that children have always needed their parents' love, time, and attention to become fully human.

Fortunately, some of us understand that it is mothers who teach their children to be human. Several years ago I came across a letter reprinted in the *Wisconsin State Journal* that expresses how critical a mother's presence is. After fourteen years on the bench, Milwaukee County Circuit Judge Leah Lampone retired in order to stay home full time with her three sons. She eloquently expressed the reasons for her decision in her resignation letter:

> As I write, I gaze upon my newborn son—an answer to our years of prayer, unexpectedly granted late in life. Patrick is napping now, exhausted from his morning's work—viewing the world from his mother's shoulder. He sleeps secure in the knowledge that upon his waking cry he may reclaim his rightful perch. The burden of his weight on my no-longer-youthful back

1 7

is lightened by the knowledge that this tender nurturing will have a lifelong impact on his perception of himself and the world around him.

My decision to leave the bench after fourteen years was not easily made. I have enjoyed the challenge and hope I have served well the trust that the people of Wisconsin have placed in me. Yet the job I leave has changed dramatically from that which I undertook when I first donned a robe.

In each of my judicial assignments over the years, I have seen, heard, and felt the unraveling of society as palpably as a slap in the face. Caught in the trap of lifelong welfare dependence, generations of impoverished and dysfunctional mothers, ignorant of the need for nurturance and incapable of adequate parenting, have produced children bereft of hope and vision and without the capacity for empathy for another human being. (I omit reference to fathers only because in most of the cases we see, they have seemingly become superfluous after conception.)...

As a substitute for the structure, control, and education the family once provided, people now turn to the government. Ancient values of self-reliance and responsibility for, and to, family are seemingly dying....

With these thoughts in mind, questioning how important my work on the bench truly is, a reordering of my priorities is perhaps overdue.

Looking back upon my years as both judge and mother, I have come to realize the greatest impact I have made in any life is that which I've made in the lives of my children.... While I suppose I could continue as both judge and mother, at age 44, after the stress of a hard day, I doubt I could be all the mother that two young boys and an infant deserve....

Patrick calls and hence I must close—both this letter and my career on the judiciary....

I leave with alarm at what I have daily seen. I leave with the warning that we as a culture must end the cycle of procreation without committing to parenting, dysfunctional household units, and abdication to the government of the family's role in teaching moral, spiritual and social values....

Hopefully, by investing more of my time in my own home, I will look up at the end of my life to see three young men, emotionally vibrant and self-reliant, ready to face their life's drama.... With that solid foundation, perhaps they will be better equipped to meet the challenge in their future of putting back together the pieces of society we let crumble in our hands.

Former judge Leah Lampone is a wise woman—she understands that by investing her time and her presence in her children's lives, she will not only be able to rear emotionally healthy sons, but they will be able to help reshape a crumbling society. Any mother is wise who chooses to tend her home fires, love her children well, and put her family's needs ahead of personal achievement.

Life is short. Time is fleeting. Our children will only grow up *once*. Will we be there for them? The choice is ours.

BRENDA HUNTER, PH.D.

ASHEVILLE, NORTH CAROLINA

2000

Introduction

THE INNER HOME

> *"Hello, is mother at home?"*
> *No one is home today.*
> *"But Father—he should be there."*
> *No one—no one is here*
> WILLIAM STAFFORD

> *In the ordinary course of events, a child*
> *takes in love with his mother's milk.*
> ANTHONY STORR

Little Austin, my only grandchild, stood in front of the withered bush collecting berries dried by the winter sun. "Bew-wies!" he exclaimed in that charming way two-year-olds have as they acquire vocabulary. He and I had taken a walk to see "the hosses and the cows" while his parents packed their car after the Christmas holiday. They were heading home, and I had just these few sterling moments left with a child I love dearly. A child born during a time of deep winter in my own life, just three weeks after I was diagnosed with breast cancer. A child who gives me joy and helps anchor me to life.

"Let's go back up the hill and see Mommy and Daddy," I suggested to this boy who finds wonder and beauty every few steps.

"Animal hole," he said as he squatted over a mole hole,

21

examining it intently. "Bew-wies for the rabbits to eat," he muttered as he carefully let each berry fall into the hole. I watched the sunlight dance on his golden hair and sweet face.

Just when I wondered if we would ever make it up the hill, Austin's father appeared and called his son's name. Dropping his remaining berries, little Austin ran up the hill and flew into his daddy's arms.

"We're going home," his father said.

"Yes," said Austin, smiling, "home."

Home. What diverse images and deep longings that simple word conjures up. For Austin and other well-loved children, home is the place they live with parents who love each other, where empathy and affection reign, and where deep-seated emotional needs are met on a daily, even hourly, basis. Home becomes, as these children mature, a place of refuge and repair. Comfort is readily available, and the restoration of the self is possible.

For others, home is an empty shell where no matter how sunny the weather is outside, it is always gray and chilly inside. Said one twelve-year-old boy whose parents, both lawyers, work long hours, "I don't like coming home after school. Nobody greets me when I come through the door. Nobody says, 'How was your day?'"

Loneliness chills the heart and withers the soul. Yet millions of American children spend eleven fewer hours with their parents each week than they did in the 1960s.[2] While loneliness is the name of the game for increasing numbers of American children, others grow up in homes that resemble a war zone, where conflict reigns, and the threat of violence lingers in the air.

Our children internalize the atmosphere of our homes based on the way we treat them and our spouses. Spongelike, they absorb our home's emotional atmosphere, which is conveyed through tone of voice, words of derision or encouragement, and the presence or absence of tangible affection. And when they become adults, they will remember, *just as we do,* what home was like.

Robin recalls that as a teenager she slept with an overcoat thrown over the foot of her bed and her window ajar during the coldest Maine nights, ready to flee if she heard the heavy, rapid footsteps of her father approaching her room. Many nights she went to bed trying to block out the sound of her parents' angry voices in the room beneath her, destroying each other's self-esteem. Too many nights Robin was awakened abruptly by a slap in the face. One of five children, it was she who served as the lightning rod for her father's unreasonable rage. Robin did not realize that her father, also abused as a child, was perpetuating a pattern of violence. All she knew was that as a young adult she dreaded returning home, even at Christmastime, fearful that she would once again become the victim of his violence.

Although the thought of home generates anxiety for those who grew up in homes punctuated by violence, many view their childhood home as the best place to be. Home was a place where good things happened; it was a safe place of love, warmth, action, and laughter. Or as one Vietnam veteran said, "At home I felt a sense of being protected. Nothing could happen to me there—no harm would come to me. Even if I was home alone, I still had that feeling."[2] Fortunate indeed are those who had reasonably "whole" parents. Remembering a happy and secure childhood, they speak of their earliest home with great warmth and affection.

Phyllis, an opera singer with warm, compassionate eyes, grew up on an Iowa farm with her sister, Eleanor, and two parents who loved each other. Her father, a burly, soft-spoken farmer, and her mother, a red-haired librarian, loved and nurtured their daughters. Consequently, Phyllis internalized a rich, deep sense of "home" during her early years. "Even when my mother grew feeble in her eighties, long after my father had died and she had left the farm to move into town, I always felt I could go home if I needed to. I know this sounds crazy—after all, my mother was *old*—but she personified 'home' to me, and the thought that I could go home if life ever became unmanageable has always comforted me."

Having received sufficient love and nurture from both parents during her childhood, Phyllis has been "at home" on this earth throughout her fifty-four years. Moreover, she has been able to create a safe place for herself, her husband Larry, and for their two children. Says Larry, "Phyllis is the most secure person I have ever known."

Those of us, then, who were well loved and nurtured by our parents carry around inside a positive inner home. But what about those of us who were deprived of essential love and care, especially from our mothers, during our earliest months and years? According to British psychoanalyst Anthony Storr, while a loved child incorporates "a lively sense of his own value" that enables him to cope with life with a strong and happy heart, the child who is "unwanted, rejected or disapproved of" has no comparable inner strength. Says Storr, "Although such a child may experience periods of both success and happiness, these will neither convince him that he is lovable nor finally prove to him that he is worthwhile." As someone said, he "may feel a little homeless all his life."

Mary Beth, a forty-seven-year-old graphics designer, knows

she missed something vital during her early years. "All my life, I've felt a deep emptiness inside. I guess when you aren't loved as a child, you grow up feeling that there is something wrong with you." Abandoned by her mother and father when she was a toddler, Mary Beth was raised by relatives. The middle-aged couple had already raised their own two children and was less than eager to begin all over again. "Oh, they fed me and gave me a place to live," says Mary Beth, "but they didn't give me what I so desperately needed—love and acceptance."

Parental rejection may not only generate adult depression, but the rejected child may also grow up feeling alienated and alone. His heart's cry as he wanders from place to place is: "Is there any place on earth for me?"

Edward Lear, nineteenth-century British creator of nonsense verse, was abandoned to the care of his elder sister after the family split up because of the father's indebtedness.[4] Lear's mother never again involved herself in his upbringing even though the family was later reunited. Lear was "bewildered and hurt by her unaccountable rejection of him" and was subject to recurrent bouts of depression, which he called "the Morbids."[5] Having failed to establish intimate ties with his parents, Lear became a lonely adult, always searching for what he felt he had missed. He longed for "someone who would want him as a person in the way his parents had not wanted him as a child."[6]

Throughout his adult life Lear wandered from country to country, living a nomadic existence typical of the maternally deprived. These souls find it "difficult to create a place which they consider 'home.'"[7]

"Children learn early in life," said the late British psychiatrist John Bowlby, addressing the American Psychiatric Association in 1986, "that life is either a gift to be enjoyed or a burden to be borne."

Is the child welcomed in the family by both parents and adequately nurtured? Does his mother sensitively respond to his signals in the early months and years of life, creating a sense of security? Or is the mother harried, preoccupied, or physically absent so that her baby comes to feel he cannot trust anyone to hear his cries or meet his deepest emotional needs?

Our children's sense of emotional security—that's a lot to put at risk for any reason. Yet we are doing just this in America today by creating a cultural climate that wars against mother love.

For more than three decades mothering has been devalued in America. In the nineties it even became a status symbol for many first-time mothers to take as little time as possible away from work for full-time mothering. Some spoke with pride of working up to the day of delivery and indicated they planned to be back in the office posthaste. One woman I met delivered her baby on Tuesday and was back at the office on Friday. So much for taking time to forge a loving bond with her baby! How can a mother create a sense of *home* for her baby in a few short days, weeks, or months?

But there are other mothers—and their number is legion—who are home by choice, providing their children with their continuous presence and love. These mothers are home because they know that they, and not a child-care provider, can best nurture their children and give them a sense of home. They know that children thrive in their mother's presence and suffer greatly if they are too often absent.

Some women elect to stay home because they carry inside a rich, warm sense of home and wish to pass the good parenting on. Said one careerist who came home when her son was born, "I grew up in a large, close-knit family, and I want to give my child what my mother gave me."

Still others are home because they wish to give their children the sense of home they were denied. They grew up in dysfunctional families and refuse to perpetuate the generational cycle of inadequate nurture. Having worked through early neglect or rejection, these mothers strive to give their children a richer sense of home than they themselves experienced.

Writer Joyce Maynard is one of these. Writing in *Elle*, Maynard says that having experienced both an early dysfunctional family life and career success, she sought "a far more elusive and mysterious commodity—success on the home front and the security of home and family."[14]

It is possible to give our children more love and nurture than we received. It is also possible (as millions of families prove) for a mother to stay home either part time or full time to care for her family, even in a situation that is very tight financially.

With a voice that's beginning to be heard, men and women across this land are reaffirming the value of home and of their ultimate human connections. Home, viewed by early radical feminists as a prison, is now being seen as a refuge for family members beleaguered by the world, as well as a necessary school for life. Many women, feeling trapped in the workplace, yearn for more hours with their children. Increasingly, child development experts are saying what many mothers and fathers have known all along—that to be fully human a child needs to be intensely loved and cared for by someone who won't "pack up and leave at five o'clock." *That someone is the child's mother.*

As we move into a new millennium, the ranks of mothers

at home are swelling. Not only are countless women quietly at home nurturing their children, developing their gifts, and forging their intimate connections, but others who have spent years in the workforce are also listening to the logic of the heart. They are quitting their jobs, packing up their briefcases, and coming home.

Brenda Barnes, one of the highest-ranking women in corporate America, is one of these. She quit her job as president and chief executive of Pepsi-Cola North America. Why? She had, in twenty-two years of devoted service, missed out on her three children's lives. She had missed too many birthday parties.[9]

Is mother at home today?

Yes, increasingly she is home.

Because I believe the future of our society depends on a close mother-child bond, I have written this book to take a deeper look at mothering. Part 1 examines the psychological research on attachment, the emotional bond each baby forges with his parents—especially his mother—early in life. Additionally, it looks at recent day care research and the genesis of the present cultural denigration of mothering, as well as the needs of older children for a mother's presence. It also examines the frightening increase of juvenile violence and why kids kill. Part 1 offers ammunition for the troops in the trenches, as well as evidence about the effects of mother's absence.

Part 2 is all about helping the mother at home get the most out of life so that she can meet her children's needs. It addresses some of the problems she faces (isolation, depression, lack of husband's support), yet it also challenges a woman to develop her gifts and understand she is home only for a season. To illustrate that we have "world enough and time" for nurturing children, I've written about women who have made significant contributions to their culture after age forty.

Finally, for consistency of style and ease of reading, the masculine has been used to include the feminine throughout this book.

PART ONE

Chapter One

HOMEWARD BOUND

Children are the anchors that
hold a mother to life.

SOPHOCLES

T alk show host Sally Jessy Raphael was in her glory.
Seated with her in the television studio under the
relentless glare of overhead spotlights, six mothers
were heatedly engaged in debate—any TV host's dream. The
controversial topic of the day? Working versus staying home.
Three of the mothers had given up prestigious careers to come
home, while the other three had elected to combine career
and motherhood. It was the early '90s, and the Mommy Wars
were in their heyday.

As the women clamored for a chance to speak, one in her
midthirties sat quietly. Sally Jessy addressed Helen Jackson
directly: "You were slated to become the first female black
astronaut, yet you gave it up. Why?"

"My oldest son was having trouble in school," said Helen.
"He was severely withdrawn and depressed. He had failed
sixth grade. My son was fast becoming a statistic, another
black male headed for trouble." Helen told the television audience she had *willingly* relinquished her enviable career at
NASA to become a full-time mother.

What made this woman feel that caring for her hurting child was more important than making history as the first black woman in space? Helen, who now has five children and lives with her second husband, John, in Boone Hill, Tennessee, has a compelling story.

Her parents separated when she was young, and her mother was hospitalized for emotional illness when Helen was five. Helen's grandmother, who proved to be the most stable parental figure in her life, came to Alabama to care for Helen and her siblings. Throughout her childhood Helen lived in a variety of homes with different relatives. When she was fifteen, she moved in with her grandmother, a domestic, who left Helen alone while she worked during the week and came home only on weekends. Helen admits that during her adolescence she had to forage for food, sometimes stealing when she was hungry. Yet Helen's grandmother loved her and motivated her to achieve academically.

"My grandmother bought me a set of encyclopedias when I was eight," said Helen, "and she rewarded me with fifty cents for every A I received on my report card. That was a lot of money for her to give."

By the time Helen had graduated from high school, she had won a scholarship to Massachusetts Institute of Technology. Instead of attending MIT, she married her first boyfriend and had three children in rapid succession. After her marriage ended, she enrolled as a full-time student at the University of the District of Columbia, and upon graduation she found a job with NASA. NASA later paid for her to attend Johns Hopkins where she worked toward her graduate degree in electrical engineering.

During her years at NASA, Helen says she was an exhausted, employed mother who ran a disorganized household. Meanwhile, her oldest son, Malik, was floundering. "He was never a behavior problem," says Helen, "but he did sometimes sit in the closet during class. He would go for days without talking. I tried to solve his emotional problems by transferring him from school to school."

Unlike some parents who blame their child or his teacher when the child falters, Helen felt responsible for her son's failure. "After all, I went back to work when Malik was three weeks old. It really tore me up. I tried to find a baby-sitter close to work so that I could breast-feed him at lunch. But Malik had a lot of baby-sitters growing up. As a little boy he was never real bad, just timid and underweight."

Feeling compelled to come home, Helen told her second husband about her growing conviction that her children needed a full-time mother. John, then a graduate student, agreed with her and promptly got a job to support his family.

So Helen came home and began homeschooling her children. After only nine months of homeschooling, all three children had soared by two or more grade levels in all academic areas. Malik, who had previously performed at the fourth grade level, now tested at the ninth grade level. No longer withdrawn and depressed, he began to develop socially and in time became a leader among his friends at church. Having passed his high school equivalency exam at age sixteen, Malik went on to attend the University of Alabama.

Under Helen's tutelage, all three finished high school by age sixteen. Her daughter Baqiyyah, once an aggressive, difficult girl, has been the recipient of numerous honors and awards. Another son, Isa, attended a chemical engineering program in Oak Ridge, Tennessee. Interviewers for this program said he was the best-adjusted student out of the forty-two attendees. Isa then won a scholarship to the University of Tennessee.

During the seven years that she has been at home, Helen has channeled her abundant energy into caring for her family. Not only has she educated her children, but she also has helped her husband and children build their log house in Boone Hill. Moreover, she and her husband have started an engineering firm in their home, and Helen works on this joint venture in the evening.

A candid, open woman, Helen admits that her family is far from perfect. She is grateful that her family, even with its problems, is far healthier than the one she grew up in. Has she any regrets that she traded a place on a space shuttle to come home for her children? "I'm not sorry that I gave up my career. Sure, I was doing my thing, but my kids were suffering. And I could never feel good if my children were unhappy."

The Swing Back Home

Helen is among the myriad women leaving the marketplace for home. The media call this phenomenon "the swing back home." Some, like Helen, come home because a child is floundering; others are tired of being torn by the multiple demands of career and family. Others simply yearn for more time with the kids.

Tanya Coble spent ten years working as a secretary on Capitol Hill. Although she came home during the early months of her firstborn son's life, Tanya gradually returned to full-time employment.

"After we bought our house, I was forced to go back to work full time," says Tanya, who now has two small daughters as well. "I had to put Brandon in day care. He cried when I dropped him off, and he didn't want to leave at the end of the day." Tanya says the day-care worker used to bring Brandon to the window to wave good-bye to her as she pulled out of the driveway. Too often, her son turned his head, refusing to look at his mother.

"That really bothered me. I felt it was unnatural to leave my son every day. My husband, Clyde, and I knew that the hours we spent with Brandon each day weren't enough, so we both felt guilty. Also, I couldn't concentrate at work because I didn't really know how Brandon spent his day. Finally, I just couldn't stand it any longer, so I quit." Tanya admits her family has continued to struggle financially, but she has no regrets.

Another mother, Judy Dungan, left her job as legislative director for an Illinois congressman when she learned she was pregnant with her second child. Judy's decision is not unusual. Numerous women who believe they can manage the demands of home, job, and a first child—no sweat—come to feel it is not worth it after the arrival of the second child. Judy admits: "I didn't think it was worth the time pressure and fatigue."

Although she had reduced her workload to three days a week after her first daughter, Madeleine, was born, Judy made the decision to stay home full time after Hillary's birth.

Judy, who admits that several years ago she could not imagine being home full time, says that now she can't imagine a return to work. As she awaits the birth of her third child in a few weeks, Judy watches Hillary hugging her doll and realizes that Hillary is doing only what she has seen her mommy do. "That makes me feel I'm doing a good job," says Judy. "Besides, some things are beyond economics."

SECURE ATTACHMENT: THE KEY TO EMOTIONAL HEALTH

Any woman who gives her child her heart, her time, and her presence is giving him a priceless gift. She is shaping her child's self-concept and teaching him lessons about love and intimacy that last a lifetime.

In his 1969 book *Attachment,* the late British psychiatrist John Bowlby wrote about the centrality of the baby's emotional bond or attachment to his mother. Bowlby, the only psychiatrist to have twice received the American Psychiatric Associations highest award, the Adolph Meyer award, believed this attachment is the "foundation stone of personality."[1] Bowlby stated that "the young child's hunger for his mother's love and presence is as great as his hunger for food" and that her absence "inevitably generates a powerful sense of loss and anger."[2]

Freud, writing years earlier, had also emphasized the singular importance of the mother or mothering figure in the child's early life. In *Outline of Psychoanalysis,* he described the relationship a young child has with his mother as unique, without parallel, established unalterably for a whole lifetime as the first and strongest love object and the prototype of all later love relationships for both sexes.[3]

This most powerful early relationship between a mother and her baby begins before the moment of birth. However, the formation of attachment—or the emotional bond between a mother and her baby—is a critical developmental milestone that occurs during the baby's first year of life.[4] Psychologists Alan Sroufe and Everett Walters call this enduring bond to mother a "psychological tether, which binds infant and caregiver together."[5] It is the baby's attachment to his mother that allows him to explore his environment with a feeling of safety, using the mother as a focal point of security or a "secure base."[6]

Not only does a child learn about love from his attachment to his mother, but he also develops a sense of self-worth based on his attachment to both parents.[7] Simply put, if a child's parents are consistently loving and sensitive to his needs, the child incorporates the message: "I am loved, I am worthy. Others will love me just as my parents love me." If, on the other hand, the child's parents are rejecting, emotionally inaccessible, or absent, then a child may come to feel: "I am unloved. Therefore, I am unworthy. How can I expect others to love me if my parents don't?"

Several years ago a television camera crew and interviewer came to my house to tape a program on infant day care. In the interview I spoke about the importance of a secure parental attachment in the formation of a positive self-image. After the program had been taped, the young cameraman said, "You spoke about me today."

"How so?" I asked. (I have learned that nearly everyone personalizes the information on attachment.)

"I never felt that either parent truly loved me, and I've always struggled with low self-esteem." Jim then recounted a bit of his family history. One of five sons of a New York City stockbroker, Jim attended prep school and failed miserably. Unable to win his mother's love (he never understood why she couldn't love him), he disappointed his ambitious and successful father by repeated academic failures. Jim then became a silent, depressed adolescent who left home in his late teens. Oppressed by suicidal thoughts, he traveled to Miami where he became involved with drugs and an Indian guru. Several years later, Jim met and married Rene.

"How's your marriage?" I asked Jim at the end of his story. "We're struggling," he said honestly. "It isn't easy for either of us to trust. We want to be close, but we don't know how to be."

Jim's story illustrates a central premise of Bowlby's attachment theory; namely, that the child who feels unloved may later have great difficulty thinking well of himself and establishing intimacy with those who matter most—a spouse and children.

PARENTAL ABSENCE

But what about something that doesn't appear as toxic to children—parental absence? What happens when parents have the capacity to love their children but are absent due to death, divorce, or career demands? For a child, absence does not make the heart grow fonder. Instead, absence generates profound feelings of rejection and a yearning for love that can dominate the whole of life. Harvard psychiatrist Armand Nicholi says that those individuals who suffer from severe nonorganic emotional illness have one thing in common: All have experienced the "absence of a parent through death, divorce, a time- demanding job or other reasons."[s] A parent's inaccessibility, either physically, emotionally, or both, "can profoundly influence a child's emotional health."[9]

It matters, then, that a mother is present, both physically and emotionally during her child's early life. If she is lost in depression, exhausted by the multiple demands of her life, or absent for long hours each day, her relationship with her child will be greatly affected.

A PERSONAL STATEMENT

I know what it is to have a maternally deprived mother who has always found it difficult to establish and sustain intimate bonds. My maternal grandmother, Martha Callie Bradford, died when my mother was four years old. One of eight children vying for the attention and affection of an alcoholic father, my mother, the second youngest child, missed out. In truth, there was little to be had. What care and affection

Mother did receive came not from the stepmother who eventually arrived to care for the brood, but from her older sister Geneva. But Geneva was only a few years older than my mother. She, herself a child, had little mothering to give. However, Mother remained intensely bonded to her sister as long as Geneva lived.

Married at eighteen, Mother lost a second significant attachment when my father drowned some three years and two children later. With her early legacy and this second tragic loss, my mother was unable to be a nurturing presence for my sister or me. In reality, my only sense of home and stability came from my paternal grandparents, with whom I lived between the ages of two and five.

Those three years were the heyday of my childhood. I roamed the farm with the security that came from knowing Granny was either in the house or garden and Granddaddy was driving the tractor or milking the cows. My granny said I often sang out, "Where's my granddaddy? Oh, where can he be?" This man, my dearest childhood attachment, always had time for me. He was the one who stepped in to fill the void left by my deceased father and absent mother.

Even after I left the farm and went to live with my mother, I was never happier than when I boarded the bus for the farm. My granddaddy, a slight man with a jovial smile and a shock of wispy white hair, perpetually clad in overalls, would stand by the side of the road as the bus ground to a stop, waiting to take my hand and walk up the long, winding lane. When we entered the farm kitchen where Granny stood, a tall woman in bonnet, faded cotton dress, and apron, concocting her mouthwatering pies and frying chicken, I knew I was *home*.

The farm, with its white frame house, red barn, and grove of sugar canes, remained a place of warm affection, open communication, and safety for me. I always had this extended family to return to on holidays. I spent every Christmas and a golden month each summer with these beloved grandparents and my sister, Sandy, who lived with our grandparents on the farm. Sandy said recently that all her Christmas memories are happy ones because she and I were together. Despite our life circumstances, we are emotionally close to each other.

With my own attachment history, it is not surprising that I struggled with feelings of homelessness much of my life or that I worked full time when my daughters were infants. Research shows that our early parenting history influences marital choice and self-esteem, as well as our ability to be emotionally close to our marital partners and children. It should not be surprising that a woman's earliest parental attachments also influence her willingness to separate from her baby.

Must History Repeat Itself?

Does this mean, however, that those of us who didn't receive the nurture we needed are trapped into repeating our own attachment history? No—it is possible to give our children more than we received. The late psychoanalyst Selma Fraiberg noted that it is not inevitable that parents pass on to their babies the suffering they experienced in childhood: "The parent says, 'I want something better for my child than I have had,' and he brings something better to his child. In this way we have all known young parents who have suffered poverty, brutality, death, desertion, and sometimes the full gamut of childhood horrors, who do not inflict their pain upon their children."[10]

According to Fraiberg, what is central is that the parent remembers the *feelings* from his own injured childhood, not just the facts. By remembering his feelings, the parent refrains from inflicting his past upon his child.[11]

This has, in great measure, been true for me.

As it happened, I was a mother long before I became a psychologist. Ironically, I, who refused to learn about child development in college, studied it as a woman in her forties when my children were nearly grown. Then older and wiser, I learned why babies are fascinating. They are born with highly complex perceptual, emotional, and intellectual equipment, ready to learn about their world, ready to bond to their parents. I marvel at babies now—at how beautiful and smart they are—but I never considered staying home full time with my own. I was, after all, the daughter of an employed mother and the daughter-in-law of a woman who earned a graduate degree in her fifties so that she could become a high school librarian. Though my mother-in-law had stayed home with her two sons when they were young, she never suggested that I stay home with Holly and Kristen.

Like other intelligent, educated women, I felt I should be in the workplace. I didn't believe then that my continuous, daily presence was essential for my babies' emotional development. Had I been honest, I would have said that while I loved my children, I viewed them, not as life's invaluable gifts, but as small people I could wedge in around the edges of my life.

I did try staying home with Holly for several months, but I felt lonely, depressed, and empty. My husband, Thomas, and I thought the best solution was to put Holly in child care so that I could find a job and function more adequately. So when Holly was nine months old, I went to work full time, teaching English at a local college.

Neither my husband nor I were aware that the birth of the first child is a significant psychological event in a woman's life. In giving birth, a woman suddenly confronts her parenting history. She reflects on *her* early childhood as she cares for her baby. Moreover, a woman identifies with her own mother when she becomes a mother for the first time.[12]

This poses few problems if a woman has a warm, close, and loving tie with a mother who is emotionally healthy. In this case a new mother will have a deep reservoir of maternal love to draw from, since she herself was well cared for. But what of the mother whose supply of mother love is nearly depleted or dry because of maternal deprivation? For this woman, mothering infants will not be easy. When the baby cries and demands constant attention during those early months, the new mother with a depleted reservoir may feel desperate. She has no warm memories of physical closeness to her mother to draw on. Unlike one woman who said her mother's lap was the safest place in the world during childhood, the maternally deprived mother looks back but senses a void.

Like other new mothers, I thought about my own mother a lot. (She and I had never been emotionally close, but earlier I did not understand why.) I can still remember as a young girl watching a friend interact with her mother. Martha, who lived in the brick house next door, had a relationship with her mother that I simply could not fathom. These two people spoke an intimate language my mother and I had never learned. I envied Martha and spent as much time with her and her mother as they would allow. As I matured, I realized something was broken in my relationship with my mother, but I tried not to think too deeply about it.

Thus, when I became a mother for the first time, I didn't have the emotional resources to manage full-time mothering. Also, Thomas, an intern on call every third night, often fell asleep right after dinner on those nights he was home. Without emotional support from my husband or significant inner resources, I willingly chose to go to work. How much better it was, I thought, to challenge students to read Shakespeare and love Chaucer than to stay home alone with Holly.

My self-esteem soared as I donned new clothes purchased in the preppie college shops in Chapel Hill, North Carolina. Now I had interesting conversations with coworkers and friends and was available for lunches out. Moreover, I could talk about my job when Thomas and I went to parties with other doctors and wives. Teaching gave my life structure, meaning, and exposure to stimulating people. It also propped up a vulnerable sense of self too dependent on externals for a sense of worth and value.

WHAT ABOUT MY CHILD?

How did Holly fare? Ah, there's the rub. She had three baby-sitters between the time she was nine and eighteen months old. I fired the first sitter because I worried about how many hours Holly spent alone in her crib while Mrs. Jones ironed my husband's uniforms and vigorously cleaned our apart-ment. I left the second sitter, an impassive older woman who lived next door, when I learned about a third woman who had been given the "baby-sitter stamp of approval" by a Duke University psychologist. As Thomas's internship neared its close, Holly went to Mrs. Tate's bungalow and became one of nine charges. (So much for staff-to-infant ratios.)

By the time my second daughter, Kristen, was born, my husband and I had moved to New Haven, where he became a psychiatric resident at Yale. Since it was more difficult to cart two children to sitters and we had only one car, I stayed home most hours, teaching part time at a community college some forty miles away. Having moved to a new locale with no emotional support, I felt myself tottering over the pit of depression. Within a year my marriage was in deep trouble: My husband decided he wanted to marry someone else. Suddenly I became a single parent with two babies.

Ironically, at this time I began an inner journey that would eventually involve confrontation with my unnurtured past, my relationship with my mother, and the healing of my inner self and my sense of homelessness. Along the way and with each advance, I became a more sensitive, caring mother. During this time of turmoil, a simple event strengthened my resolve to come home to my children. One day when I stopped at Margaret McCarthy's house to pick up the girls, Margaret walked me to the car, carrying twenty-month-old Kristen. As I reached for my daughter, she turned away from me and put her arms around Mrs. McCarthy's neck. I was stung. *My child preferred the sitter to me.* Years later I learned that often young children do establish attachment relation-ships with their baby-sitters, and sometimes these ties are more secure than the parental bonds. From that moment, I determined I would do whatever I needed to do to become more emotionally accessible and to deepen my children's trust.

Within a year, I was on board an airplane in the middle of a summer night flying to London with my small, scared chil-dren, then two and four. Holly was confused and troubled at leaving our home and at having her father disappear. (He had taken a job in the Southwest.) I was frightened as well. I wasn't at all sure what I would find in London; all I knew was that I was pursuing a better lifestyle for the children and me.

A friend had sent me a book by Edith Schaeffer called *L'Abri. L'Abri,* which means "shelter" in French, is an account of the Schaeffers' desire to offer spiritual shelter to the various people who came to their home in Huemoz, Switzerland.

I was struck by the faith the Schaeffers exhibited in their willingness to open their home to people who were searching for intellectual answers to questions of faith, meaning, and purpose, as well as to those in need of emotional healing.

I went to the London L'Abri because of a conversation I had with Dr. Schaeffer at the first American L'Abri conference in Lookout Mountain, Tennessee. One night after Dr. Schaeffer spoke to a large gathering, I lingered, hoping to speak to him about the possibility of coming to Switzerland. Empathic, he suggested that my children and I could profit from time in a Christian community. "Go to London," he said. "God is bringing Christians there from all over the world. There you will find the Christian community you long for."

London? Sell my house and car and resign from my position as an English teacher? Teaching jobs in the humanities were already becoming scarce in 1970. I flew back to Connecticut after the conference, pondering Dr. Schaeffer's words. I knew I could no longer endure the sterility and loneliness of being a single mother in suburbia. I had few friends, and the bar scene was not for me. Moreover, my children needed more nurture than I, emptied by the collapse of my marriage, could give them. After wrestling with this decision for several weeks, I decided that my daughters and I belonged at L'Abri.

Soon the three of us were nestled in the caring L'Abri community in Ealing, London, and I had what every mother at home needs daily: emotional support from other women. Two mothers of older children took the three of us under their wings. As Katie and Judy nurtured me, I was in turn better able to nurture my daughters. No longer trapped alone in a suburban house, no longer living the frenetic life of the employed mother, I spent time several days each week with those two new friends and with others in the L'Abri church community.

That was thirty years ago.

Out of my own unnurtured past I have come to care passionately about mothering and to believe that good mothering is "every child's birthright." But I am not naive. From my own experience as a mother and a psychologist, I know that not every woman, whether she works or stays home, is emotionally equipped for the task of parenting. When my own children were born, I lacked the emotional support of other women. The result? I was not capable of giving my children the nurture they needed. I ran from my deepest self—I went back to work.

Yet I believe in personality change and healing for the unnurtured self. Not only have I experienced this in great measure, but I have known other women who have confronted the wounded child within and gone on to achieve greater self-acceptance and wholeness. Not surprisingly, their relationships with their children and husbands became more intimate and less conflicted.

Let's examine in greater detail what the studies reveal about attachment and how the sensitive mother works her magic. How does she forge those intimate ties with her children—bonds that last a lifetime?

Chapter Two

FORGING ATTACHMENTS

She shone for me like the Evening Star.
I loved her dearly—but at a distance.

SIR WINSTON CHURCHILL

IN SPEAKING ABOUT HIS MOTHER

The baby emerges from the darkness of her mother's womb into the brightly lit delivery room as her father watches—nervously, eagerly, proudly.

"It's a girl," says the obstetrician, holding the baby aloft so the mother can see the result of nine months of pregnancy and seventeen hours of labor.

"She's darling," the mother murmurs. "Just look at those chipmunk cheeks." The new mother glances at her husband, who smiles, nodding his affirmation. The baby starts to cry, and the doctor places her on her mother's abdomen to be caressed. "There, there, it's going to be okay," coos the mother to her daughter.

This woman and her baby are taking the first hesitant steps of what child psychiatrist Jack Raskin calls "a beautiful ballet." As the mother sensitively provides for her baby's physical needs, she and the baby will communicate with intricate interactions that involve sound, touch, imitation, facial expressions, and body language.

Like Raskin, child psychologist Evelyn Thoman believes

that the apt metaphor for the dialogue that ensues between babies and their mothers is "the dance." According to Thoman, "babies are born dancing," which is the title of a wonderful book she has written with Sue Browder.[1]

What does Thoman mean by this? The kind of dance she writes about "is a timeless form of communication, infinitely more complex, subtle, and meaningful than a polite ballroom waltz. The baby's dance—which is actually communication at its most basic level—comprises rhythmic arm movements, eye shifts, head tilts, coos, cries, fusses, gazes, and dozens of other behaviors."[2]

A baby moves rhythmically in response to his mother. Through her voice pitch, tempo, and facial expressions, a mother communicates her emotional state to her baby, and he dances synchronously in response to the messages he receives.

The late Boston University researcher William S. Condon found, in watching videotapes of mother-baby pairs, that babies danced rhythmically "in unison" with their mothers' words. Studying babies who were a few hours old, Dr. Condon and his colleague Dr. Louis Sander found that no matter what language the baby heard, a baby moved some part of his body in synchrony with human speech. For example, in the fraction of a second it took an adult to utter the "kk" sound of "come," one baby moved his head to the right, extended his elbow, rotated his right shoulder upward, his left shoulder outward, and circled the big toe of his left foot. Says Thoman, this is this baby's dance step for the sound "kk."[3]

A baby not only moves rhythmically to his mother's speech and voice inflections, but newborns are also adept at imitation. At a psychology conference on infancy I attended several years ago, one researcher showed the audience photos of a baby just a few days old imitating the researcher's facial

HOME BY CHOICE

expressions. When the researcher made a big "O" with his mouth, the baby did the same. When the researcher stuck out his tongue, the baby followed suit.

Since a baby dances with his mother from birth, he needs a dependable and accessible partner—someone who picks up on the baby's signals and over time becomes skilled at decoding the messages the baby sends long before he is verbal.

OUR HUMAN CONNECTIONS

As a mother and her baby engage in the "dance," the baby is establishing his first vital human connections. According to Bowlby, over the first year of life, but particularly between the ages of six and twelve months, every baby forges intimate bonds or attachment relationships with his mother first, then with his father.[4] Although Bowlby states that all babies (even abused babies) attach to both their parents, he believes in a hierarchy of relationships, with mother at the top of the pyramid. While the young child expands his world to include other attachments by the second year, the mother is the "touchstone," the one the baby goes to when he is tired, ill, or distressed.[5] Psychologist Michael Lamb found that until the baby's second year, when he is upset he will usually make a beeline for his mother.[6]

My daughter Kristen's experience certainly validates Lamb's observation. While Austin prefers his daddy, Greg, as playmate, when he is hurt, tired, or hungry, he chants: "Mama, Mama!" Then no one but Kristen will do as he crawls onto her lap.

While Bowlby advocates that the mother's role is primary, he acknowledges that the father plays an equally vital role in child development.[7] Lamb, who has written extensively about the role of the father, agrees. Lamb says that in the early years fathers and mothers play different roles in a child's life: Fathers become important attachment figures through playing with their children, while mothers act as nurturers.[8]

Bowlby also notes that the child forms a different attachment relationship with each parent. A child may be securely attached to one parent and insecurely attached to the other.[9] One study found that children judged to be securely attached to both parents exhibited the most confidence and competence; those judged to be insecurely attached to both parents, the least.[10] Those children who had a secure relationship with one parent but not with the other fell midway between the other groups on their scores.

BOTH PARENTS PROVIDE A SECURE BASE

Bowlby believes that, even though their roles differ, *both* parents provide "a secure base from which a child or an adolescent can make sorties into the outside world and to which he can return, knowing that he will be welcomed, nourished physically and emotionally, comforted if distressed, reassured if frightened."[11] Bowlby adds that it is only as children become confident of their parents' dependability that they can afford to explore their world and take essential risks.

I remember going to a local mall with my friend Jennifer when her son David was a toddler. She and I sat in a small amphitheater while David sauntered off to explore his surroundings. David often looked back just to make sure his mother was still there. Finding that she was, he happily wandered up and down a few steps, observing the people passing by. But he never forgot about his mother for long. He didn't need to run back; he just wanted her in view. It was obvious that Jennifer was her son's secure base—the love of his life.

Bowlby writes that as children mature, they venture further from home and the secure base their parents provide, but they still check in from time to time. Even adolescents and young adults need parents to function as a secure base.[12]

One summer when our daughters Holly and Kristen were in their early twenties, they traveled to Europe together. Before they left, in the name of economy, Don and I decided they should call home only twice on our nickel. However, after receiving a few frantic letters about their near emergencies, we relented, agreeing that funding frequent calls was a small price to pay for everyone's mental ease. Holly and Kristen still needed a secure base and were much more confident as travelers knowing we could be reached weekly by phone. We had horrendous phone bills, but it was worth it.

Both Parents Provide Patterns for Later Relationships

Not only do both parents function as the child's secure base (the mother especially so at first), but *both* parents also provide the child with a pattern, an emotional template, for all future intimate relationships. According to Bowlby, a young child forms "internal working models" of himself, his parental attachments, and his world out of the raw material of his parental relationships.[13] Based on the way his parents treat him, a child will form certain expectations about how others will treat him. If the parents are warm, loving, and emotionally accessible, the child comes to believe that *he* is lovable and worthy. As he matures, he will possess high self-esteem; he will be able to trust others and, later in life, will have the capacity to be intimate with a spouse and children. Secure in his parental attachments, this individual will expect others to treat him the same way his parents have.

What about the child whose parents are rejecting, cold,

violent, or physically present but emotionally absent? Bowlby believes it is likely this child will come to view the world through a lens of mistrust. Having low self-esteem, such a child may suffer from profound feelings of unworthiness.[14] As he matures, the individual who is insecurely attached to his parents will have difficulty being close to those who matter most. For example, he might wake up one day to a wife, now in her forties, who has decided she is tired of trying to get close to a man who has a wall around his heart. She may create a parallel life and cease looking for closeness, or she may leave.

What proof exists for the validity of Bowlby's internal working models? A number of researchers have found that the security or insecurity of a child's earliest attachment relationships relates to his later social competence and sense of personal power. For example, children who are securely attached to their parents possess more social skills as preschoolers and kindergartners than those found to be insecurely attached. As kindergartners, securely attached children possess greater coping skills and can handle frustration better than their insecure counterparts.

What is more, securely attached children usually become cooperative preschoolers and kindergartners, able to forge friendships and adapt well in their school setting. Insecurely attached children often become aggressive, hostile, and uncooperative with their peers, or they retreat from others, becoming passive and withdrawn.

RYAN AND JONATHON

I know two children who possess opposite characteristics, in part because of their differing parental histories. Ryan, a five-year-old, saunters into his kindergarten class each morning with the *savoir-faire* of a future statesman. "Hello, Johnny," he calls to another boy. "Good morning, Sally," he says to an approaching classmate. Ryan exudes self-confidence and good will.

Ryan's mother, Cecelia, who worked for a U.S. senator, left her job on Capitol Hill when Ryan was born. She says that other people often remark on his self-confidence. "They can't believe he's so at ease with adults and other children," she adds, laughing. Ryan's father, Chap, a statistician with the federal government, is convinced his son is destined for future leadership. "Why, he might even become president some day," he says, amused at his own presumption.

While Ryan possesses the high self-esteem of the secure child, Jonathon is an angry, troubled little boy. During his first year of life, Jonathon's mother, Marlene, returned to work, leaving Jonathon in a neighborhood day care center. Apparently Jonathon tried to form attachments to his various child-care providers, but no sooner had he forged a bond than his caretaker left for a better job. After a while Jonathon didn't seem to care about forming ties at the center, rather he became the preschool bully, snatching toys from other children, hitting and kicking peers and even teachers on occasion.

Jonathon's mother works as a C.P.A. for a local accounting firm, and his father is a young lawyer hoping to make partner in several years. Both feel guilty about mortgaging their son's early years, but they also feel trapped—they believe they need both incomes to fund their upper-middle-class lifestyle. Marlene feels particularly uncomfortable each time she has to leave Jonathon and his father for her frequent business trips.

Jonathon's parents have tried to ignore his hostility, but recently his kindergarten teacher called them in to say that Jonathon has few friends and that he seldom cooperates with her or other adults. "You have an angry son," Mrs. Jacobs said quietly to Marlene and John. "I believe he needs more of your time and attention."

The Impact of Early Experiences

What's the prognosis for Ryan and Jonathon? Can their early experiences be easily erased, or is each likely to continue down a particular developmental pathway? While a number of attachment psychologists believe that change is indeed possible (particularly as children mature intellectually), most agree that personality change is hard to achieve.

Bowlby believes that once we form our internal working models or mental expectations of how others will treat us, they exist outside our conscious awareness, resisting dramatic change.[15] Even when we encounter others who treat us in more positive, loving ways than our parents, we may have trouble believing this new treatment is either deserved or real. We may revert to our old, familiar thoughts about others and ourselves and simply exclude new information, especially in the area of our key attachments. Bowlby says we practice "defensive exclusion"; that is, we reject information that doesn't fit our perceptions of ourselves. Only the securely attached child updates incoming information.[16]

For example, a child who is securely attached to his parents as a result of their consistent, affectionate care will develop an unconscious belief that should he ever need help, a trustworthy individual will come to his aid. This strong conviction that the world is a friendly place occupied with helpful people gives the child confidence when he encounters stressful situations. He feels he can cope with what life sends.

Suppose, on the other hand, a child loses a parent to death or divorce. Or suppose one or both parents are rejecting. Or perhaps a parent tries to control the child's behavior by threatening abandonment. The child then develops quite different internal working models. He finds the world "comfortless" and people "unpredictable." Bowlby believes that this individual will eventually respond to life by "shrinking from it or by doing battle with it."[17]

Doug, an only child, grew up in an eastern, middle-class family with two stable, responsible parents. He remembers feeling loved, always aware his parents were *there* when he needed them. Doug's father, a teacher, was as emotionally accessible as Doug's mom. "He was a good father; I knew he loved me," says Doug. "Both he and my mom encouraged me to talk about my feelings honestly. They were people I could trust." As an adult, Doug has confronted life with a trusting, confident demeanor. He expects others to treat him as his parents did—with kindness and respect—and he handles stress confidently and with resolve. In his marriage he is cooperative, and with his wife and children he is openhanded and affectionate.

Natasha, on the other hand, grew up with an alcoholic mother and a father who abandoned the family when Natasha was twelve. At thirty-five, Natasha often finds life overwhelming. Recently, her husband broke his leg, and Natasha had to care for him in addition to her two daughters. "Why does God do this to me?" she asks, feeling that an insensitive Providence has dealt her a series of nearly lethal blows. Never having received sufficient love and nurture as a child, Natasha feels unable to cope with the exigencies of life. In her mind, God—as well as others—bears the cold parental imprint.

Although some consider attachment theory the best-researched theory of child development,[18] and Bowlby as well as numerous other researchers believe our early parental attachments influence all others, attachment theory has its detractors. We will discuss this in greater detail in the next chapter.

OTHER ATTACHMENT FIGURES

At this juncture you might well ask, but what about other caregivers? Why isn't a grandmother or a father just as good as a *mother* when it comes to caring for a baby?

A child needs at least one person he trusts and feels is in charge. That figure is the baby's "touchstone"—the one he goes to when he is sick or frightened or sad. All others are secondary.[19] Bowlby has said that a child can establish a secure attachment relationship with any caregiver—as long as that person acts in a mothering way. In *A Secure Base* he has said fathers can be as effective as mothers if in the early months they act like mothers. What matters to the child is that he has a caretaker who is sensitive and consistent, one who loves him passionately. Only then will he feel loved and learn to love in return.[20]

But let's look for a moment at some of the implications of this.

Suppose a child does spend most of his waking hours with a father, grandmother, or other relative he comes to love dearly. Who will become that child's psychological mother—the person he is closest to? When I asked one woman about her relationship with her mother, she replied, "Which mother?" Her mother had worked full time when this woman was very young, and she was closest to her grandmother, who had cared for her. While it is wonderful that a child can be emotionally close to the substitute caregiver, I wonder if most mothers are willing to play second (or even third) fiddle in their child's emotional life. Occasionally children come to forge closer bonds with their baby-sitters than their parents. A recent study found that some children who spend long days in day care may be insecurely attached to Mom and Dad but securely attached to a young, sensitive caregiver.[21]

One woman, concerned about this very thing, deliberately moved her daughter to a new care-giving situation every three or four months to prevent her from forming close ties to anyone save herself and her husband. The mother did this without any apparent knowledge that she might be wreaking havoc on her baby's emotional life.

Additionally, some mothers discover they are jealous of the closeness the father establishes with the child in families where role reversal has occurred. One mother who continued working full time after her son's birth said she envied her husband, a writer, who stood, holding their baby, waving good-bye as she climbed onto the bus, headed for the office. "It wasn't too many months," said Jan, "before I felt Tom knew more about Danny than I did."

Even if a woman is willing for her husband to assume the primary care-giving role, he is unlikely to remain at home over the long haul. An Australian study by Graeme Russell illustrates this.[22] Russell recruited fifty families in which both parents shared the care-giving responsibility. In some of these families the father stayed home while the mother worked. Although this arrangement seemed to work well initially, when Russell did a two-year follow-up study of twenty-three of these families, he was disappointed with what he found. Only four of the families had maintained their nontraditional lifestyle.

Why did these Mr. Moms go back to work? Several said they were bored at home, some said they needed the money, and still others complained of lack of adult company as well as pressure from their male peer group. What about the mothers in this study? They willingly reverted to their traditional roles because life at home was "less rushed and more relaxed."[25] Moreover, they felt that the mother-child relationship was stronger after they returned home.

While it is advantageous for any child to have a more involved father, complete role reversal is still rare and may not be long lasting. As one psychologist said, "Men just aren't wired the same as women." In support of this, a southern university recently voted against parental leave for its male faculty members because the faculty committee felt the men would use their leave to stay home and publish. Apparently the committee believed that working toward achieving tenure would prove more compelling than changing diapers.

So mother, it seems, is not off the hook.

No matter how much feminists have tried in the past three decades to erase sexual differences, biology dictates that a woman carry her baby inside her body until birth. Her breasts provide milk. (Her husband's never do.) Moreover, a woman's baby is programmed to fall in love with her. During that first year, a mother isn't just feeding, diapering, and playing with her baby. She is teaching him lessons about love and intimacy he needs to know his whole life long. If a mother is absent too often, he will fall in love, or try to, with whomever she has left in charge. A mother who elects to reenter the workplace full time needs to think carefully about this. Upon reflection, she may decide that no paycheck is large enough to justify depriving her baby of her consistent care.

The baby needs someone who will consistently meet his needs month after month. Psychologists generally agree that consistency of care is best in the earliest months. Who is less likely to pack up and quit the job of mothering than the child's mother?

Of course, if Mother is depressed or preoccupied with her own painful past, her baby will not be able to dance with her and fall in love with her as he needs to. But does this mean, as is sometimes suggested, that a wounded mother should simply return to the marketplace since she finds full-time mothering so difficult? To suggest this implies simplistically that eight to ten hours in the workplace will "fix" whatever is wrong with mother psychologically, and that she will be able to give her child sufficient love and care during the few hours she has left each day.

While it may be hard, and even painful, I believe it is far better for a mother to seek help through psychotherapy and to work through any psychological problems while she devotes herself to learning to dance with her baby. A new mother has a wonderful challenge: She has a reason (in the person of her baby) to confront her unnurtured past and grow as a person. Many women have done just this, and their lives are richer for it.

Now let's examine this evidence on day care to understand why separation is hard for a baby.

Chapter Three

MOTHER CARE OR OTHER CARE?

*My bias is that a woman's
most important role is being at home
to mother her small children.*

T. BERRY BRAZELTON, M.D.

I met Betsy, a tall brunette in designer denim, at a friend's house on a cold December morning. As we sat drinking our coffee, I asked her if she planned to return to work.

"Oh, yes," said Betsy with enthusiasm, as she cradled her ten-day-old son in her arms. "I can't leave my job for long. My boss wouldn't like it. Anyway, I've only been with this firm for six months, so I can't take much time off. Besides, I've decided to put Eric in day care when he's three weeks old. I want him to be adequately socialized, so I'm planning to expose him to other children as soon as possible."

Betsy believed her baby needed to be socialized through contacts with other adults and children. What she did not know was that during his first year, her child needed a "close, continuous, and intimate" relationship with *her* far more than the company of others. According to child development experts, children do not engage in peer play until they are about two years old, and then they engage in parallel play—

63

playing alongside each other when they are not wrangling over the same toy.

Our grandmothers knew that babies need their mothers. Until the advent of strident feminism, child development experts knew that, too, and said as much in the books and articles they wrote. Though it has become politically correct to suggest that young children are infinitely resilient, the data do not support this. The fact remains that babies thrive when they have sensitive, responsive, and consistent mothering. And they fail to develop their full potential when they are deprived of maternal love. They need their mothers during their earliest years more than they need toys, socializing with other children, or the material comforts a second income will buy.

THE GREAT DEBATE

I need to say up front that psychologists are divided on the issue of other-than-mother care. While many support full-time mothering in a child's earliest years of life, others seem more concerned about the employed mother's guilt.

I once cornered a nationally known child-development expert to ask him about his outspoken support of the employed mother. I knew from reviewing his research that he had studied mother-infant interaction, so he knew about the importance of the "dance." Yet in media interviews he failed to say with any conviction that babies needed to be cared for by their mothers. When I told him about my concern for mothers at home and their need for support from the experts, he took two steps backward and replied, "Ah yes, but mothers who work feel *so* guilty."

Other psychologists are leery of becoming embroiled in political controversy over such issues as maternal employment and infant day care. I once telephoned a researcher to ask him about the research he had conducted on infant day care. Although he was initially cordial, he instantly cooled when I told him the purpose of my call. Brusquely, he said he was *not* interested in being interviewed. "I've forgotten *everything* I ever knew about infancy," he snapped, denying the validity of his own research. (I later learned that he had been burned by the media, so he had reason to be wary of interviews.)

While some experts shun controversy, psychologist Sandra Scarr, the author of *Mother Care/Other Care,* has become an outspoken proponent of infant day care. One often reads some pithy comment in the *Wall Street Journal* or the *Washington Post* made by this well-known psychologist from the University of Virginia.

Dr. Scarr, who is herself an employed mother, believes children do not necessarily need to be cared for by their mothers at home. She writes that "day care can actually be good for children." She believes that "today's child," while sensitive to his environment, is nonetheless "resilient." Scarr suggests that bad experiences can readily be overcome by good experiences (contrary to Bowlby's notion of internal working models): "Today's child is not a china doll who breaks under the first environmental blow. Rather, our child is a tougher plastic doll; she resists breaking and recovers her shape, but she can be dented by later blows."[1]

Although Scarr is an advocate for children's resiliency, she does write about an unsettling experience involving her third child, Rebecca. Scarr, who employed baby-sitters because of her irregular hours and extensive travel as a university professor, returned home one day to find her eighteen-month-old crying. Her small daughter simply said, "Kathy hit me! Kathy hit me!" Scarr found large, red welts on her daughter's body. Says Scarr, "the sitter had beaten her badly."[2]

After she called the police and registered her complaint, Scarr learned this same baby-sitter had physically abused other small children whose parents had filed complaints, yet because no adult witnessed the abuse and could testify, the police told Scarr they were unable to prosecute. Scarr writes with obvious frustration, "No one was there to prevent the abuse or to testify about it."[3] The irony of her comment should not go unnoticed.

It is to prevent just this situation that many full-time mothers stay home with their very young children. They feel it is not always possible to effectively screen every sitter, and they don't want to pick up the pieces once abuse occurs.

The psychologist who sounded the alarm about maternal employment and infant day care in the late eighties was Jay Belsky, professor of human development at Penn State University. Based on research findings since 1980, Belsky said that placing a baby in day care during his first year might erode his sense of trust and order in the world. This could also lead to later personality maladjustment. Belsky wrote in *Zero to Three:* "Children who initiated care in the first year, the evidence suggested to me, seemed at risk not only for insecurity but for heightened aggression, noncompliance, and possibly social withdrawal in the preschool and early school years."[4]

Like Belsky, Bowlby was concerned about the effects of early child care and was accused by the feminists in Britain and America of making employed mothers feel guilty. I once observed as a young female physician holding a sleeping infant in her arms asked Bowlby when she could safely return to work. We were attending a workshop at the annual meeting of the American Psychiatric Association. Bowlby did not equivocate in his answer: "I don't recommend at all that a mother return to work during the baby's first year. What's important," he said "is what's optimal for the child, not what the mother can get away with."[5]

Bowlby acknowledged that young women who have promising careers face tough decisions when they have children, but he did not believe the answer for them was to attempt to do two jobs—manage both career and family. He did, in fact, understand the educated woman's dilemma. "The more brilliant the career, the greater the pressure," remarked Bowlby. "Women in the professions are unlucky. The problem is more acute with them."

Pausing, Bowlby scanned the room filled with bright, young psychiatrists and remarked, "If you want a job done well, do it yourself."

Clearly, infant day care is a significant national concern. Infants currently represent the fastest growing segment of the day care population. As I learned at the Clinton White House Child Care Conference, about 50 percent of American babies are in other-than-mother care. Because of early day care, a significant number of the future generation may grow up without a close maternal bond and with an insecure attachment relationship with one or both parents. But before we examine some of the recent day care research in detail, let's review how the psychologists do this research in the first place.

THE *STRANGE SITUATION*

In the late 1960s psychologist Mary Ainsworth, first a protégée and later a colleague of Bowlby's, created an ingenious laboratory experiment called the *Strange Situation,* currently the most important instrument used by psychologists to measure the attachment relationship an infant has with his parents. It is the instrument of choice in infant day care research.

Robert Karen says, "No one prior to Ainsworth had come upon a method of assessing relatedness. And no one before had found a way to assess how styles of parenting contributed to individual differences. Through this ingenious project, capping years of research, Ainsworth had begun her revolution."[6]

The *Strange Situation* consists of eight three-minute episodes that provide a window into the attachment relationship a child has with his parents.[7]

Imagine, for a moment, that you are a psychologist sitting behind a one-way mirror observing and coding maternal and child behavior. First, you watch as a mother and baby are shown into a room (a university laboratory). The floor is covered with brightly colored, intriguing toys that engage the baby's immediate attention. In a few minutes, a stranger (hired by the psychologist) enters and begins to chat with the mother. Most babies hardly notice or, if they do, are not alarmed. Soon, however, the mother abruptly leaves the room, and the baby is alone with the stranger. *Alone.* While some babies appear not to notice and keep playing with the toys, others begin to whimper or cry openly. Fortunately, the mother returns within three minutes and the baby is mollified. But alas, the mother leaves again! And whereas the first time the baby was left with the stranger, this time he is left alone. He does not know his mother is waiting just behind the door.

What do babies do when mother leaves for the second time? Some show their independence and don't cry; others go berserk, crawling after the mother or running to the door. "*Mommeee, Mommeee,*" they shriek. Finally, mother returns. It is this reunion, as well as the one before it, that captures the attention of the psychologist.

How does the baby greet his mother? Does he ignore her and keep playing with his toys? Does he cry inconsolably no

HOME BY CHOICE

matter how much his mother tries to soothe him? Does he cease crying quickly and become interested in the toys around him once again?

What happens in the reunion episodes allows psychologists to evaluate the attachment relationship that a young child has with a parent. Based on the reunion episodes and other observed behavior, Ainsworth and her colleagues at Johns Hopkins identified three patterns of attachment: secure, anxious-resistant, and anxious-avoidant.[8]

PATTERNS OF ATTACHMENT

Ainsworth found that the *securely attached child* crawls or moves toward his mother during the reunion episodes. This boy or girl wants to be picked up and comforted and protests if his mother tries to put him down too soon. Because he has found his mother trustworthy in the past, however, he is easily comforted and will eventually begin playing happily with the many toys in the laboratory. This child knows his mother can be *counted on* to meet his needs responsively and sensitively. According to Ainsworth, mothers of these babies have been "less rejecting, interfering and/or ignoring than the mothers of other infants."[9]

The *anxious-resistant child*, however, is angry with his mother for leaving him. Writes Robert Karen, "He is hooked by the fact that she does indeed come through on occasion. He picks up that she will respond sometimes—perhaps out of guilt—if he pleads and makes a big enough fuss. And so he is constantly trying to hold on to her or punish her for being unavailable. He is wildly addicted to her and to his efforts to make her change."[10] This baby has a mother who is inconsistently accessible and responsive.

During the *Strange Situation*, these babies are often inconsolable, finding it hard to stop crying once they become upset. Others are conspicuously passive. It is his mother's unpredictability that produces the child's anger. He must deal with behavior best described as "she loves me/she loves me not," and this makes him furious. I once asked Ainsworth which insecurely attached child concerned her most, and she replied, "The anxious-resistant baby."

What about the *anxious-avoidant child?* During the reunion episodes, this baby either ignores his mother or averts his gaze when she tries to catch his eye.[11] He does not want to be held and will squirm to get down if picked up. Usually he is not particularly distressed during the separation episodes, or if he is, he seems to be bothered that he is alone not that his mother has left him.

What kind of mothering has the anxious-avoidant baby experienced? These babies have had rejecting mothers. These mothers have repulsed their babies' bids for comfort and attention; they simply did not enjoy physical contact with their babies.[12]

Robert Karen describes the avoidant child thus: "He becomes angry and distant (even though he remains no less attached). His pleas for attention have been painfully rejected and reaching out seems impossible. The child seems to say, 'Who needs you—I can do it on my own!' Often, in conjunction with this attitude, grandiose ideas about the self develop: I am great, I don't need anybody."[13]

On the surface, the avoidant child personifies the American virtues of independence and individualism. He doesn't appear to need his mother at all. He is the kid who can be dropped off at the day care center and picked up *whenever.* And while the other children may look longingly toward the door, awaiting the vision of their mother's form, this child continues playing with toys. He is occupied, not with relationships, but with inanimate objects. He acts as if he has no needs. In actuality, the avoidant child has built a wall to protect a vulnerable self. For some, this wall will remain in place until someone comes along years later to dismantle it, stone by stone—possibly a psychiatrist or a trusted, patient spouse.

Mary Main, a psychologist who has pioneered attachment research on adults at the University of California at Berkeley, believes avoidance is a defense mechanism.[14] The avoidant child has been repulsed so many times by the one who should love and comfort him that he defends himself against further emotional pain by ignoring his mother in times of heightened stress and anxiety.

Think about this for a moment. Our babies come out of the womb frightfully dependent. We humans have the longest state of dependency of any of God's creatures; *a baby needs everything*. He needs to be fed, to have his diapers changed, and to be talked to if he is ever to learn language. Initially, all he can do to communicate is to cry and flail about. If he's left to cry in his crib for long periods of time, or if his mother is out of sync with him, he will be hurt and confused.

To protect himself, the baby withdraws. He avoids this mother he needs, but he is *angry*. That's a lot for a baby to have to process by twelve months of age.

The Pain That Is Separation

Let's look for a moment at an experience that conjures up powerful feelings in our babies—separation from parents, especially mothers. As Erik Larson wrote in *Parents* magazine: "Separation is serious business and psychologists now conduct their research with increasing urgency. They cite the large numbers of children who must cope with separation as their moms go back to work and as divorce breaks up more families."[15]

When Ricky's mother, Eva, initially left him in the neighborhood day-care center, he sobbed as she walked out the door. Over the next four years, Ricky, who told his parents that he didn't like going to day care, ceased to show any emotion when his mother dropped him off and collected him at day's end. Throughout his childhood Ricky spent most of his waking hours at Wee People, and his sister, Janice, who had entered elementary school, spent her late afternoons there as well.

One day a clinical psychologist came to the center to get Janice to take her to play with her daughter. As Janice put on her coat and said good-bye to Ricky, the psychologist noticed that though tears flowed down Ricky's cheeks, the little boy stood mutely by. He didn't even ask to accompany his sister on the outing.

This psychologist, who works with troubled adolescents, later told a colleague about this episode, saying that Ricky had already learned his efforts made little difference in his world. "Someday he may become a depressed teenager," she said, "and not know why. He will be suffering from 'learned helplessness,' having discovered early on that his crying, his attempts to bring his mother back, didn't work."

WHAT SEPARATION FEELS LIKE

Why is separation so painful for small children?

During his first year of life when the baby is forming an attachment to his mother (and father), he is also forming a mental image of her that will sustain him in her absence. The baby will happily accept substitute care until he begins to form this attachment to his mother (between six and twelve months of age). But from then on, until his mental image of

HOME BY CHOICE

his mother is firmly in place, her presence is extremely important to him.[16]

When eight-month-old Joey's mother, Jacqueline, walks out the door, he does not yet have the capacity to know that she will return in two or ten hours; all he knows is that she is gone. *Gone.* This woman whom he loves passionately has simply disappeared from his life. The baby-sitter his mother has left him with may also frighten Joey. Simultaneously, he has to cope with his mother's disappearance and stranger anxiety.

How do we know how babies think? The famous Swiss psychologist Jean Piaget studied babies' intellectual development and found that in the early months, babies will not actively search for toys and other objects when they disappear. If a six-month-old baby is looking at a toy, and the toy is suddenly removed from sight, as far as the baby is concerned, the toy has disappeared forever. Out of sight, out of mind. Once the baby has developed a sense of object permanence, however, he will make an active search for a missing toy or missing mother. If someone hides the toy, the child will look for it; if Mom leaves the room, he will search for her. (Some psychologists feel that babies develop a sense of person permanence before they know that objects are permanent.)[17]

Piaget also found that before the age of two, children do not form mental representations or symbols of missing objects. Think what this means for baby Joey. Until the end of his first year (and usually not before age two), a baby does not have a mental picture of his mother to comfort himself in her absence. Joey can't tell himself, "I love my mommy and Mommy's coming back. Mommy has *not* left me for good." Joey's mom has simply disappeared. Imagine the intensity of this little boy's anxiety.

I have watched my grandson Austin handle separations

from his mother. Until he was about twenty-six months old he didn't seem to understand when I told him, "Mama will be back soon." I had been saying this for months and though Austin loves me and has always enjoyed coming to "Mimi and Papa's house," he invariably started looking for his mother after a few hours in my care. Only when he reached thirty months of age was he able to have his parents go away for the weekend without any visible emotional discomfort.

Christopher Coe, a professor of psychology at the University of Wisconsin in Madison and pioneer in studies of how separation affects immune responses, offers this provocative statement about such separation: "We've radically altered the way we rear our children. It's just never happened in history that we've imposed such early separations of such a lasting duration. It's a big human experiment that may have a high price tag."[18]

Of course all babies must experience some separation from their mothers. That's inevitable. And I have often been accused by talk show hosts (especially men) of wanting to chain babies to their mothers' bodies and never give women a break. I am not suggesting that mothers need to be with their babies around the clock every day. How well I remember needing some time away from my children just to think and feel like a person again. But when separations are long and frequent, or when they occur too early in a child's life, then a child may experience intense anxiety or sadness.

"When separation imperils that early attachment," writes Judith Viorst in *Necessary Losses*, "it is difficult to build confidence, to build trust, to acquire the conviction that throughout the course of our life we will—and deserve to—find others to meet our needs. And when our first connections are unreliable or broken or impaired, we may transfer that experience,

HOME BY CHOICE

and our responses to that experience, onto what we expect from our children, our friends, our marriage partner."[19] Viorst further believes that severe separations in early childhood can create "scars on the brain."

Psychologists do not know for sure if repeated daily separations can be summed in a child's psyche to equal a severe separation. But the evidence is mounting that these separations do their damage—that the cost of separation in early childhood may be high.

I have watched a number of babies and toddlers negotiate separations from their mothers and have witnessed, on occasion, real anguish. Some mothers have heard their children's cries; others have not. The latter, perhaps because their own mothers did not hear their cries when they were infants, have left their babies sobbing. Sometimes it is all I can do to keep from running after these insensitive mothers to say, "Please don't do this. Please don't leave your child when he is sobbing or afraid. Stay awhile until it is obvious he can cope with your absence and, if he can't, then take him with you and wait until he is ready."

Ironically, while some mothers do not realize just how important they are to their young, subhuman primates are biologically programmed to keep their infants nearby. Bowlby writes in *Attachment* that the chimpanzee, the gorilla, the baboon, and the rhesus macaque all keep their infants close to them. The infants sleep beside their mothers at night and never wander far from their sight by day. They run to their mothers if they become alarmed or afraid. Primate infants, studies show, spend the whole of their infancy in close proximity to their mothers.[20]

Apparently, subhuman primates make good mothers. Not only do they stay close to their infants, but when they discipline their young, rebuffs are always gentle. Moreover, as the off-spring grow older and move away from their mothers, their mothers do not reject or mistreat them.

I remember reading years ago that Dr. Jane Van Lawick-Goodall, who spent years researching chimpanzee behavior, decided to model her own mothering of her son Grub after what she witnessed in the African bush. Said Goodall, "The female chimp is a good mother. She never leaves her young children or neglects them. I've tried to follow this with Grub. I didn't leave him at all when he was small, and I've never left him screaming. I know lot of mothers leave their children alone, but I don't believe in it. Because I've always been with him, Grub has felt secure right from the beginning. Now he'll wander off on his own confidently, and he's never gone through the stage of being worried about strangers.[21]

How many American mothers are in Goodall's camp? Probably too few. Yet the wisdom of her stance is borne out by decades of child development research. Babies and young children hunger for their mothers' presence, and once they become securely attached, they will toddle off and need them less.

America's Hottest Political Topic

Before I begin our discussion of child care, I need to say at the outset that day care is possibly the hottest political topic in America. It is certainly the most emotion-laden issue in our culture, as well as in academia today. When I was interviewed by Dr. James Dobson on Focus on the Family radio in the fall of 1999, he stated that child care was one of the most controversial subjects he ever deals with.

He added that he fully expected to get "flak" from his listeners after our interview because "the system in America is fixed so that everyone feels disrespected." Dobson continued,

"The woman who's working full time feels someone out there is blaming her for not being home more with her kids, and the mother at home feels people are saying 'how stupid that you've got this talent and you don't use it.'"

Why is child care such a hot political and cultural issue? The answer is simple: guilt and money. Not only do millions of American mothers feel guilty because their children are in child care, but day care is big business. According to U.S. Census data, in 1995 there were approximately 21 million infants, toddlers, and preschool children under the age of six in the U.S. and more that 12.9 million of these were in some form of child care.[22] Although most young children are still in a home-based setting, some 52 percent are cared for by nonrelatives or are in center-based care.[23] The bottom line is simply this: There's a lot of money to be made minding America's children.

MATERNAL GUILT

Let's look at the reality of maternal guilt. Since a mother, not a father, carries the psychological burden for the well-being of her children, she worries when little Tommy screams at the interstate exit nearing the day-care center, "Don't take me *there*, Mommy!" And if he becomes an angry, emotionally distant four-year-old or a depressed teenager, she asks herself, "Did all those years in day care have anything to do with this?"

Not only do millions of American mothers wrestle with guilt daily, but many of the female psychologists who have devoted their careers to infant day care research probably do so as well. Let me explain.

When I was working on my doctorate in developmental psychology at Georgetown University, I became aware that some of the top female developmentalists churning out infant day care research had put their own children in day care. For example, Alison Clarke-Stewart, a professor at the University of California in Irvine whom I debated on national television, wrote a book on day care and dedicated it to her son who "spent his first year in day care so this book could be written." (By the way, Clarke-Stewart contributed the idea of "quality time" to the cultural discourse in the 1970s.)

Also, Sandra Scarr, author of *Mother Care/Other Care,* had her children in child care. And when I asked Martha Cox, a researcher involved in the federally funded National Institute of Child Health and Development study (NICHD) about this, she said that most of the female NICHD researchers used early and continuous care for their babies. Is it possible that maternal guilt is, in part, driving their research and biasing their interpretation of the data? Since no scientific research is without bias, particularly in the social sciences, the fact that some of the most strident proponents of day care are female academicians who utilized day care for their babies should not go unnoticed.

Unlike some of his female colleagues, Jay Belsky has openly acknowledged that his gender and the fact that his wife cared for their two young sons at home could have affected his interpretation of the day care research.[24] Belsky, who became something of a media darling in the late eighties, reviewed the day care research in 1978 and concluded that day care did not harm children.

Belsky later reversed his position in an article in *Zero to Three* in 1987 and ignited a firestorm in academia and the culture at large. Suddenly Belsky, who had been sought after at meetings and infancy conferences, found that he was "Hamlet's ghost."[25] In the early '90s Belsky said, "I'm a pariah. I violated the Eleventh Commandment of Developmental

Psychology—'Thou Shalt Not Speak Any Ill of Day Care, Whatsoever, Ever.'"[26] Belsky has since become one of five male researchers on the NICHD team (there are twenty females), but his voice in the culture has become muted.

So when you read about some new study on infant day care that is hot off the press, remember the emotion-laden controversy surrounding the issue and look at the gender of the researchers. Simply put, many female developmentalists may have an ax to grind.

How best to raise America's children? This is the hottest political issue in this country, and money and guilt lie at the heart of it. With that understanding, let's look at some the infant day care findings.

THE DAY CARE RESEARCH

Just what does key infant day care research show? In the eighties, before it became politically incorrect to speak ill of day care, key studies found that placing a baby in substitute care for twenty or more hours a week during that critical first year of life not only increased the baby's risk of insecure attachment to mother and/or father, but this also created behavioral and emotional problems later on, particularly between ages three and eight.

What's going on here? When a mother resumes employment for twenty or more hours per week during her baby's first year, some researchers believe the baby may feel rejected as a result of the daily separations. Why? Mom is simply not there to respond to her baby's signals. This may lead to the "heightened avoidance" that researchers have found among infants of employed mothers. With this in mind, let's look at several important day care studies.

First, a 1983 study of the infants of middle-class families

by Pamela Schwartz of the University of Michigan found that no matter what the child care arrangement, those who entered full-time child care before they were nine months old were more likely to avoid their mothers during the reunion episodes than those cared for by their mothers at home.[27]

Researchers D. Wille and J. Jacobsen found this same increase in avoidance in 1984 when they investigated forty-five eighteen-month-old children in Detroit. When these toddlers were studied using the *Strange Situation,* those who were classified as anxious-avoidant had spent about sixteen hours per week in child care; their securely attached counterparts had spent only five hours in care.[28] Psychiatrist Peter Barglow and his colleagues reported similar findings of increased avoidance in their study of affluent families in the Chicago area.[29]

Also, two studies have found that boys are particularly vulnerable when mother goes to work during that important first year. First, P. Lindsay Chase-Lansdale and Margaret Owen found in 1987 that when mothers returned to work when their babies were between two weeks and six months old, sons were more likely than daughters to be insecurely attached to their fathers.[30] Jay Belsky and Michael Rovine also found that boys who spend twenty or more hours per week in substitute care are more likely to be insecurely attached to both parents than those boys raised at home by their mothers.[31]

Why are boys insecurely attached to their *fathers* when mothers return to work? Chase-Lansdale and Owen suggest that when mothers work, fathers may respond to increased stress by being negative and harsh with their sons. These little boys may not receive the love and nurture from their fathers that they so obviously need.

Boys, it seems, are particularly vulnerable to feelings of emotional insecurity engendered by maternal absence.

Long-Term Effects of Infant Day Care

Early studies, such as the one conducted by J. C. Schwarz and his colleagues, have shown that older children who entered day care before they were twelve months old are more physically and verbally abusive toward adults, less cooperative with grownups, and less tolerant of frustration than their counterparts who had no prior day care experience.[32]

Another long-term study of kindergartners and first graders found that those who had been in a high quality day care facility since they were three months old were more aggressive than those who had begun day care later on. These early care children were more likely to "hit, kick, and push than children in the control group. Second, they were more likely to threaten, swear, and argue."[33] Teachers said that these early-day-care children did not have strategies for dealing with their angry feelings; instead of talking about how they felt or walking away, they lashed out.

One of the most provocative studies to date was conducted by psychologist Carolee Howes at UCLA.[34] In a study of eighty children, Howes looked at how they were affected over time by a number of factors: age of entry into day care, the quality of care received, and family characteristics. Howes found that children in low-quality care as infants had the greatest difficulty with their peers when they became preschoolers. When they entered kindergarten, their teachers rated these children as more distractible, less task-oriented, and less considerate than later-entry children.

Possibly the most startling finding, however, had to do with what Jay Belsky has called "the power of influence."[35]

Howes found that as toddlers, early-care children were more influenced by their caregiver-teachers than were those cared for as infants by their mothers. This was not the case for those who entered day care after twelve months of age. Then, the family was the most important socializing influence.

For a parent, this is sobering news, particularly for those who want to be the leading influence in their child's life. When we give our very young children to others to rear, what is at issue is not only their attachment to us, but also our power to influence them later on. That's a lot to put at risk for any reason.

The Gold Standard of Infant Day Care Research

Since so much controversy has surrounded infant day care research, and since earlier studies found disturbing long-term effects, the federal government has funded research since the early '90s—the National Institute of Child Health and Development (NICHD) Study—to look at the long-term effects of child care.

The NICHD Study, which began to follow 1,300 families at ten different sites in 1991, released its initial findings in April 1996 and fired "the shot heard round the world."[36] In this long-term study, which planned to track the effects of child care on children's development through age seven, the results of Phase 1 seemingly rendered a body blow to full-time mothers everywhere. For example, the *Los Angeles Times* headlines read "Child Care No Risk to Infant/Mother Ties" and the London *Guardian* reported, "Child Care Report Backs Working Mums."

I groaned when I read these headlines because I know how I would feel if I were still a mother at home, trying to ensure my child's humanity in a culture hostile to mothering.

But when the Family Research Council in Washington, D.C. asked me to analyze the study, I found a different story than what was reported in the media.

Basically, Phase 1 found that early day care neither helped nor hurt the mother-child bond. In other words, the study found no effects. When I later spoke with Jay Belsky about this, he responded, "If this were a study of cocaine use and the researchers found the same effects, who would say cocaine use doesn't matter?"

The study did find, however, that if a mother was insensitive to her child's emotional needs, just having her child in day care for as little as ten hours per week increased the risk of insecure attachment. Then the study found that between 46 and 48 percent of the infants were insecurely attached.

Also, the study found that male infants, more than female infants, were adversely affected if mother worked thirty hours per week. Then some 42 percent of the baby boys were insecurely attached to their mothers. This is a hefty number in light of proven male emotional vulnerability and the risk of psychological and behavioral problems later on.

In April 1997, about a year later, the NICHD network released findings, indicating, on the positive side, that child care does not harm the cognitive and language development of children when compared to home-reared children, *but the care must be of high quality.* This is an important caveat since most day care in America is mediocre at best, and day care workers are particularly transient, with about a third changing jobs yearly. So the positive findings in this particular study are germane only for those rare, high-quality day-care settings.

The study also found, on a more negative note, that mothers who placed their children in day care in early infancy were less sensitive in their interactions with their children at six months and more negative at fifteen months. And the children responded in kind by being less affectionate toward their mothers at twenty-four and thirty-six months than were their home-reared counterparts.[17]

Then in November 1999, the NICHD team released new findings that supported the negative trend already reported. The researchers found that the more hours a child spent in child care, the less attuned mother and child were to each other. Sounds like common sense, right? When the psychologists looked at mother-child interaction at six, fifteen, twenty-four, and thirty-six months, they found that when mother worked forty hours per week and placed her child in day care from infancy on, she was less sensitive in interacting with her child, and the child was more negative toward his mother.[18]

Why is mother-child interaction so important? Since a child's relationship with his mother is the "foundation stone of personality," it is critical that the relationship be loving and warm. If it is not, the child will blame himself, and his self-worth will be diminished. Also, psychologists know that the way a mother interacts with her child is an important predictor of later child development—affecting social, cognitive, and linguistic competencies in early and middle childhood.

Well-known psychiatrist Stanley Greenspan, who has spent twenty-five years exploring how children learn and grow, says, "Emotional interactions between a child and a loving adult are responsible for the mind's growth."[19] Greenspan goes on to say that children who have healthy interactions with their parents are *twenty times* more likely to have normal or superior intelligence than children without them.

For the first two years after Austin's birth, I watched my daughter, who chooses to stay home, interact with Austin. Since his birth I have lived close by to love and support both mother and child in their "dance." My daughter comforts her little boy when he cries, gets up at night when he calls, and is warm and affectionate toward her son. Although she planned to breast-feed Austin only for a year, when she sensed that he needed the emotional comfort of the nursing, she continued it until he was two. Her pediatrician later laughed when Kristen told him this. "Anytime I see mothers nurse their babies longer than a year, the baby is usually a boy," he said.

At two and a half Austin is a happy, engaging toddler who is literally exploding with language, having already learned months ago how to operate a VCR, open and lock doors, and understand what the knobs and buttons do in a car. (This boy has a devoted father and grandfather who have allowed him hours of "car play.") As a grandmother, I am pleased by what I see in this little fellow's face and eyes. As a developmental psychologist, I believe Austin is off to a great start in life and will someday grow up to feel "life is a gift to be enjoyed" *not* "a burden to be borne."

OTHER HAZARDS OF DAY CARE

Thus far in discussing day care I have focused on the child's emotional bond and the fact that putting a child in day care too early puts attachment relationships at risk. I have done so deliberately because this is the area of greatest concern for child development experts. If a child falters in his emotional development, he falters in life.

But what about other hazards of day care? For one, day care is a breeding ground for disease—for children of any age. Children in day care are exposed to a host of diseases, ranging from bacterial meningitis to cytomegalovirus, and hepatitis A. In addition, children in day care are at much higher risk for gastrointestinal disease, especially diarrhea, than are home-reared children.[40] Add colds, ear infections, and other upper respiratory infections, and the result is a child who is often sick.

Many children find the long day in day care oppressive, regimented, and antithetical to their needs as children. Wendy Dreskin, who along with her husband, William, founded and directed a high-quality day-care center in San Francisco, became so concerned about the stressful effects of day care on the children that she and her husband closed their center.

Dreskin felt the children missed their parents and had to deal with a day that was far "too long for them." The long day pushed some of the children, hungry for parental attention, over the edge. Dreskin says of one child: "One day when another little girl was sitting in a teacher's lap I heard Alison cry, 'I want teacher's lap.' When the other child did not move, Alison attacked her, raking her nails across the child's face. She reminded me of a starving urchin fighting for a scrap of bread."[41]

Dreskin explodes the myth that children stop crying the minute parents leave. She says this is often what directors tell the day-care workers to say to make parents feel better.

Dreskin notes that at the end of the day the children eagerly awaited the sound of mother's car coming up the hill. "The children would listen and say, 'Cathy, I hear your mother coming.' They were so anxious to be reunited with their mothers that they were tuned in to the motors in their parents' cars."[42]

In addition to the longing to be at home with their parents, one of the silent costs of years spent in highly regimented day care will be a longing for the freedom of lost childhood. Play is the work of childhood. To play freely children need unstructured time. They need to be able to concentrate on building houses with blocks, coloring, dressing their

HOME BY CHOICE

dolls, and waging mock warfare without the constant interference and regimentation that day care requires.

My daughter Kristen told me that during the two years she attended day care half-days, she was bored and longed to come home directly after morning kindergarten. She was never happier than when I picked her up at 2:00 P.M. to take her home to play.

GUIDELINES FOR OTHER CARE

As has been shown, babies and young children do not profit from long hours of other-than-mother care. Many studies show that it is better for children to spend their infancies at home with their mothers. But how long does a mother need to provide on-site care? Obviously, parents need guidelines as they think about returning to work and placing their children in child care.

At an infancy conference, I once asked the experts how long a mother should stay home with her baby. While one said, "as long as the mother wants to," the consensus was that a mother should stay home, if at all possible, until attachment was consolidated at two to three years of age.

The late psychoanalyst Selma Fraiberg, famous for her intervention work with wounded mothers, would agree: "A baby can tolerate brief separations at two and a half more easily than he could at one year. But prolonged separations for several days will still create anxiety for him. This anxiety is a measure of his love and a measure of his incapacity, still at two and a half, to grasp fully the notion that mother, though not present, must be some place and will certainly return."[43]

Fraiberg believes that while a baby needs his mother most of the time before age three, "around age three, but sometimes later, most children can tolerate a half-day's absence."[44] Once a child has learned to trust his mother, he can transfer some of that trust to others. As stated earlier, a child of three also has the cognitive capacity to know his absent mother will return. Moreover, at this stage of development, a child is interested in playing with other children.

But this may be small comfort to mothers employed ten to twelve hours per day. About this Fraiberg is clear: "When a child spends eleven or twelve hours of his waking day in the care of indifferent custodians, no parent and no educator can say the child's development is being promoted or enhanced, and common sense tells us that children are harmed by indifference."[45]

So, what's a mother to do if she needs to earn money? I suggest she consider part-time employment or working from home (see chapter 8).

THE PART-TIME SOLUTION

Few women can work full time and still have enough energy or presence of mind to be emotionally accessible to their children. Too often they are exhausted, hungry, and irritable when they enter the door at night, wondering what to cook for supper, if anyone fed the dog, and how many chores will need to be done before bedtime.

Part-time employment can be a boon for a mother and for her family's income. When a mother works part time, she is able to keep her skills honed, earn additional income, and provide care for her family. Charlene Canape, author of *The Part-Time Solution,* points out that while being a good mother is a woman's most important job, working part time increases self-esteem and allows a woman to grow professionally should she desire to return to full-time employment.

I said as much to Larry King when he asked in an interview: "And you think the mother should stay home all the time, right?"

"No," I laughed, "but part-time employment is better for children than full-time. It's better for the mother, too." Part-time employment allows a woman to maintain her skills and still go grocery shopping, attend Little League games, volunteer at school and church, and have something left in her emotional bank for her children and husband on a daily basis.

Myriad women find that part-time employment lends structure to their week, adds zest to their lives, and provides essential income. "I have the best of both worlds," says Amy, who leaves her three-year-old with a sitter eighteen hours per week. "As a social worker I'm able to earn half of my old salary and enjoy Jason the rest of the time. Plus, I maintain my professional identity."

Granted, part-time employment has its downside. Joanne Alter writes in *A Part-Time Career for Full-Time You* that part-timers have lower earnings, fewer fringe benefits, limited job possibilities, and fewer promotions. While this is so, Alter points out fields providing great opportunities for part-timers: accounting and word processing.

Susan Dynerman and Lynn Hayes, authors of *The Best Jobs in America for Parents Who Want Careers and Time for Children Too,* believe that a quiet revolution is occurring in this country. Men and women are insisting on work options that include flex-time, shortened work weeks, part-time hours, job sharing, telecommuting, and work done at home. Dynerman and Hayes state that women jump "in and out of the job market like wildfire in response to their families' needs." Corporate America needs to deal with this and offer women flexible work solutions that acknowledge the reality of children in their lives.

But what about the single mother who has fewer options?

MOTHER CARE OR OTHER CARE?

What about the Single Mother?

There are no easy answers for the single mother. Her lot is the hardest of all. I know. For five years I was a single mother, worried about all that my children were missing due to their father's absence. I was also afraid my ex-husband would decide not to send the modest child support check. Fortunately, the girls and I did receive child support regularly. Many single mothers are not so lucky. Too often, a husband flees and leaves nothing behind except wounded children and a mountain of financial obligations. Or women have children out of wedlock, and the children legally have no father.

Thus, the American landscape is populated with millions of struggling single mothers. As of spring 1992, some 9.9 million single mothers had children under the age of twenty-one living with them.[46]

According to Census Bureau data, of the 6.2 million custodial parents awarded child support, only half were fortunate enough to receive what they were due. The rest? About half received partial payments. The rest got nothing at all. *And yet it's that child-support payment that helps lift a woman and her children out of poverty.* Child support is important even though the mean amount of child support received by *all* women in 1992 was $3,011.[47]

What has happened to the idea that fathers help conceive children and then stick around to rear them? We could blame men and excoriate them for abandoning their wives and children—and many men do just that. But women have had a lot to do with the erosion of male commitment to marriage and children.

Beginning in the late sixties when the divorce rate started to escalate, feminists encouraged women to leave lackluster marriages, take the kids, and refuse alimony and child support. Repeatedly, I read that only weak women needed alimony because all self-respecting women needed to work and let their vanishing husbands off the hook. The result? Divorced women and their children rapidly became "the new poor."

Of course, economics are only one facet of the divorce experience. But a Washington, D.C., economist had it right when he said, "Parents who can't afford to maintain their child's predivorce lifestyle can't afford to divorce."

I sympathize with single mothers who must juggle the dual roles of working and parenting alone. I know this is a demanding life. And I believe something must be done to make American divorce laws more equitable to women and children. No-fault divorce has sounded the economic death knell for women and children.

The Never-Married Mother

What about the woman who chooses to have a child although she's unmarried? Celebrities like Madonna, Rosie O'Donnell, and Jodie Foster do it. Why not the rest of us? According to some women in this society, men are an expendable part of the family unit.

I had the curious experience of driving back to the Los Angeles airport after the *Home Show* with three unmarried women: a recent college graduate (the driver), a divorced writer for the *New York Times* who had a twelve-year-old son, and a computer expert who had just adopted a Guatemalan son. The three chatted happily. Then someone said, "Men aren't really necessary. We can support ourselves, and we can adopt children."

Should I rise to this challenge? I wondered. I had an intense head cold and felt physically ill-equipped for any debate. But I couldn't remain silent. "Men are necessary. Children desperately need fathers for self-esteem and achievement." Their response? I was "retrograde," an Ozzie and Harriet throwback.

As I persevered, trying to answer their arguments without anger, I felt growing concern about this popular belief among liberated women that, because they don't need husbands, their children don't need fathers. Psychological research shows that nothing could be further from the truth. Moreover, women with children need the fathers' economic provision, and in the case of divorce, as Judith Wallerstein's *Second Chances* so powerfully shows, children need an ongoing relationship with their fathers to succeed in life.

When a Single Mother Must Work

Since it is a given that the single mother work to supplement her child support check or support her family single-handedly, is it necessary that she work full time outside her home so that her children end up losing both parents at the time of divorce? Some feel they must, but there are other mothers who desire to be with their children so strongly that they start a home-based business.

One mother started a business cleaning houses when her husband left her with three sons ages seven, five, and one. She wanted to keep her baby with her, and she felt she had few other marketable skills. Christine made this venture a success, displaying courage and ingenuity as she paid her bills and spent time with her young children.

During my book tour when I was on radio and television talk shows, I was surprised at how many single mothers called in to say that they were working from home. One mother in Tucson, Arizona, said that she had recently come home because her teenagers were floundering.

"I couldn't continue my high-pressured job and watch my kids mess up their lives," she said. She worked from her home as an accountant.

Another mother called in when I was on the radio in Chicago. She said she worked from home so that she could be more emotionally and physically available to her preschoolers. The interviewer, who admitted that his young son was in day care, said, "Oh, well, you're just lucky." Without missing a beat, this mother replied, "No, I'm not lucky; I'm resourceful. When I knew I was going to have children, I decided I wanted to be the one who would raise them, so I developed marketable skills for a home-based career."

While it is not my intention to heap guilt on single mothers who find they must work, they too need to know how maternal (and paternal) absence affects their children. Children's needs do not change when their family structure changes. Babies still need that one-on-one relationship with their mother—that unhurried time when both learn to know each other. Young children still need that close emotional bond with at least one person in order to develop a conscience, empathy, and a sense of self-worth. Our teens need us to supervise their after-school hours. And this is tough to do if we are gone ten to twelve hours per day and then are tired and harassed when we are home.

I would challenge any man leaving a marriage to give his wife and children their fair share of his income. I would challenge any single mother, if at all possible, to investigate job sharing or part-time employment or to use her wits and ingenuity to turn her skills into profit at home.

ONE WOMAN'S CHANGE OF HEART

Sometimes changing circumstances and a change of heart bring a mother home. When Dana experienced a family move and allowed herself to see what was happening to her toddler, she decided to come home.

Dana, who feels her story is representative of other mothers of young children, was a sales representative for a Fortune 500 company and had a stable job to return to after her first child, Miriam, was born. When her baby was just six weeks old and beginning to establish a routine, Dana went back to work, never dreaming how disruptive this would be to her baby's routine and to their relationship. After all, her baby had already begun to sleep through the night, so Dana thought that Miriam could handle her mother's daily absences just fine.

But when she began her long days at the sitter's house, Miriam cried most nights. "Miriam went ballistic after I went back to work, but I told myself that she was just a difficult baby. Truthfully, I didn't want to think about what was happening to her because my self-image was wrapped up in my job," says Dana.

She and her husband knew something was wrong when Miriam's temper tantrums gained in intensity as she grew older. According to Dana, Miriam was capable of "biting, hitting, kicking, and spitting" for long stretches of time. Also, Dana had a growing awareness that she didn't really know her daughter.

When Miriam was three, the family moved from California to Virginia, and Dana decided not to go to work right away but instead to begin to get in touch with her daughter emotionally. Besides, both mother and daughter were exhausted by their fast-track lifestyle. "We slept for three months," says Dana, "and I spent the early days dealing with Miriam's behavior problems. I remember not getting out of my bathrobe one whole day as I spent hours teaching her *not* to slam the door."

It took Dana nine months to get close to her defiant little

daughter. "Although she was still angry with me, she began responding and allowing me to be physically affectionate. I had tried to be affectionate earlier," says Dana, "but she pushed me away."

Are there residual problems from the early years in substitute care? Dana admits her daughter is still prone to tantrums, and she also suffers from separation anxiety. Each morning when Dana drops her off at school, Miriam needs "twelve kisses and tons of hugs before she is ready to go."

At this point Dana has been home with Miriam for four years, longer than she ever intended to be. What's different about their relationship? Dana feels comfortable with her child and is committed to being there with Miriam over the long haul; Miriam is beginning to trust her mother to meet her emotional needs. When Dana remembers the emotional distance the two experienced and her daughter's rage, she is grateful that she came home when she did. "Because we have been able to repair our relationship, I believe the whole of my daughter's life will be different," says Dana. "I know it will be better."

Not only has she worked hard on repairing her relationship with her bright, sensitive child, but Dana has also had the courage to look at her own parenting history and seek healing.

Final Thoughts

When Dr. James Dobson and I taped the program entitled, "The Value of Motherhood," he shared a story I had never heard before. At one point in the program after we had talked about child care he said, "Well, we lived it. We were going that route, too. I was a student at USC, and we were trying to pay an enormous school bill and struggling to keep the bills paid. My wife was teaching, and I took our little girl, Danae, to a nursery school each day. But one morning I took her there, and she just began crying and weeping. She was about three. She was just clinging to me, saying 'Don't make me go. Don't make me go.' I had to go to work, so I left. But when I picked her up that night, I said, 'Danae, you'll never go back.' So we sold our Volkswagen and ate it. I don't regret it. It allowed Shirley to stay home."

How moving and profound is this deceptively simple story told by America's most famous psychologist—a father who actually *heard* his daughter's cries and responded, even though the response entailed a lifestyle change and no little personal sacrifice. Sadly, we live in an era when too many parents are deaf to their children's cries and when all too few are willing to make the requisite sacrifices to rear reasonably whole children.

Yet when all is said and done, what truly matters in life? The love and affection that roll across the generations through our children, or how much money we leave behind?

Chapter Four

DO OLDER KIDS NEED MOTHER AT HOME?

*Today's children are living
a childhood of firsts.*

RICHARD LOUV

I n her 1998 book, *A Tribe Apart,* Patricia Hersch profiled eight teenagers who live in an affluent area of northern Virginia. In an interview for *Newsweek* magazine she stated: "Every kid I talked to at length eventually came around to saying without my asking that they wished they had more adults in their lives, especially their parents."[1]

While American teenagers may long for more parental time, currently millions have parents who deem them old enough to come home daily to empty houses—to microwave frozen dinners or to feast at McDonald's with peers. But children and teenagers cannot survive psychologically and spiritually without sufficient parental time and attention. And when we become parents in absentia, requiring our children to raise themselves, they, and eventually we, suffer.

According to *Newsweek,* of all the problems that teens cite, loneliness heads the list.[2] One study of 7,000 teens found that, on average, teens spend three and a half hours alone each day and only 25 percent have a mother at home when they walk through the door after school. Is it any wonder that only 35 percent of the

97

teenagers interviewed by *Newsweek* felt understood by their families? While 85 percent said that mom cared about them a lot, only 58 percent said the same about good old dad. How do lonely teens fill up their time? Some 98 percent watch television for eleven or more hours each week.

I think it is safe to say that many older children in this country are not faring well. In fact, Dr. Joseph Zanga, president of the American Academy of Pediatrics, believes that the emotional health of America's older children is worsening.[3] Writing in the *American Academy of Pediatric News*, Dr. Zanga had this to say: "By every measure our children are *physically* (italics his) healthier today than they have ever been. But their emotional health is poor and getting worse. That's reflected by the rising tide of substance abuse, violence, sexually transmitted diseases, and teenage pregnancies."[4]

WHAT'S THE BOTTOM LINE?

So what's the bottom line? Our children need our time, attention, and presence to grow well into themselves. They need someone at home who's passionately concerned about them, not just during the early years, but also over the long haul. Even beyond infancy and toddlerhood, children need *someone* to be present during most of the hours they are at home. That *someone* needs to be available on a daily basis to educate, love, nurture, discipline, and guide. My conviction is that that *someone* needs to be mom.

If a mother wants to rear a child who will leave home with a sturdy sense of self, she needs to be there for him during the years he is growing up. Mothering is simply not a job she can turn over to baby-sitters or teachers or to the child himself, especially in this culture. With drugs, empty houses, violent video games, Internet pornography, and sex all too readily available, how can parents be naive enough to believe that their children will escape temptation and harm?

Coming of Age in America

It's tough to grow up in the land of the free these days. In *Childhood's Future*, journalist Richard Louv writes movingly about the lack of nurture in modern family life. A columnist for the *San Diego Union*, Louv interviewed some three thousand parents, children, teachers, and other professionals across America. His findings are sobering: America's children feel a pervasive sense of sadness due to a fragmented family life. Many of the children Louv interviewed lamented the absence of family meals, family rituals, the loneliness of coming home to an empty house. Many felt abandoned by their superstressed, superbusy parents. A common refrain among the parents was, "I'll play with you tomorrow."[5]

Said one third-grade girl, "My parents say, 'I'll spend time with you tomorrow,' but they don't."

Said a boy, "My dad works morning till night, and my mom often works afternoons and nights, so they say, 'Tomorrow we're gonna do something,' but tomorrow comes and they go to work."[6]

The children in Louv's book spoke poignantly of parents who left home for errands and their own pursuits just as the children returned home from school, and of turning to gangs or early sexual partners for companionship and solace.

One child was mature enough to recognize that his younger sibling was out of control because their mother worked during her second son's early years and because of their father's frequent absences. Said this boy, "My brother's morals and mine are different because my parents brought me up, and my brother is getting brought up by a lot of his friends, along with me."[7]

According to Louv, increasing numbers of American children are raising themselves. He calls those who come home daily to empty houses, "children who own themselves." Although he notes that older children are generally positive about self-care, he says parents are embarrassed when they pick up their kids at the school or library late in the day. Many sense judgment from the disapproving librarian or teacher. One librarian Louv interviewed spoke of her unease when she locked the library doors at night while youngsters waited in the dark for working parents to pick them up.

THE LATCHKEY CHILD

Not all children like coming home to empty houses. I certainly didn't. From the age of seven onward I came home to an empty apartment after school. In her defense, my mother was a widow who felt she had to work. Since we had no car, she often walked the two miles home on her split-shift days as a telephone operator just to be with me when I arrived home after school. I was grateful on those occasions when Mother was home and I did not have to be alone. Unfortunately, she would often have to walk back to work while I kept my lonely and frightening vigil at home alone, sometimes until ten o'clock at night.

I can distinctly remember sitting on the floor in the living room of our caboose-style duplex, looking back through the bedroom and kitchen to the back porch on warm summer nights. A nine-year-old home alone, I was ostensibly reading a book, but I was ever aware that it was late at night and that only flimsy latches on the front and back screens protected me from nighttime prowlers. My heart thumped loudly as I listened to the noises of the night.

Days alone were better. After tossing my books on my

bed, I would grab a snack and join the neighborhood children on the street outside, riding a friend's bike up and down the hill. But no matter how sunny the weather outside, our empty duplex was ever in shadows when I turned the key in the door to let myself in. And I felt fear stab my heart as I quickly dropped my books and searched under the bed, in the closet, and behind doors before I relaxed. Since this was the late forties, I had no phone friend to call to share my news and worries.

"Hello, Phone Friend."

"My teacher said to call if I hear a strange noise."

"What did you hear?"

"The door knocked, and I thought somebody was in there."

"Are you on your own right now?"

"Yeah."

"Do you want me to hold on while you check the doors and windows?"

"Yeah." A couple of minutes pass.

"I'm back. There's nobody there."

"I think you were very sensible to call."

"Okay, 'bye."⁸

Sometimes I called my mother at work, but most days I told no one about that day's events. I became a girl who seldom revealed her private thoughts or feelings. I certainly did not share my feelings with either my girlfriends or my preoccupied mother. Sometimes I shared my heart with my sister when I visited my grandparents' farm where Sandy lived, but most of the time I hid my vulnerable self behind a wall of silence or superficial friendliness.

I did glean one important legacy from all those years home alone. When my own children entered school (after my

DO OLDER KIDS NEED MOTHER AT HOME?

values had changed at L'Abri, and I became more emotionally involved in mothering), I determined that they would never become latchkey children. I would be present most of the time when they walked through the door, so they would have a mother to talk to. I believed that any child, whether seven or seventeen, needed someone to listen to words spoken from the heart. Since I didn't have that growing up, I made sure my girls did.

Besides, I knew that once children entered school, they became citizens of a rough, tough world, and few, if any, can manage all the assaults on self-esteem by themselves.

SCHOOL: A WAR ZONE

Jenny, a tall, thin girl with thick glasses, walks to her junior high school blocks away from her home in a New Jersey lakeside community. She becomes aware that two girls are following her. Slowing down, she decides to wait and walk with them, until they chant in unison, "Jenny, Jenny, who cut your hair? Bet you got it cut by a lawn mower." Stung, Jenny speeds up, hoping she can disappear inside the school building before she starts to cry.

Henry, eleven, has a facial scar from an automobile accident when he was five. One day as he walks into his fifth-grade classroom, another boy hails him, "Hey, Scarface. Where'd you get that ugly scar?" Henry slumps in his seat and tries to become invisible.

Roland, fourteen, boards a school bus on a fall afternoon in rural Ohio. His unruly hair sticks up from the crown of his head. "Alfalfa, Alfalfa," teases one of the popular girls. Roland's heart beats fast, and he pretends not to notice. Others smell the scent of wounded prey and begin chanting, "Alfalfa, Alfalfa, just look at your hair!"

Nancy, twelve, sits down at her table in the lunchroom with her four friends, only to be told by the ring leader that she can't sit with them anymore. The other girls giggle. Nancy feels a stab of fear. Where can she go? Cliques occupy all of the other tables. She remains seated beside the very girls who have just rejected her and silently, painfully, eats her lunch.

Don recently took me to the small town of Clinton, Illinois, to show me the grain silo beside the railroad tracks where the twins, Merle and Berle, used to wait to beat him up after school. They only did this once because Don later out-witted them, but he clearly remembers the fear he tasted. And my husband is in his sixties!

These are real tales from the war zone called school. It's the nature of the beast for some children to torment others mercilessly. British writer William Golding captured the heart-lessness of children in *Lord of the Flies,* and we have recently witnessed a gruesome massacre at Columbine High School in Littleton, Colorado, where the jocks tormented the "Trench Coat Mafia." The word from the school front is that, as parents have removed themselves increasingly from their children's lives, physical assaults and verbal abuse from peers have only gotten worse.

Our children and teens need us to occasionally protect them from abusive peers and to shore up a wounded self-esteem. Psychologist David Elkind told a radio audience that he had once trimmed the edges of his picture in what he thought was an artistic manner—artistic, that is, until his teacher said, "Why did you ruin it?" Elkind, a professor of child development at Tufts University, said, "I never took up art again."

If we are not there when our school-age children return home, we may never hear about the pressures or triumphs of the day. Many mothers find that by the time they arrive home from work, aerobics, or volunteer activities at five or six o'clock, their children's hearts are closed to them. Don used to ask the girls to wait until dinnertime so he didn't have to hear warmed-over news. He felt, and rightly so, that Holly and Kristen were reluctant to recount the news of their day twice, having told me earlier. I explained that Holly and Kristen couldn't sit on hurt feelings or exuberance for hours after coming home.

But that's what happens when a mother is too often absent. The child then learns to internalize his feelings. Said one successful executive who has difficulty with intimacy in his marriage, "I was always alone in the house. Consequently, I never felt my parents were interested in me. They both worked long hours and had a lot to do when they finally got home. Now it's hard for me to tell anyone what's going on inside."

I believe that one of the most valuable gifts any mother can give her child is the sense that she cares passionately about him and that the child's concerns are her concerns. If a mother does this, she will not only be emotionally close to her child, but she will also be creating a foundation for closeness in adolescence when children naturally pull away from parents. When a child feels that his parents care and want to know about his inner life, he is less susceptible later to drug abuse and self-destructive behavior.

DRUG USE AND EMOTIONALLY DISTANT PARENTS

Harvard psychiatrist Armand Nicholi has conducted research on drug users. He says that young people who use drugs have one thing in common: emotional distance from their parents.[9] Also, drug users spend a lot of time away from home, relying on peers for emotional support. Other studies of drug users, says Nicholi, show that they differ markedly from nonusers in that drug users come from homes where parents smoke, drink, or use psychoactive drugs.

Nicholi believes that when children use drugs (and some begin to use marijuana as early as sixth grade), it's because they feel lonely or isolated and suffer from "a moral and spiritual void."

"In essence, people take drugs to alter or escape from a less than tolerable reality," says Nicholi, "and to meet intense emotional needs."[10] Where do these "intense emotional needs" originate? Nicholi blames parental absence due to divorce, death, or time-demanding jobs. Parental absence contributes to "the anger, the rebelliousness, low self-esteem, depression, and antisocial behavior" of the drug user.[11]

Other research found that eighth graders who were home alone for eleven or more hours per week were *twice* as likely to engage in heavy use of alcohol, tobacco, and marijuana than those teens who had a parent home after school. This pattern persisted even when the sex, social status, and ethnicity of the child were considered.[12]

In spite of such movies as *Home Alone* and *Home Alone 2* and the greater cultural acceptance of latchkey children, children are *not* infinitely resilient. While the nineties witnessed the emergence of the myth of the resilient child who can rear himself, excel academically, secure admission to an Ivy League college, and make his absent parents proud, reality presents a different story. Bored, scared, and lonely at home, teens often fill up the void with self-destructive behavior. One boy who turned to speed when his parents divorced and later remarried suffers neurological damage into his thirties. He feels the price he continues to pay for his years of drug use is inordinately high.

DO OLDER KIDS NEED MOTHER AT HOME?

MOTHER AS FIRST TEACHER

But a mother is not only a sensitive, empathic presence to keep her teenagers on course, she is also her child's first teacher and, along with the child's father, the transmitter of family values and eternal verities.

I determined when Holly and Kristen were young to teach them about life, and one good way to do this was to expose them to excellent children's literature. Great literature not only helps in character formation, but it hones the intellect as well. As a former teacher, I knew the best way to foster reading and writing skills was to read aloud to the children as well as to provide an intellectually stimulating environment. I was better able to do this, of course, when I stopped working full time and could concentrate on my children's needs.

When each girl was one year of age, I sat beside her on the couch and opened the beautifully illustrated *Mother Goose.* I began my children's education with nursery rhymes. Sometimes I made up tunes and sang their favorite rhymes. I read as long as the girls would sit still. Eventually this evolved into the ritual of reading for a half-hour before bedtime. Over the years we worked our way through anthologies of Bible stories, poetry, C. S. Lewis's Narnia tales, and classics such as *Heidi, Little Women,* and *The Wind in the Willows,* to name a few. I loved those warm, happy times when the girls leaned into me, and I could feel the pressure of their warm, cuddly bodies as we read stories that no one had ever read to me. What a marvelous opportunity to fill in some of the holes in my own education, and what a nurturing experience it proved for all of us!

After Don and I married, he joined us for the nightly reading ritual, taking his turn reading aloud. We sat through years of evenings, four upon the couch, sitting close together as he and I read *Two Years Before the Mast, The Swiss Family Robinson, A Christmas Carol,* and *Robinson Crusoe,* among others. When he read *Uncle Tom's Cabin,* the girls and I wept over Tom's death. This ritual of reading aloud continued year after year until the girls reached junior high and mutinied. "We can read books ourselves," they proclaimed.

Now in this season of my life I have the pleasure of reading aloud to little Austin. He loves books, and when he visits our mountain retreat, he climbs onto my sleigh bed, books in hand, chanting "Mimi, read books!" So we read and read and read again. Austin, at thirty months of age, already knows his colors and the alphabet, and he can count to fifteen and back again. He loves to name the plants and wild animals for me in his jungle book. "Go-riga...octopus...anemone...bobcat...sea horse...dolphin...rhinoceros," he says patiently, pointing to the pictures. And when we finish reading, we sing several of those simple children's songs I once taught his mother.

I love reading to my grandson because I know just how important good literature is for character formation and in teaching skills. Reading builds vocabulary, develops imagination, enlarges comprehension of ideas and concepts, shapes attitudes, and teaches values.

Years ago, when I taught English in various high schools and, later, writing and literature in several colleges, those students who were good readers were also good writers. And those who read seldom watched television. In one class of high school juniors in Middletown, Connecticut, I had some deplorable writers. When I asked what they did after school, they all said they went home to lounge in front of the television and while away the hours. Of course, I had them write and rewrite essays for me, but on the home front I sold our television and never bought one again until Kristen, my younger daughter, had, like her sister, achieved a stellar score on the SAT exam.

What did this emphasis on reading do for my daughters? By the time Holly and Kristen entered school, each had a jump start academically. Both were in gifted programs throughout their years in school (atypical for children of divorce), and Holly was one of four (and the only girl) chosen to attend the Governor's School for the Gifted after her junior year in high school. After high school, both girls entered the University of Virginia as Echols Scholars, an honor bestowed on 10 percent of the incoming freshman class. Kristen graduated Phi Beta Kappa and Holly bested my Georgetown G.P.A. when she got her graduate degree from American University in film and communications. Do I believe that reading aloud daily had anything to do with this? You bet I do. Genes, the cognitive research shows, only account for so much of brain development. Then environment steps in and takes over.

I share this personal account not only because I am a proud mother and grandmother who values the education of the mind, but also to show that reading is foundational to academic success.

I am not suggesting that all children will become scholars if they grow up in families that value books and reading. Our children possess different gifts, just as we do. But whether children have mechanical, musical, mathematical, athletic, or artistic skills, all can profit from a time of structured family reading. The person who is exposed to great literature early on will come of age with a larger worldview, an appreciation for the arts, and an understanding of human nature he otherwise might not have. And as he is exposed to ideas that have shaped Western civilization, as well as to heroes and heroines who have resisted temptation and made good choices, not only will his character

HOME BY CHOICE

be influenced by this exposure, but he is also likely to read to his own children when he becomes a parent.

In addition to reading aloud, when the girls were four and six, I bought each a weekly paperback. I was influenced in this decision by a friend who is now a university professor in New Zealand. One day I asked Bill how his parents had fostered his intellectual development. He said that, though they had never attended college, they had wanted him to excel academically and had encouraged him by buying him a book every week.

Though I was a divorced mother at the time, I took the girls to a bookstore every Friday and bought each a paperback of her choice. (Of course, I guided their selections.) When I eventually could no longer afford this practice, we visited the library frequently and subscribed to excellent children's magazines, such as *Highlights* and *Cricket*.

But all of this takes *time*. Family time. Personal time. If parents rush in at 6:00 P.M., tired and hungry, and the children are waiting with clamorous needs, it is unlikely the family will linger at dinner for a leisurely time of reading aloud. Besides, who will have had the presence of mind to obtain the books in the first place? A family needs to have leisure, structure, and a certain peacefulness to do something as simple as reading aloud each evening.

Thus, on-site, interested mothers oversee their children's intellectual development, offer help with homework, and give their children the message that they have caring, involved parents. This is important if children are to achieve academically. Studies of maternal employment generally find that sons of employed mothers perform less well academically than sons of full-time mothers. Why is this so? Boys may need more guidance and supervision than their "time poor" working mothers are able to provide. Psychologist Ann Crouter and her colleagues write that to achieve academically, a child needs "an effective monitor" who knows about his day and is aware of his experiences.[13]

Homeschooling Parents

Since some parents are not satisfied with educating their children informally, myriad families are engaged in homeschooling their children to foster creativity, independence, and academic success. One family in California has received national press attention for its efforts. David and Micki Colfax were so successful in teaching their children at home that their three oldest sons—Grant, Drew, and Reed—were accepted at Harvard.[14] Encouraging their children to assume responsibility and learn independence, David and Micki fostered each child's intellectual interests. The parents guided their children's reading, provided a large library at home, and encouraged them to use the public library. They helped their children take their interests and run with them. Said Drew, who built his own telescope, "If we had any sort of interest, if we didn't already have the materials we would get them."[15]

Cecelia Gleason, who used to run a U.S. Senator's office, has homeschooled Janise and Ryan for years. Not only have both performed well on standardized tests, but they are also thoughtful, polite, engaging teenagers. At seventeen, Ryan is a regional champion at Bible memorization, having committed entire books of the Bible to memory. His mother is his coach, and she chauffeurs Ryan and other homeschoolers from their home in rural Purcellville, Virginia, to Pennsylvania monthly to compete. Cecelia, who quit her job on Capitol Hill when Ryan was born, used to worry that she wouldn't be an effective homeschooling mom, but her kids have proved otherwise.

DISCIPLINING OUR CHILDREN

Of course, more is involved in a child's development than just intellectual stimulation. Children need to develop physically, emotionally, spiritually, and morally. I have written extensively of a mother's role in these various aspects of child development in *The Power of Mother Love*. Since mothers teach their children to be human, theirs is a time-consuming and challenging job with consequences that last a lifetime.

After a child has established attachment relationships with his parents, he needs to become a disciplined human. He will learn as his parents patiently teach him the rudiments of self-discipline and as they model disciplined lives before him.

Although children need to be disciplined by their fathers also, the mother at home is a primary source of discipline for her children during the workday. She is on-site, so she is elected to shape her children's behavior. If she doesn't, her life will be chaotic. Who can wait until Daddy comes home when Junior decorates the walls of the family room with his new magic markers? Mom is in charge, whether she wants to be or not. If she does a good job, the reward *is* a well-behaved child who likes himself and is well liked by others. If she doesn't, she will help create a hellion who is unpopular with his peers and who will have a hard time controlling his impulses as an adolescent, giving his parents grief.

When a parent fails to control his child's behavior, this may signify that the parent has minimal investment in parenting and is putting his energies elsewhere.[16] Or it may mean that the parents grew up in families that failed to establish healthy boundaries, so they feel guilty putting boundaries in place.

Poorly disciplined children don't believe their parents are committed to them, and most feel unloved. I have a friend, a

111

DO OLDER KIDS NEED MOTHER AT HOME?

lawyer educated at Dartmouth, who was turned over to baby-sitters for rearing while his mother played golf and his father poured his time into a successful medical practice. "I never really felt my parents loved me," said Zachery. "They seldom disciplined me for *anything*. I was just an ornament in their middle-aged lives."

It takes time and energy to love and discipline our children, starting when they are about fifteen months old. I had no idea when my babies were born just how many hours I would spend in the next eighteen years shaping their behavior. Yet what better person than Mom to teach them to speak respectfully to adults, to care for their pets responsibly, to clean their rooms, to handle their angry feelings, to develop good study habits, to obey curfews, and to show compassion? So most of the time, especially in their early years, I was that someone. I found Dr. James Dobson's *Dare to Discipline* an invaluable tool when the girls were young, and now I see my daughter Kristen pouring over *The New Dare to Discipline,* trying to find the magic bullet for her strong-willed little boy.

I watched the mother of a toddler in a restaurant recently. The boy sat quietly next to his older sister until he had eaten, and then he started to climb over the back of the booth. His good-natured mother quietly grasped his leg and placed him back in his booster chair.

"There, Brad," she said. "Remember? We're working on good manners today. We don't climb in restaurants. Besides, I have a gold star for your chart at home if you sit quietly until I finish." Then this wise mother deftly whisked a box of magic markers and paper out of her backpack for her energetic boy.

Whether you have a toddler or a teenager, there are some simple principles that produce good behavior. *First,* mean what you say and be consistent. Wishy-washy parenting produces wild kids. *Second,* reward good behavior (praise, stickers, stars) and weed out bad behavior (time out, spanking, or withdrawal of privileges for older kids). *Third,* rear likeable children—kids you can be proud of. If you don't like your kids, chances are, others won't either. *Fourth,* remember we get the kids we deserve. The responsibility of rearing well-mannered kids rests squarely on our shoulders.

Of course, when fathers are home, they need to take over the task of disciplining their children. Not only do mothers need a break, but clinicians know that children have greater self-control when they have involved fathers who are authoritative and give firm but not harsh discipline. Fathers are even more important as disciplinarians when the children become obstreperous teens. Then fathers protect their wives from mouthy daughters and make their strapping sons toe the line.

Teaching Values

Have you ever wondered why some children have the same values as their parents, while others rebel and become diametrically opposed to everything their parents hold dear? Psychologists have found that this doesn't happen by chance.

Psychologist Kevin MacDonald says children who have a warm, affectionate relationship with their parents will adopt their parents' values, while those who have grown up in conflict-ridden homes subject to a daily barrage of negativism will not.[17] Yet when children and adolescents reject their parents' values, they are at risk for later behavior problems. Adrift, alienated, and rebellious, these young people tend to be isolated as well.

This whole area of values becomes strategic when our children begin to walk the high school corridors with adult bodies and raging hormones. Gone is the adoring daughter of the latency period, gone the dutiful, quietly obedient son. Instead our adolescent sons and daughters are often mercurial, difficult, and intractable.

Norman Kiell suggests that adolescence is a psychological state "as definitely characterized by domestic explosions and rebellions as typhoid is marked by fevers."[18] And while the hormones in adolescent children rage, parents are themselves prey to midlife angst. At the same time an adolescent is struggling with his identity, his parents are confronting their mortality and renegotiating their marriages. This often creates a volatile mix.

Yet what our teenagers need is for us to hold the line, recognizing that while adolescence is a time of turbulence, it is also the time when identity is forged. Psychoanalyst Erik Erikson wrote in *Childhood and Society* that adolescence is a psychosocial stage when adolescents are involved in a difficult identity crisis. Erikson believed that creating a sense of identity was so difficult that most adolescents exhibited some degree of psychopathology.[19]

Adolescent Depression

Today all too many adolescents in our society are struggling with emotional problems. Some adolescent depression is normative because self-esteem drops precipitously at age twelve and slowly begins an upward climb, reaching some kind of stability at age eighteen.[20] Also, girls begin to menstruate and suffer from hormonal fluctuations with accompanying mood changes. But the level of depression we are witnessing today among American children and teenagers is unprecedented. The *Wall Street Journal* states that in 1996 five hundred thousand children and teenagers received a prescription for either Prozac, Paxil, or Zoloft.[21] This is serious business because no research currently exists that tests the safety of antidepressant usage with children. Yet both parents and some physicians would seemingly rather use powerful drugs with troubled youth than deal with the root causes of the depression.

I worked with depressed patients for years; in fact, it was my specialty as a psychotherapist. I know that when someone is depressed, he has overwhelming feelings of helplessness, hopelessness, and hostility. He feels inferior, isolated, and alone in his pain as he stares out on a world that is unbelievably bleak and lonely. He may also be preoccupied with thoughts of death and fantasies of retribution against those who have hurt him. To make matters worse, the depressed person is often suicidal.

Now I need to say that some psychologists believe that ideas about suicide are common during adolescence and not just among depressed teens. Many teenagers feel inferior as they struggle with questions of identity, sibling rivalry, or separating from parents.

In fact, one study of 407 high school students found that 32 percent of the males and 46 percent of the females had thought of taking their own lives. And the females in this study reported more emotional problems, lower self-esteem, and less parental support than did the males.[22] Other surveys of high school students indicate that one in four considers suicide each year.[23] But why do we think it's "normal" for teens to ponder suicide? What has happened to families in this country to foster this morbid preoccupation among our children?

Psychiatrist Larry Brain, director of Child and Adolescent Services at the Washington, D.C., Psychiatric Institute, believes adolescents today have greater stresses to deal with than adolescents of an earlier era. As proof, he cites the changing family structure, dual career marriages, divorce, and lack of extended family.[24] He adds that many young people feel alienated and detached from their families as well as from society.

Which adolescents are at risk for suicide? Those who have lost parents early in life (due to death or divorce), those who have no strong inner core or sense of self, those who are frightened by life, and those who were maternally deprived are particularly vulnerable. These teenagers may become walking time bombs. Also, adolescents with perfectionistic parents whose standards are impossible to meet are at risk. Some adolescents snap under the strain, feeling they must get A's in every academic subject to please their demanding parents. Others who are at risk include loners who feel empty inside, substance abusers, and those who are accident-prone.[25]

At-risk teenagers often come from families that have severe marital conflict. Fathers are usually absent or ineffectual. Moreover, one or both parents may be alcoholics who utterly fail to meet the children's needs for emotional support.[26]

Given that adolescence is an increasingly stressful and confusing time, this is no time for Mom and Dad to retreat and retrench. Nor is it a time for Mom to be so involved in her career or volunteerism that she has too little time and energy to stay the course. If we either cave in to our adolescents' demands or absent ourselves from their lives, we force our kids to seek solace from their peer group. As one high school teacher says, "I don't believe kids turn to their peers because they are close to them or even because they like them that much. Sometimes they go to their peers by default."

WHAT TEENS NEED

What teenagers need is a strong parental coalition that can stand firm in the face of adolescent misbehavior. This is hard to provide since parents, who have been "dethroned" by their teenagers, are bombarded daily by their adolescents' fluctuating moods. Yet a united front is essential.[27]

We cannot give up even if some days we want to. Especially then our children need us to be emotionally available, to hold firm. Though we give our older children greater slack, we still need to know where they are after school, whom they are with, and when they will return home. Said one mother, "I believe in giving my son greater freedom; then if he handles that responsibly, I give him some more. You can't be rigid and authoritarian with teenagers." This same mother is present when her son walks through the door in the afternoon because she knows an empty house can be a dangerous place.

Parents are naive if they assume that their teenagers will never use the empty house for drugs or afternoon sex. Remember the divorced mother in the movie *Parents*? Conned by the wild thumps of her daughter's heavy metal music, this mom wises up when the local photo processor mistakenly swaps her daughter's Kodak-recorded coitus for her bank promotion photos.

Having observed adolescents and listened to them over the years, I know that many find empty houses a convenient place to engage in self-destructive behavior. Consequently, I made sure I was home most afternoons. Did I distrust my daughters? Once a teenager myself, I remember how seductive and intense peer pressure can be. I did not know then what psychologists have discovered—that parents, not peers, are the primary moral influence for their teens. Had I known this, I would have relaxed but still would have chosen to be home when the girls arrived after school.

Not that either girl always appreciated my presence. I

remember having a conversation with Kristen when she was in the tenth grade and using her abundant energies to gain popularity. She told me in a snippy tone, which she knew would infuriate me, "Why don't you go to work full time? Most of my friends' mothers work."

I looked at her and grinned. "Well, for one thing I'm working on my doctorate in psychology so I can better understand you. But why don't you want me around? Is it that you don't like having me at home keeping track of your activities?"

"Right!" she said, smiling.

"But you need me here, whether you know it or not," I said, giving her a hug.

And so I manned the fort, even after I returned to graduate school. I simply planned my schedule around the girls' after-school activities. This paid off in spades when Kristen became a senior and went through a period of turmoil with several of her friends. For weeks she and they were estranged, and I, who had earlier been a pariah, became a valued support player. Often when she roared up the driveway in our old Suburu after school during that period, Kris needed me to apply first aid to her wounded ego.

During her freshman year in college, Kris said to me, "Mom, I'm glad you were home during that time. I really needed you. I hated it on those rare days when I drove up the driveway, and your car was gone. If you hadn't been there for me, I don't know what I would have done."

Would Kris have been okay if I had been absent every afternoon? Maybe. I had *been there* for her and Holly for years. But she was under great pressure from her peers to engage in self-destructive behavior, and I didn't know the full extent of this at the time. In any event, I'm glad I was home during those years to reinforce the values of abstinence and sexual purity for my girls, to encourage them to excel academically, and to be a friend. Besides, I wouldn't have missed the chance to deepen the bond with my daughters for the world. And the fact that we phone each other long distance nearly every day has probably grown out of those daily, after-school conversations.

As you man the fort and become CEO of your at-home empire, you need to understand why your culture gives your so little encouragement and support. You need to know why mothers at home in America ever experienced such a massive fall from grace.

DO OLDER KIDS NEED MOTHER AT HOME?

Chapter Five

FALL FROM GRACE

What I have seen in many full-time mothers gives me
great pride in women. It has made me see
that they come through the
very difficult task of raising children riding only on a deep belief
that what they are doing is worthy and important.

DEBORAH FALLOWS, PH.D.

For almost four decades, the mother at home has experienced a massive fall from grace. In their press for equality of the sexes, feminists, beginning in the sixties, launched a wholesale assault on marriage and motherhood that continues today.

It began in 1963 with the publication of Betty Friedan's *The Feminine Mystique,* in which Friedan stated that home was a prison for all those mothers in suburbia who, having devoted themselves to child care, still felt empty inside and unfulfilled. Friedan wrote that many American women in the fifties and early sixties suffered from "a problem that has no name," which produced feelings of restlessness, loneliness, and desperation.[1] Friedan felt that being "just a housewife" destroyed women's potential and caused brain rot. That she hit a nerve was evidenced by the media sensation this suburban wife and mother caused and by the subsequent huge book sales. Once Friedan had delivered her broadside on housewifery, it wasn't long before motherhood came under attack, and the mother at home, once the keeper of the family dream, came to be regarded as a societal pariah.

Listen to psychologist Michael Lamb articulate the eighties' view of the mother at home: "Just a generation ago, for example, the working mother (especially one with young children) was considered selfishly derelict in her maternal responsibility and her husband (if there was one) was considered a shamefully inadequate provider and/or a weak husband because he 'permitted' his wife to work."[2]

Lamb stated that any woman who wanted to maintain any feelings of self-worth felt that she must be employed in order to do so. He wrote, "Especially in professional and middle class circles, it is often rather shameful to admit to being 'only a housewife and mother.'"[3] He warned that educated women just might become overprotective mothers if they stayed home too long with growing children who needed them less.

Writer Anne Roiphe, an early feminist and mother, states in her book *Fruitful* that the term "just a housewife" became "as dirty and derogatory a term as 'spinster' had once been." Roiphe adds, "In some feminist circles children were plucked from their place of honor in their mothers' lives and seen as albatrosses hanging from the neck."[4]

Not only did early feminists view children as incredible burdens, but giving birth was considered a curse. "Pregnancy is barbaric," wrote Shulamith Firestone in her radical treatise *The Dialectic of Sex*. Roiphe states that once the radical feminists started churning out their diatribes against marriage and mothering, it wasn't long before the "sugary sweet image of motherhood had been debunked, de-aproned, dethroned."[5]

How well I remember the early feminist onslaught on housewifery and mothering. When I initially read Friedan's book, I was married to my first husband, a young physician-

HOME BY CHOICE

in-training. At the time, I was teaching at a local college to help support the three of us while farming Holly out to a succession of baby-sitters. I remember giving assent to many of Friedan's ideas because I was then committed to balancing career and motherhood. Of course, at that time, I had no idea that my own restlessness at home and diminished sense of worth during the early months when I stayed home with Holly had anything at all to do with my early life history. That would come years later.

After my two years at London L'Abri and remarriage, I made the commitment to be home with the girls, but it wasn't easy. Don and I made significant financial sacrifices, and when I read women's magazines and news dailies, I often felt devalued by my culture and desperately alone, which robbed me of a lot of joy. I wonder if Friedan ever anticipated that she would increase the loneliness and desperation of those mothers who wanted to stay home, when this was the very disease she said she was trying to cure.

At that time we lived in a small lakeside community in northwest New Jersey, and from my home I watched the cars head out in the morning for the "real world" of the office, while I headed for my dining room table to write. (Eight books later I still choose to write at my dining room table.) Although I knew in my heart that my children needed my emotional availability and my presence, it was hard to stand against cultural pressures. Whenever I faltered, Don encouraged me to be wholehearted about my mothering and to trust my perception that the girls needed far more love, time, and attention than I had received from my harried, employed single mother.

In time, I mothered my children from a sense of conviction that arose from the deepest part of my being, and this eventually made me strong. Strong enough to pursue a Ph.D.

in my forties so that I could take on the feminists whether on national television talk shows or in public policy debates. Strong enough to write and speak about a politically incorrect topic called day care and not care about pleasing others. Strong enough to fire an oncologist and surgeon who told me that I would die if I went the alternative medical route for cancer treatment and did not take their drugs of choice.

I owe a lot to those years at home when my convictions were continually tested and tried by fire.

A Sea Change Is Coming

Fortunately, a sea change is coming in American attitudes toward the mother at home, and women of my daughters' generation are not only finding more compatriots at home, but they feel less stigmatized for choosing to stay home. The sea change started in the midnineties and quietly continues in the new millennium as the ranks of mothers at home swell and as my daughters' generation espouses little interest in feminist ideology. While this is so, print media and New York City publishing houses, those bastions of unmarried female feminists and working mothers, would have us believe that most mothers are in the workplace and that only those who couldn't make it at the office are hiding out at home.

Most Mothers Still Stay Home

Even though the mother at home has been devalued for decades, and women's magazines and newspapers would have her believe she is part of a vanishing breed, is she home alone?

Sara, mother of baby Josh, alternates between discouragement and anger when she reads in her women's magazines or hears newscaster Tom Brokaw say that some 62 percent of all mothers of children eighteen and under are in the workforce. "I'm twenty-five," she says softly, "and already I've become an anachronism."

But *are* the majority of mothers in the workplace? Hardly. In fact, the 1996 Bureau of Census Report, "Who's Minding the Preschoolers?" indicates that mothers *still* provide daily care for 53 percent of the 20.5 million children under the age of five in America today.[6] When we look at the data on children cared for in a tag team arrangement with mom and dad supplying the child care, then some 61 percent of all preschoolers are still cared for by their parents.[7]

As for older children, nonemployed mothers at home care for 39 percent (21.9 million) of the children in this country between the ages of 5 and 14. Thus, mothers at home are faithfully providing care for 32.1 million children (or 41.8 percent) of America's 76.6 million children under the age of 15.[8] Let's hear it for moms!

As for the media's attempt to have us believe that no self-respecting woman is at home all day with her children, sometimes we have to become sleuths to find out the true situation. First, we need to understand just how the Department of Labor defines maternal employment. DOL considers a mother to be employed if she works as little as one hour per week, if she works from home or on the family farm, if she provides child care for other mothers in her own home, or if she is employed full time for any period of the year. That means that a mother could work forty hours a week during the Christmas holidays and still be classified by the DOL as a working mother. So that's how the overall working mother statistic gets to be so high. What is more, Census Bureau data indicate that out of 26.4 million married mothers with children, some 15.9 million either stay home with their children full time or work only part time.[9]

What Do Mothers Want?

So there's comfort for Sara and for all the other mothers who temporarily put their career aspirations on hold in order to be at home with their children. And there's even more comforting news on the home front. During the nineties, *poll after poll indicated that parents want more time at home with their children, not more time in the office.*

For example, in a 1997 Wirthlin Worldwide survey conducted for the Family Research Council, 1,004 adults were asked what type of child care was best for preschoolers. An overwhelming majority said that mother care was the most desirable form of child care. The least desirable form of child care according to the respondents? You guessed it—center-based day care.

Then in May 1997, the Pew Research Center surveyed 1,101 American women, and 41 percent of those surveyed said that a traditional family with an employed father and a stay-at-home mother was best for kids. Only 17 percent of the women polled felt it was beneficial for children and society to have Mom in the workforce.

When *Parents* magazine polled readers in May 1996, 43 percent of the 18,000 mothers surveyed said they would prefer to stay home, and 68 percent of the working mothers said they did not feel they had enough time for their families. Also, when asked which they preferred—home or the office—*only 4 percent said they would choose to work full time.* Think of that! Where are the vaunted majority of mothers who want to leave their children with just anybody and go off to work? What is more, some 61 percent opted for part-time employment, and 29 percent didn't want any paid employment at all.

Finally, a 1996 national survey of women's awareness, attitudes, and opinions conducted for Concerned Women for

America by Wirthlin Worldwide found that eight out of ten women agreed with the statement, "If I could afford it, I would stay home and be a full-time mother."

So what are we to conclude from these and other surveys about parental attitudes? American mothers know in their hearts what's best for the kids—and it is mother care, not other care. Moreover, there are myriad mothers whose bodies are trapped in the workplace, while their hearts are home. And the fact that many feel they cannot afford the luxury of caring for their children indicates that they and their spouses may have chosen unwisely to mortgage their children's emotional well-being by living to the hilt on two incomes. Or the mother may be divorced. But what's the end result? A whole lot of free-floating mother yearning in the culture.

As a psychologist, I know that whenever a mother suffers emotionally, a family suffers. While husbands may be able to handle the fallout of maternal angst because of tradeoffs such as money, a bigger home, or status, children have no such capacity. When their mothers are too often absent, tired, grumpy, or exhausted, they end up being hurt. I have found it painful to watch children attempt to relate to anxious, harried mothers who aren't taking care of their own emotional needs. How can they possibly have anything rich and wonderful in their mother bank to give to their children?

Said one mother of four children under the age of fourteen, "I don't know why I'm angry all the time. Lately I've been yelling at the kids, and I told my husband, Ron, 'for the past two weeks you can't do anything right.'" This forty-something mother juggles a demanding career, carpooling, soccer matches, swimming meets, church activities, and home renovation, then wonders why she falls into bed at midnight, exhausted.

When she complained to me about her schedule, I told

her what I, as a psychotherapist, say to my patients. First, I ask, "Are your choices helping you or hurting you?" If they respond negatively, I counter, "Which choice would you like to change?"

It takes courage to change our lives when we feel we are running in the wrong direction. But sometimes we must, particularly if our current choices are hurting us or our marriages or our children. Whenever we feel we are on the wrong path or not being true to what we believe, that is the time to make new choices.

The Feminist Fallout Continues

In an article in *Time,* Claudia Wallis asks if women who bought the feminist sell in the sixties, seventies, and eighties, concentrating on career and neglecting to have children, are burned out and nostalgic for the fifties: "Is the feminist movement—one of the great social revolutions of contemporary history—truly dead? Or is it merely stalled and in need of a little consciousness-raising?"[10]

Wallis notes that many women blame the feminist movement for emphasizing the wrong issues—the Equal Rights Amendment, lesbian rights, hairy legs, and bra burning. Moreover, many who bought the image of the superwoman discovered that a careerist with a small child must make significant sacrifices. Wallis tells of one successful careerist, Carolyn LoGalbo-Goodfriend, the mother of a five-year-old and manager of over $300 million of Kraft accounts, who cornered Gloria Steinem at a party and asked, "Why didn't you tell us it was going to be like this?" To which Steinem responded, "Well, we didn't know."

Additionally, women nearing forty who put their careers before family are finding that they are childless and demoralized because of it. I have talked with a number of unmarried women—from the White House to the corporation—who find themselves in successful careers more by default than choice. Said one attractive professional in her late forties who runs a congressman's office, "I never thought I'd end up like this— unmarried and childless. I used to laugh at women like me— women who spent their days and their lives working on some-one else's agenda." Then she grew quiet and added ruefully, "I have become the woman I laughed at."

Wallis quotes disenchanted Elizabeth Mehren, forty-two, a writer for the *Los Angeles Times,* who said, "Our generation was the human sacrifice. We believed the rhetoric. We could control our biological destiny. For a lot of us the clock ran out, and we discovered we couldn't control infertility."

Recently, I spoke with Ellen Paris, former writer for *Forbes* magazine and the *Washington Times,* who interviewed over a hundred childless women ages thirty-nine to forty-nine and uncovered a lot of angst. While about 25 percent never wanted children in the first place, the women Paris inter-viewed, who hit their late forties still desiring children, were "really regretful." "Then they felt adoption wasn't an option," said Paris. She added that the never-married women in her study were the "most regretful." Sometimes the married women had simply postponed childbearing, whereas others who were single felt they "never had the chance."

Paris undertook this project because she felt there was a "huge audience" of women struggling with childlessness, and she was working through the issue in her own life. As a result of her conversations with other women, at forty-five Paris got off the fence, and she and her husband Mark adopted Sim, a Vietnamese baby, when she was nine months old. "I knew if I didn't become a mother, I would have regrets," said Paris.

Then she added, "This has certainly stopped the aging process. I can't think about approaching fifty when I have a toddler underfoot."

Ellen Paris is a fortunate woman. When she decided to become a mother, she and her husband were able to adopt a baby. Other women aren't so lucky. I have spoken to numerous attractive single women who want to marry and have children but feel that men of their generation—children of divorce and day care—are commitment phobic. Said one thirty-year-old unmarried professional, "A lot of men in my generation have grown up in day care without a close relationship with their mothers. They've had to contend with parental divorce and absent fathers. They begin dating, if they date at all, only to have to deal with women who can support themselves, have sex when they want it, and pay for artificial insemination. No wonder they're scared."

The Dawning of a New Day

Fortunately, a new day is coming in America. In the mid-nineties, the venerable *Wall Street Journal* proclaimed that stay-at-home mothers are fashionable again.[11] Indeed, they are downright chic in some neighborhoods, having become the newest status symbol, the equivalent of a BMW a decade ago. "It's not something you brag about, but it's a source of pride," says David Seckinger, a Merrill Lynch broker in Atlanta whose wife gave up a job in publishing to stay home.

In pockets of middle- and upper-class America, stay-at-home motherhood has become something to die for. Why is this so? Many couples are mortgaged to the hilt and feel they can't afford the luxury of having a mother at home. The *Wall Street Journal* calls these mothers who have come home from the workplace "Power Moms" and indicates they are anything but apologetic about their choice. "The 'I'm just a housewife' with apologetic overtones is going away," says Ann Clurman, a partner at Yankelovich consulting firm, which studies societal trends. Mothers at home, according to Clurman, see themselves as CEOs running the family household.

They also believe fiercely that their children are better off when they stay home. One mother interviewed by the *Journal* even referred unkindly to day-care centers as "those little meat factories." Another spoke proudly of being around "to reinforce values." And when Jane Seckinger, a former magazine ad salesperson, was interviewed, she said her children were smarter because she's at home. "My youngest was retested because he scored so high on a test for the gifted program. That has a lot to do with my being at home."

According to a series of polls conducted by the *Washington Post,* Harvard University, and the Henry J. Kaiser Family Foundation, two-thirds of the people surveyed said that although it may sometimes be necessary for mother to work, it would be better for her family if she could stay home to care for the house and the children, even into the children's teenage years. This point of view was expressed by both men and women and across age groups, with older people feeling the most strongly. In addition, half the respondents said that they respect mothers at home more than mothers who work outside their homes.[12]

Gratefully, cultural attitudes are changing, and increasing numbers of mothers are listening to their hearts and coming home. And many who feel trapped in the workplace are honest about their yearning to spend more time with their children. But how did we get here in the first place? How did we arrive at such a wholesale rejection of motherhood?

If we look beneath a feminist's rhetoric to her attachment

history, we discover that a woman's attitudes toward marriage and particularly toward mothering have their roots in her infancy and early childhood. As a psychologist who has done research on women's attachment histories and their attitudes toward childrearing versus career, I know that whenever a mother makes a decision to sacrificially give herself to her child, she is being influenced by more than cultural attitudes or even economics. She is, first and foremost, affected by what happened to her in childhood and her own nurturing history.

When it comes to motherhood, the past is prologue.

Chapter Six

WHY DO SOME WOMEN REJECT MOTHERHOOD?

If men could menstruate,
abortion would be a sacrament.

GLORIA STEINEM

As early as the 1970s, researchers were asking why some mothers chose to stay home while others opted for a career. Was the stay-at-home mother simply hiding out at home, intimidated by her more competent, employed sisters, or was something else going on—something on the psychological level perhaps?

In the early seventies, Rhona and Robert Rapoport, a British husband and wife team, looked at this issue and found that most of the employed mothers in their study grew up in families where they were "lonely, only children."[1] Their homes were filled with tension and frequent episodes of marital strife. Moreover, most of the women did not have emotionally close relationships with both parents. Of the five women studied, two had highly conflictual relationships with their mothers, and a third woman with her father.

Another theme that emerged from the seventies' research was the father's profound influence on his daughter's career decisions. Psychologist Laurel Oliver found that a warm, accepting relationship with her father encouraged the development of a daughter's femininity and the acceptance of the traditional lifestyle.[2] That is, those daughters who felt emotionally close to their fathers identified with their stay-at-home mothers, and they wanted to stay home as their mothers had done.

On the other hand, Margaret Hennig and Anne Jardin conducted a now famous study of twenty-five successful corporate achievers and found that women who excelled in business also reported close, supportive relationships with their fathers. In *The Managerial Woman,* Hennig and Jardin wrote that the fathers in their study were nontraditional, and so they encouraged their daughters to achieve in the world of work rather than pursue the traditional lifestyle their mothers were living. Most of the women in this study expressed the desire to outstrip their conventional mothers in the achievement arena as they identified closely with their fathers. And their fathers encouraged this mentality. The authors write that the fathers wanted their daughters to experience life in ways their mothers had not.[3]

Not surprisingly, many of the women in this particular study held negative views of their mothers: "They remember their mothers as comfortable necessities, 'warm, fluffy pillows,' who were not terribly exciting or magnetic."[4] One woman even decided as an adolescent that she didn't like women because they were "stupid." She spoke of her adolescence as a time of "reducing dependency on my mother, by rejecting some of her—and other women's—traditional ideas about women's roles. My relationship with my dad changed very little. Perhaps it broadened and deepened if anything. I was always the center of Dad's attention."[5] Another woman harshly evaluated her traditional mother thus: "I wanted to be more of a person than my mother was."[6]

Why did these fathers disparage their wives as role models

for their daughters? While the authors did not examine the parental marriages, it is possible to speculate that these fathers had unsatisfying marriages and looked to their daughters for love, admiration, and female companionship—qualities that were missing in their own marriages. Having worked for years as a therapist, I know that whenever a father turns away from his wife and allows the daughter to supplant her mother, a sterile marriage usually exists. And the father usually has his own psychological problems that cause him to turn to his daughter for more emotional support than she should give. This unhealthy triangle also creates an unbridgeable gulf between a daughter and her mother that will cause the daughter problems later on in her relationships with other women and any daughters she may have. She may also have contempt for other women and fail to develop close female friendships. When she has children, she may prefer her sons to her daughters.

In any event, a woman pays a high price when she rejects her mother and identifies too closely with her father. As the achievers in Hennig and Jardin's study show, a woman who rejects her mother also repudiates certain aspects of her femininity, particularly her need to nurture children. None of the women in this study married before the age of thirty-five. None ever bore children.

But is the rejection of a traditional lifestyle always equated with the rejection of motherhood? And does identification with her father and achievement in the workplace automatically mean that a woman rejects her feminine, nurturing self? Or is something else operative? Mary-Joan Gerson of the New School of Social Research investigated these issues in her study of 184 female undergraduates. She discovered that those who wanted to become mothers reported that they had experienced happy childhoods and especially warm relationships with their mothers.[7] These college women had memories of mothers who enjoyed child rearing and devoted a lot of time and energy to their children's care. Family life was also happy. Unlike the corporate achievers in Hennig and Jardin's study, Gerson found no collusion here between father and daughter resulting in the rejection of mother. And what of those women who wished to remain childless? Their earliest memories were of maternal deprivation and a lack of warmth and nurture from their fathers.

Moreover, Gerson found that the women in her study who held strong feminist views had little desire to ever become mothers. Why was this so? Gerson speculated, "It may be that motherhood is associated with inferior status for liberated women."[8] Yet when she looked at those women who held antifeminist views, Gerson found that they remembered their mothers as loving and happy at home.

Lack of Parental Nurture and Feminism

Gerson was not the only psychologist who found a connection between the presence and absence of nurture in childhood and the desire to have children. B. E. Lott studied undergraduate men and women, finding that those who wanted to become parents themselves had experienced warm, nurturing parenting in early childhood.[9] Their fathers, as well as mothers, had devoted a lot of time and energy to caring for them. When these men and women were asked their views on feminism, they were not in favor of women's liberation. The feminists in the study, on the other hand, said they were not interested in having children. Nor did they remember that either parent had been warm, affectionate, loving, or involved during their childhood. Fathers received particularly low marks.

These studies, which would be politically incorrect in academia today, indicate that an individual's own attachment history strongly influences his attitude toward parenting the future generation. Moreover, one's earliest relationship with one's parents affects one's attitudes toward feminism.

What can we learn from this early research that is germane today? Hennig and Jardin's study suggests that women who identify with their fathers (and not their mothers) often become committed careerists, particularly if their fathers reject the mother's traditional lifestyle. Also, as Gerson and Lott discovered, for a woman to even desire to become a mother, she needs to have been well nurtured as a child by both parents.

Obviously many women become mothers by default—because their husbands want children or it's the thing to do—but to truly desire to carry, bear, and nurture a child, it helps greatly if the woman herself was loved and valued by her parents. If she was deprived of sufficient parental warmth and emotional support, she may wish to remain childless and feel, as some feminists do, that marriage and the family are oppressive to women.

ATTACHMENT HISTORIES OF FIRST-TIME MOTHERS

Intrigued by these studies when I approached my own doctoral research, I chose to investigate the relationship between a mother's memories of her earliest parental attachments and her decision to leave her firstborn baby to return to work. I wanted to look at a mother's level of maternal separation anxiety as well as her attitudes toward career and motherhood. I chose to link the research in adult attachment with research in maternal employment—something that hadn't been done before.

So one summer I made my way into three metropolitan hospitals in the Washington, D.C., area, armed with a battery of questionnaires. My task? I had to convince weary, sleep-deprived first-time mothers—and eighty-nine of them, at that—to participate in my study.

WHY DO SOME WOMEN REJECT MOTHERHOOD?

I well remember pushing open door after door at Georgetown University hospital to find women in various states of dress and undress, many suffering from the pain of their C-sections. I remember one who had her baby propped up on a pillow while she tried to give him the breast. She was tentative and a little scared. But it was wonderful seeing all those glorious newborns and talking to their mothers shortly after they had given birth for the first time. Such a cataclysmic event!

What did I learn from my research? First, let's look at those mothers who said they preferred to be employed rather than stay home with their newborns. These twenty-three women had the highest scores of any group on father rejection. When asked about their relationship with their dads in childhood, *these women had poignant memories of father rejection.* These mothers also valued career more highly than did those mothers who preferred to stay home, and they valued the maternal role less.

What about those mothers who preferred to stay home with their babies? They reported positive, idealized memories of their own mothers.

While I as a psychologist can only speculate about what these findings mean, I believe that women who prefer employment may be attempting to gain their father's love and approval by means of a career. These mothers indicated that, in childhood, they could not always trust or count on their fathers. According to Bowlby's attachment theory, women who had trouble trusting their fathers in childhood may also have trouble trusting their husbands in adulthood. Remember— they learned "attitudes and expectancies" at their father's knee. Without trust, these new mothers would have difficulty depending on their husbands to provide for them financially after the birth of their first child—a time when women, because of their raging hormones, invariably feel dependent and vulnerable.

I also discovered that *the more a woman remembered feeling rejected by her father, the less she was interested in the mothering role*. It is possible that early rejection by a father interferes with a woman's ability to focus on the highly feminine task of nurturing her child and giving herself wholeheartedly to mothering. For a woman to interrupt her career, she needs to feel comfortable with the men in her life: her father and her husband. And if she doesn't? She will cling to her job like a lifeline.

I remember one attractive thirty-five-year-old who said she was not emotionally close to her father. A diehard, she had worked until hours before her delivery. When I walked into her room, she was hovering over her gorgeous son, who lay sleeping in his isolette. After I introduced myself, she started to cry. "I've always worked. And I planned to go back to work in just a few weeks, but my baby is so vulnerable. So small. So dependent on me. I had no idea I would feel this way. I don't know what to do." And then she wailed.

But what about that other group of new mothers I studied, those who preferred to stay home and who idealized their mothers? While parent idealization may indicate personality maladjustment (the defensive blocking of painful memories), in my study I do not feel this was the case. I believe the home preference group consisted of traditional women who idealized mothering and felt love and warmth toward their own mothers. Several called their baby "a miracle" and "a blessing." Many mentioned closeness to their mothers and that their mothers had enjoyed staying home. A number came from large, Roman Catholic families.

WHY DO SOME WOMEN REJECT MOTHERHOOD?

As stated earlier, the birth of the first child is a significant psychological event in a woman's life. One woman called new motherhood, a "psychic earthquake." Many of the women I interviewed were euphoric about motherhood, although some seemed subdued. Several indicated they had never expected to feel such a strong desire to nurture their babies, and some were already struggling with their decision to return to work.

When I asked these women how they would have felt had they never become mothers, the two groups gave quite different responses. Among those women who preferred employment, many said children were not essential for a fulfilled life. If they had children, fine. If not, they would have found other outlets for their nurturing needs—nieces, nephews, work. Said an attorney, "My life would have been complete [without children]. I am happily married. I have a good job. I would have missed motherhood, but it's hard to miss something you have never experienced."

This was not the case for the home preference mothers. For them, motherhood had long been an integral part of their life plan. Some had wanted to have children since they were very young. And many said they would have been devastated had they been childless.

These two groups of mothers also had significantly different attitudes toward leaving their babies to return to work. Even at two to five days postpartum, the mothers who preferred to stay home had greater anxiety about leaving their babies for work-related reasons than the employment preference mothers. Also, their belief that their babies needed *their exclusive care* only increased over time. This was not true for those mothers who preferred to return to work. By the time their babies were four months old, these moms (all twenty-three were back at work) had significantly less anxiety about leaving their babies than did those mothers who preferred to stay home.

What's going on here? Why did the employed mothers have significantly less separation anxiety than the mothers who preferred to stay home? It may be that their life plans included both career and motherhood, or it may be that they had to deny their maternal feelings so they could return to their jobs with less guilt.

In speaking about mothers who withdraw from their babies emotionally—for work or military deployment—the well-known pediatrician T. Berry Brazelton said in the *Detroit Free Press* on January 27, 1991: "They withdraw not because they don't care, but because it hurts to care."

It hurts to care. But don't babies need their mothers to care, to refuse to be self-protective, and to fall in love with them? How far we have come in this culture that some mothers have to shut down emotionally to be able to leave their babies for work or war!

Is any job worth the pain a mother feels when she wrenches herself away from her baby to go to war? Is any career worth the price a child must pay his whole life in terms of emotional insecurity and lack of self-worth if he fails to forge a secure, loving attachment with his mother? I think not. The fact that this happens repeatedly and unthinkingly in our society indicates that our priorities are skewed and that we have lost track of what really matters in life.

My research and other studies suggest that the fact that some women put their children's well-being ahead of career is not, as the culture has suggested for decades, because they are gutless or inferior to employed mothers. Rather, the research shows that a woman's childhood relationships with her parents not only shape her maternal feelings, but also her feelings

WHY DO SOME WOMEN REJECT MOTHERHOOD?

about feminism, her investment in career and the mothering role, and her level of maternal separation anxiety.

In this arena, as in many others, things are not what they seem.

THREE FAMOUS FEMINISTS

It is one thing to read about psychological studies in the abstract; it's something else to see their meaning played out in real life. Let's look for a moment at three women who have profoundly shaped American culture and motherhood in the past three decades, women who came from troubled families and who are ardent feminists: Betty Friedan, Germaine Greer, and Gloria Steinem.

- Betty felt like an outcast as an adolescent and grew up in a home where marital conflict reigned. She arrived at adulthood furious with her rejecting mother.
- Even as a child, Germaine felt sure that her mother never liked her, and she later wrote a poignant book stating that she never really knew her father. Greer, one of the most flamboyant and outrageous of the early feminists, was a psychological orphan.
- Gloria was abandoned by her father when she was a child and was left to care for her mother, a woman later hospitalized for mental illness.

So writes Marcia Cohen in *The Sisterhood*. In her book, Cohen not only writes of the flowering of the second wave of the feminist movement, but also examines the families of origin for three famous founders of modern feminism.

Betty Friedan, founder of the National Organization of Women, grew up in a household short on mother love.

According to Betty's sister, Amy, their mother, Miriam, had "a complete inability to nurture…we really absolutely did not have a mother loving us."[10] Cohen remarks that Betty's mother was intensely critical of her and made Betty feel both unwanted and ugly. Said Betty's brother, "My mother still thinks Betty has worked as hard as she could to make herself as ugly as possible."[11] As an adult, Betty went into psycho-analysis to work through her deep-seated rage at her mother.

Not only did Betty Friedan have to contend with her mother's cutting remarks growing up, but she also witnessed her parents' heated marital battles. Her father, Harry Sr., had a difficult time funding the expensive upper-middle-class lifestyle his wife Miriam demanded. "The children remember the arguments between their mother and father, remember Harry very angry, his face reddening, banging his fist on the table, storming out of the room."[12]

What was Friedan's response to her conflict-ridden family and her own lack of nurture? Although she had children, she and her husband had a violent, abusive marriage. She later wrote a book articulating her own dissatisfaction with the housewife's lot, suggesting that all traditional women in America lived lives of "quiet desperation."

Friedan's own marriage was punctuated by ugly verbal and physical battles. Shortly after Betty's children were born, "her marriage was growing stormy and during arguments, things, sugar bowls, books and the like—seemed to fly."[13] Friedan was later divorced, but not before she had published her now famous *The Feminine Mystique*. Friedan said in this book that educators, psychologists, and women's magazines—as well as Madison Avenue—conspired to keep women chained to the kitchen stove, where they developed only half a self. She termed the isolated, suburban home "a comfortable concentration camp, filled with unhappy, restless prisoners." The rest, as they say, is history.

Betty Friedan was not the only important founder of the modern feminist movement to emerge from a family that resembled a war zone. Australian born Germaine Greer, author of the rebellious *The Female Eunuch,* was born to an absent father and a mother who openly rejected her.

When Germaine Greer was born, her father was off to war. It was World War II, and Reg Greer, an army intelligence officer, had joined the Australian Air Force. He returned six years later visibly aged by the experience. So for the first six years of her life Germaine was raised by her mother, Peggy, who delighted in flirting with the American servicemen who stopped off in Melbourne en route to the Pacific. Greer later wrote of women who teased men sexually but failed to deliver promised favors. Cohen writes: "Eventually Germaine Greer would analyze flirtatious, manipulative behavior with her own dramatic flourish. She would shock and entrance with her graceful, philosophical account of warped female sexuality, labeling it the performance of a 'female eunuch.'"[14] Was this a veiled attack on her mother?

According to Cohen, Greer would come to describe her childhood as filled with pain and humiliation. Not only did her mother beat her viciously on occasion, but she also hit Germaine with "passion" and "for no good reason." "If she lost a ball or coloring book, Peggy would never allow her to have another. That was that. And so her imagination began to paint possibilities. Perhaps she was not really her mother's child. She didn't feel like Peggy's child."[15]

In reflecting on her relationship with her mother, Greer said: "I thought about the children who did, obviously, not only love their mothers, but actually like them, hang out with them.... I thought they were faking, I thought it was a thing you did for outsiders. You pretended to be good chums."[16]

As Germaine Greer grew older, the antagonism between mother and daughter continued. Greer, a bright woman who later earned her doctorate at Cambridge University, was forced by her mother to pay room and board as an adolescent. The summer she was seventeen, however, she was ill and not working.

Opening the refrigerator one day to pour herself a glass of milk, Greer was stopped by her mother, who said harshly, "Leave that alone. That's for my children."[17] Stung by her mother's overt rejection, Greer immediately left the house, taking only the clothes she had on her back. Forced to return home a month later, she found her mother in the garden. This influential feminist writer has never forgotten her mother's first words upon her return: "Who let all the flies in? Oh, it's you. You're home."[18]

While Cohen's *The Sisterhood* chronicled Germaine Greer's maternal rejection, Greer herself writes of her father's rejection in her book *Daddy, We Hardly Knew You*. Her father "never once" hugged her. "If I put my arms around him, he would grimace and pretend to shudder and put me from him. It was a joke, of course, a tiresome, hurtful, relentless, stupid joke.… I clung to the faith that he was not genuinely indifferent to me and did not really find me repulsive, although I never quite succeeded in banishing the fear of such a thing."[19]

Greer states that shortly before his death, her father accepted all the "kissing and hugging" from his nurses that he had never permitted her to give him. It is not surprising that Greer once said, "At bottom, I've always thought I was unlovable."[20]

Fellow feminist Gloria Steinem also experienced a lack of parental love and nurture. Her father, unable to keep a steady job, later abandoned his wife and daughter when Gloria was only eleven years old. This was several years after her mother

WHY DO SOME WOMEN REJECT MOTHERHOOD?

had suffered "a nervous breakdown." From then on, Gloria not only had to cope with her father's absence, but she also had to care for her disturbed mother. The two lived in a run-down house overrun with rats. Writes Cohen: "The poverty was ugly, and years later, after Gloria had catapulted to stardom as one of New York's 'beautiful people,' she would talk about the rats, about waking up at night and pulling her toes in under the covers in fear, about actually being bitten by one of them."[21]

To deal with the pain and humiliation of living with a mentally ill mother who once painted the windows of the house black, Steinhem developed a protective wall around herself, detaching herself from her impoverished existence and the embarrassment of her mother's condition.

As an adult Steinhem wrote, "My ultimate protection was this: I was just passing through, a guest in the house."[22] Cohen notes that Steinem, like Greer, had fantasies that her biological parents were actually her foster parents and that someday her real parents would arrive to rescue her from her painful existence.

What was the possible psychological impact of having to care for a disturbed mother? John Bowlby states in *The Making and Breaking of Affectional Bonds* that when parents exact role reversal from their children—when they require their children to parent them—they create profound feelings of insecurity. The child becomes "a compulsive caregiver" when the child has a mother "who due to depression or some other disability" is unable to care for the child while insisting the child care for her. Then the individual grows up believing "the only care he can ever receive is the care he gives himself."[23]

When parents act like children, and their children function as parents, children deny their own needs for love and nurture. They may cry out, as did one young mother who experienced role reversal, "nobody took care of me," or they may become detached from their own inner needs, as Steinem seems to have done, denying both their anger and their pain. Yet she who cared for her mother later helped launch the feminist revolution, caring on a national scale for the plight of oppressed American women.

Thus the caregiver child became the caregiver revolutionary.

The point of this brief foray into the lives of these influential feminists is to understand that all three grew up in starkly troubled families. Friedan and Greer had openly rejecting mothers, and Steinem had an abandoning father and a mentally ill mother. As a psychologist, I believe that these women projected their painful attachment histories onto the culture at large, believing they spoke for the majority of American women.

While Friedan has been able to overcome her parenting history to some extent, in mothering her own three children, Greer wrote in *The Female Eunuch* that she "despised women." That Gloria Steinem's father abandoned her and her sick mother helps us understand the origin of her pithy slogan, "A woman needs a man like a fish needs a bicycle."[24] It stands to reason that her mother's illness and her father's failure to love and protect her during her own vulnerable adolescence may have affected Steinem's views of marriage and parenting. While she has had lovers, Steinem has never had a husband.

Like Greer, Steinem has never had children, though she made her abortion famous.

THE IMPACT OF FEMINISM

How ironic that these three highly intelligent women, none of whom is currently married, have so profoundly influenced our current notions of family and motherhood. Speaking out of the pain of their own nurturing histories, these three have disparaged marriage and the mother who chooses to stay home to care for her children. They, and other outspoken feminists, made her first a cipher and, in recent years, invisible.

Sadly, their ideas continue to influence women around the world and social policy even as I write. Though Betty Friedan has attempted to soften her message in recent years, acknowledging that the feminist movement has largely ignored the importance of the family and women's need to nurture their children, countless mothers at home have struggled with low self-esteem, loneliness, and feeling devalued because of feminism's disparagement of marriage and mother care. And those women who answered feminism's clarion call and left home for the office? Some have watched their children spend summers in day care, return home during adolescence to empty houses, leave home seldom to return because of weak emotional ties. Was it worth it?

In the past decade, whether in my office or on the road speaking and being on talk shows, I have had my finger on the pulse of mothering in this country. My conviction is that those mothers who have allowed themselves to fall in love with their babies and enjoy the role of motherhood are growing stronger in this culture and that those who have denied their maternal feelings have paid quite a price. Take the mother who called in to the Dick Staub show in Chicago when I was a guest promoting *The Power of Mother Love*. This mother said that her four-year-old son, who had been in day care since birth, was angry, remote, and did not like to be touched. She wanted reassurance that he would be okay emotionally, but sadly, I couldn't give it. There's no quick fix for a weak or absent emotional bond. I did tell her to spend more time holding her son (though he would be uncomfortable at first) and talking to him face-to-face.

But I knew from years of reviewing child development research that this little boy was on a high-risk developmental trajectory. And in my travels I have heard increasingly of lost, angry, detached little boys, some of whom may become walking time bombs, as we shall see in the next chapter.

Obviously Betty Friedan touched a nerve when she published *The Feminine Mystique* in 1963. How else could she have started a revolution? What is more, millions of American women responded to her rhetoric. And yet, as Dr. Deborah Fallows points out in her book, *A Mother's Work,* part of the reason for this radical response was that at first the workplace seemed like a quick fix for all that ailed the woman at home. Writes Fallows: "On a personal level the workplace seems to offer an answer for just about all the problems and complications of women's lives. Dependent upon your spouse? Get an income, become self-sufficient. No power to back up your opinion? Get equal power with a paycheck—money talks. Bored? Get out of the house and in with interesting people…. Lonely? Get out of the house and into an office."[25]

Only one thing was missing from feminist rhetoric, notes Fallows: the effect of a mother's absence upon her children.

The effects, America, have been enormous.

FINAL THOUGHTS

When I reflect on these three famous feminists' lives, I feel some compassion and a whole lot of anger. I feel compassion, particularly for Germaine Greer, who at fifty-one took an anguished look at her relationship with her father. Not only did Greer finally confront her father's rejection, but she also discovered that his whole life was a lie: Reg Greer was not the man he had claimed to be. Greer found that her father had lied about his origins and had even taken a pseudonym. At the end of her search for her father's past (and love), Germaine felt devastated. She writes, "In finding him I lost him. Sleepless nights are long."[26]

Who would not feel sympathy for a woman who has looked at parental rejection with such rigor?

Nevertheless, I am angry that these women used their impressive intellects to shape social policy without first examining and understanding their own personal histories. Generations of women worldwide have marched to their antimarriage, antimale, and antifamily drumbeat. Yet we women can only blame ourselves for ceding the vast territory of the heart and abandoning our children for something as small and inconsequential as a career.

As I approach sixty and battle breast cancer, I have thought deeply about the meaning of life—my life—and about what lasts. Let me tell you, achievement doesn't last. When Dr. Dobson, in a *Focus on the Family* interview, asked if I were suggesting that a woman bury her talents and substantial gifts to stay home with her children, even for a season, I responded that when one is faced with a life-threatening illness or the end of life, what matters is *not* career, accomplishments, possessions, or status. *What matters is what lasts.* Our relationships—with God, our families, and those whose lives we have touched deeply.

And it's these meaningful relationships, which have always defined our lives as women, that feminism forgot or chose to ignore. This has not been without enormous societal consequences. As we shall see in the next chapter, the impact of our mothering choices can sometimes be frightening.

Chapter Seven

WHY KIDS KILL

---

*Juvenile violence is no longer a stranger
in any ZIP code.*

FORMER SENATOR DAN COATS

This may be an uncomfortable or even frightening chapter for some to read. I have included it because we have a cancer growing in our society, threatening the lives and emotional well-being of our school-age children. Some parents have disturbed, angry children, and they need help in understanding how to help them. In addition, this chapter provides a needed answer to the question the culture is asking: Why do some kids kill?

On a warm May day in 1998, a fifteen-year-old boy entered Thurston High School in Springfield, Oregon, pulled a rifle from his trench coat, and opened fire on two boys outside the cafeteria. Kip Kinkel, who had already shot his parents, then propped open the door of the cafeteria with his foot and started shooting. Eventually, he walked up to a boy who had dived under a table and shot him in the head at point-blank range. Kinkel's parents and two students died.

Later, when Kinkel was tried on four counts of murder and

151

WHY KIDS KILL

twenty-six counts of attempted murder, detective Pamela McComas read from his journal while Kinkel, ashamed, hid his face in his arms. Kinkel's journal was filled with threats of violence and feelings of profound loneliness and hatred. He wrote:

> I sit all alone. I am always alone.... In the end, I hate myself for what I've become.... I hate every single person on this earth. I am so consumed with hate all the time. Could I ever love anyone?... I am so full of rage.... Blowing the school up or walking into a pep assembly with guns...that is how I will repay all you.[1]

On another page of his journal he wrote menacingly: "They won't laugh after they are scraping pieces of their mothers and sisters off the wall of my hate."

Unfortunately, Kip Kinkel is only one of a growing population of severely disturbed, lost boys who choose to vent their hatred on teachers, peers, and parents. The "Kids Who Kill Hall of Fame" also includes the following:

- Luke Woodham, 16, of Pearl, Mississippi, who reacted to parental divorce in 1997 by stabbing his mother to death and killing two students and wounding seven others;
- Michael Carneal, 14, of West Paducah, Kentucky, who walked into a Bible study in 1997, killed three students and wounded five others;
- Barry Loukaites of Moses Lake, Washington, who killed one teacher and two students and wounded another on February 2, 1996;
- Andrew Golden, 11, and Mitchell Johnson, 13, of Jonesboro, Arkansas, who opened fire in their school in

1998, killing one teacher and four students and wounding ten others;

- Eric Harris, 18, and Dylan Klebold, 17, of Littleton, Colorado, who killed one teacher and twelve students and wounded twenty-three others in 1999—the worst school massacre to date;[2]

- An unnamed boy, 6, who took a gun to school in Michigan on February 29, 2000, and shot a six-year-old classmate, Kayla Roland, in the neck. She died, and he became one of the youngest killers on record.[3]

WHENCE THIS RAGE IN THE HUMAN HEART?

How could such rage and violence exist in the hearts of America's children? What kind of parenting could possibly have produced such vicious killers? Or can we just blame external forces like television, Hollywood, and video games? These were a few of the questions I set out to answer as the keynote speaker at a conference attended by school administrators in southern Virginia this past summer. I spoke on the unsettling subject of why kids kill. Following my presentation, an FBI agent came to the podium to talk about what these principals of elementary and high schools could do if, heaven forbid, another school shooting should occur.

In his introduction the assistant superintendent of schools said that five years ago he would not have dreamed of having such a conference. "But times have changed," he said, "and today no area in America is safe."

The assistant superintendent is right. Times in America have changed, and the school shootings, which started in 1993, have only escalated since then. Moreover, these shootings didn't happen in ghetto areas among African-American and Hispanic students, but in suburban and rural areas and

153

among white males age eighteen and under.

America, more than any other country in the world, is experiencing an epidemic of juvenile crime.[4] Because of the seriousness of this problem, on July 18, 1996, former Senator Dan Coats held Senate subcommittee hearings on youth and violence and invited criminal justice experts to come to Washington, D.C., to testify. When I asked Senator Coats how these experts felt about this epidemic, he replied, "They're scared."

Although we've been lulled into complacency as a nation by hearing that the crime wave is down, the truth is more complicated. In reality, while adult crime has decreased, juvenile crime is on the rise. For example, between 1985 and 1994, the arrest rate for murders committed by adults rose 11 percent, while during the same time period, the arrest rate for murders committed by juveniles rose by 150 percent.[5]

Not only are we rearing a bumper crop of young criminals who lack a conscience, a capacity for empathy, and a sense of remorse, but these kids who kill also possess a heartlessness— an inhumanity—that terrifies adults. According to Chuck Colson, president of Prison Fellowship, older prison inmates are frightened by the ferocity of younger inmates.[6] I heard of one guard who retired after a career in a West Virginia prison who said that older inmates often asked to be transferred to other areas of the prison, away from their more rapacious, heartless, younger counterparts.

Everyone needs to understand why some children in our country are engaging in unspeakable acts of violence. Not only are some parents struggling to understand their own remorseless, angry kids, but none of us lives in a vacuum. We may live next door to a deeply troubled child, or we may have children who attend public school rubbing shoulders with these sons and daughters who are consumed with rage.

The safety of our children as they walk into their schools each day is uncertain. As demonstrated by the recent incident of a first grader shooting another first grader, even our youngest children are at risk. Even if they are never hurt physically, children who witness a school shooting will be severely traumatized and need significant psychological help. They will most assuredly experience a loss of innocence at having witnessed such an atrocity.

In this chapter I want to give you information that will help you understand why some of these neglected and emotionally deprived children commit such heinous acts of violence. As you are forewarned, you will be better equipped to protect your children and even work with your child's school to identify and help the severely disturbed child.

Another reason we need to face this issue head-on is because criminal justice experts predict that the worst is yet to come.

WHAT'S COMING, AMERICA?

In 1996, James Fox, Dean of the College of Criminal Justice at Northeastern University in Boston, testified before a Senate subcommittee. He stated that by the year 2005, America will have a bumper crop of fourteen- to seventeen-year-olds sauntering down the halls of its high schools—the segment of the population now committing the most crime.[7] Fox stated, "We now have in this country 39 million children under the age of ten. There are more young kids than we have had since the fifties when the Baby Boomers were kiddies. But these young kids will not be young for long; they will be teenagers before you can say 'juvenile crime wave.'"[8] According to Fox, this generation of poorly supervised teens (57 percent have moms in the workplace) will be the best-armed generation in American history, and they will be everywhere. No area in America will be safe.

I've been forecasting a similar scenario for years, based on my understanding of how kids become human. I have taken to the airwaves, given numerous speeches, and talked to the power brokers on Capitol Hill about what's coming to America based on the way we are choosing to rear our children. In the early nineties, few understood the message. Now, as a talk show host in San Francisco said to me, "Everyone's worried about the kids." And well they might be. We are apparently unique in the entire world in rearing so many heartless, conscienceless children.

Understanding Why Kids Kill

So why do some kids kill? Maryland attorney Sol Sheinbein and his wife, Victoria, have repeatedly asked themselves the same question: How could their quiet, obedient son Samuel have viciously murdered another boy? In 1997 Samuel Sheinbein killed, dismembered, and burned the body of an acquaintance in Maryland, leaving his upper-middle-class parents bewildered. Said Sol of his son, "Today I speak to myself and try to understand how it is possible that my son—quiet, obedient and talented—could kill. I never raised a hand on Sam. There was never tension between us. His brother and sister are so talented. So why did I fail with him?"

As a psychologist, I was intrigued by the mother's statement that her son Sam rarely laughed or cried. Both parents acknowledged that they didn't have as close a relationship with Sam as they did with their other children. I think their statements contain the key to understanding how this emotionally repressed, obedient boy could commit such a monstrous crime.

We have to look beyond the fact that this was an affluent, white, intact family to the emotional bond Sam had with his parents. It's significant that they were never close. Also, while normal babies smile at four months and laugh soon thereafter, Sam did neither. In fact, at his trial in Israel (his father, an Israeli citizen, sent him there after the murder, possibly hoping for greater leniency), Sam sat stone-faced through the proceedings, never cracking a smile or shedding a tear.

Something obviously went awry in Samuel's emotional development that prevented him from establishing an emotional bond or attachment relationship with either parent. It appears that Sol's first two children were able to do so. This is key to understanding why Samuel killed another boy. Something happened in Sam's infancy that prevented him from him laughing or crying, something most children do with abandon. When a baby, who has all of his human emotions available for expression by eight months, does not laugh or cry, he is usually severely depressed and unable to get his mother or primary caretaker to meet his most basic emotional needs. It could be that his mother struggled with postpartum depression.

I need to say at this point that I am not trying to exonerate Samuel Sheinbein by blaming his parents, nor do I know the circumstances surrounding Samuel's infancy. Whenever a child commits an adult crime and maims or destroys another human being, he needs to bear the consequences for his actions, and in many states this means that children and teenagers are currently being tried as adults. This is as it should be.

But if we are ever to stem the tide of youth violence, we need to understand the origins of such rage and hatred. We must change the way we rear children and come to value mothering and the first two years.

Origins of Rage and Violence

Child killers are made, not born. Now I know that in saying this I will raise hackles and antagonize many who would like to blame Hollywood, guns, the media, television, and video games for the upsurge in teen violence. Obviously, these influences are bombarding our children and teenagers daily. And it is true that most of the kids who kill have had access to guns in their own homes. *However, when a child grows up to be a killer, something has gone dreadfully awry in his nurturing history. Since personality is shaped from the womb, the child who kills has had an impoverished or abusive attachment relationship with his parents, particularly his mother.* Unable to establish an emotional bond with the first person he ever tries to love, he grows up with weak or absent parental attachments. He is at risk for becoming a kid who kills. This absence of attachment is the key to understanding why some kids are so destructive.

Granted, each of the young, white male teenagers involved in recent school shootings was influenced by his culture and involved in dark, dangerous activities. The teen killers listened to music by Marilyn Manson, had heroes like Hitler and Nietzsche, and spent hours playing video games like Mortal Combat, Doom, and Quake. Several also watched movies such as *Natural Born Killers* and *The Basketball Diaries.*[10]

But the fact that these lost boys chose to fill their minds and hearts with the influences of darkness and evil attests to the fact that all possessed an inner void. Where did this emptiness, this heart of darkness come from? It grew out of the soil of their earliest attachment relationships.

Children who feel loved and valued by their parents do not kill. Nor are they sitting ducks to dark and perverse cultural influences. Loved children who are emotionally close to their parents develop a core sense of self and want to please their parents. They also possess a resilience to peer pressure that unloved, unattached children lack. Moreover, they are not severely depressed, walking time bombs waiting to explode.

So when we start to look for causes, let's clean up the culture, yes, and let's lobby for better gun control, but let's also look to parents for the way that children turn out. And let's look at the child's earliest years and his attachment relationship to his mother. I was quite distressed after the Columbine massacre at the media's attempts to absolve Harris's and Klebold's parents from any responsibility for what had happened. Even neighbors came forward to exonerate the parents of blame.

I was a guest on *Janet Parshall's America* shortly after the Columbine tragedy, and when I tried to take some of the responsibility for this massacre *home* to the parents, several angry women called in wanting to absolve them of guilt. Instead of holding the parents' feet to the fire, the callers blamed video games, the media, and guns. I understand that parents in this country are uncomfortable with looking for causes on the home front. Many feel guilty about neglecting their children. But home is where we must go if we're ever to understand why kids kill and change this negative cultural trend.

Children who kill do not spring up on the cultural scene overnight. That kind of antipathy and rage is years in the making, and it starts in infancy. Whenever parents are neglectful, abusive, or nonresponsive, they will have troubled kids who are angry and out of control by two or three years of age. These kids are impulsive, have frequent temper tantrums, attack siblings, and have little frustration tolerance. By age five they are often at war with the world.

Many of the parents of the teen killers knew their kids were in trouble long before the killings. Kip Kinkel's parents were about to send him away to a troubled youth program.

Loukatis, Carneal, Kinkel, and Harris were severely depressed, and several of the kids were on antidepressants. Johnson, who was mourning his parents' divorce, and Golden, who spent most of his after-school hours with his grandparents while his parents worked, were both tough, mean-spirited kids.[11]

How to Spot a Troubled Kid

As stated earlier, in normal human development, a baby forges a deep and enduring emotional bond with his parents by twelve months of age. The baby then becomes an emotionally secure child able to trust his parents and others. He possesses high self-esteem and resilience in the face of adversity, learning to manage his emotions and modulate his impulses.[12]

When a mother tells her two-year-old, "Don't hit me or Johnny," she is teaching her child the rudiments of self-control. When she comforts her little boy who has fallen, she is teaching him lessons about empathy. And when she catches her son in a lie and says, "Mommy knows you took the cookie. You need to tell Mommy the truth," she is working on developing her child's conscience. Out of the abundance of a warm, affectionate attachment relationship a child learns to love in return. He or she desperately wants to please. Soon the child generalizes that loving parental treatment to others, expecting that all others will treat him as his parents have done. He feels loved; he feels worthy. His world is a safe, exciting place.

This is not the case with those children who experience a disrupted or disordered attachment to mother first, then father. Whenever a child is unable to forge a loving emotional bond with his parents *for whatever reason,* the whole of his life will be different. These children are at risk for attachment disorder, and some of them, at the extreme end of the scale, may become children who kill.

ATTACHMENT DISORDER

What do I mean by the term "attachment disorder"? It is the designation that clinicians give children who possess certain characteristics due to a weak or absent emotional bond with parents. According to clinicians Terry Levy and Michael Orlans, authors of *Attachment, Trauma, and Healing,* these children possess an unstable sense of self-esteem that fluctuates between feelings of abasement and grandiosity. They decompensate in the face of adversity and have poor peer relationships. Incapable of genuine trust, intimacy, and affection, they develop, starting at ages three and four, oppositional relationships with authority figures. Because they have a weak or absent emotional bond with their mother, they never learn to modulate their emotions, and they lack impulse control.[13] Their aggression may be overt in terms of physical violence, or it may be passive—manipulative and surreptitious. These "trust bandits" see their parents as hurtful and unloving and the world as a bleak and dangerous place. They must be ever ready to engage in battle with it while feeling in their hearts that life is not worth living.[14]

Whereas securely attached children are capable of compassion, empathy, and genuine remorse, the attachment-disordered souls lack these golden, humanizing capacities. Those who experience the most severe attachment disorders develop no meaningful relationships—ever—unless or until they receive outside intervention that turns their rage into love.

According to criminologist Curt Bartol, the unattached or severely attachment-disordered will become true psychopaths in time, exhibiting "an absolute lack of remorse or guilt for anything they do, regardless of the severity or immorality of their actions and irrespective of their traumatic effects on others."[15]

What traits do attachment-disordered kids share with

adult psychopaths? According to clinical psychologist Terry Levy and therapist Michael Orlans, these traits include "glibness and superficiality, egocentric and grandiose thinking, lack of remorse, guilt, empathy, deceitful and manipulative behaviors, emotional shallowness, impulsivity, need for excitement, irresponsibility, not learning from experience and lacking meaningful relationships."[16]

Of course, all children will sometimes lie to protect themselves, but the future psychopath lies when he doesn't have to. Lying for these children is a way to gain control in any given situation. Longing for love, these attachment-disordered children are afraid of their parents, whom they view as hurtful and insensitive. Therefore, they are only comfortable if they have the upper hand through lying and manipulation.[17]

Unfortunately, as I told the school administrators, teen killers are not always easy to identify. Sometimes neighbors and teachers view them as normal, though peers regard them as "geeks" or "nerds." Although they may be totally out of control at home—hitting parents and putting holes in walls—future psychopaths often are not violent or overly explosive at school. In fact, they are likely to be superficially charming, outgoing, and articulate.[18] They may, like Harris and Klebold, possess above average intelligence. But they are chronic liars who have no internalized moral sense, and these future killers are preoccupied with blood, fire, and gore. Extremely narcissistic, severely attachment-disordered kids are self-destructive, even burning and cutting themselves.[19] They deeply resent their popular, successful peers. While cars, proms, and mainstream music fascinate normal teens, these kids are interested in guns, bomb making, assassinations, and violent Internet web sites.[20]

In an interview, Michael Orlans, who has worked with severely attachment-disordered children for years, said that future psychopaths share several characteristics. "They are cruel to animals; they engage in fire setting; and they wet the bed." When I asked him about bed-wetting, or enuresis, he replied, "They're pissed off at the world, and by wetting the bed they know they will hassle adults. They're very angry kids."

FAMILIES OF TEEN KILLERS

What kind of family produces an attachment-disordered child? While the family may appear normal on the outside, inside the home the family may be abusive, violent, neglectful, or chaotic. The mother may be severely depressed when the child is an infant or have other serious emotional problems. Either parent may be a substance abuser. Also, the parents themselves may be emotionally crippled by unresolved issues from their own families of origin, such as sexual or physical abuse, and the child may have experienced a history of separation or prolonged parental absences.[21] If he has had multiple caregivers, he has learned at an early age that to love is to lose. Again and again. This withers the heart.

When we look at the school shooters, we see that Barry Loukaitis had a suicidal mother who was planning to divorce his father. Luke Woodham was abandoned by his father when he was eleven; Mitchell Johnson had divorced parents.[22] On the other hand, Andrew Golden, Michael Carneal, Kip Kinkel, Eric Harris, and Dylan Klebold came from intact families—normal to the outside world. Of course, we don't know what went on inside these families, but as Michael Orlans said in an interview, "Something was wrong, deeply, seriously wrong."

Two forensic psychologists, James McGee and Caren DeBernardo, who have examined the lives of the school shooters, whom they call "classroom avengers," state that these lost boys come from dysfunctional families characterized by frequent hostility and explicit or covert anger.[23] Both the parents and the kids have lots of power struggles and battles for control, and when the parents attempt to discipline, they are either overly harsh or inconsistent.

The way these kids have been treated by their parents and the losses some have sustained is why they suffer from severe depression. I suspect that all have been depressed since infancy when they tried to fall in love with their parents and failed. Consequently, by the time they reach adolescence, they want to die—to kill or be killed.[24] On December 14, 1999, officials released footage from videotapes made by the Columbine killers, Harris and Klebold, three months before the massacre. The videotapes were filled with hatred and rage, as well as the boys' awareness that they would die.

"I'm going to kill you all," sneered Klebold, pointing an imaginary gun at the camera as Harris watched while he swigged Jack Daniel's whiskey. Harris and Klebold blamed years of taunting by schoolmates, rejections by girlfriends, and other snubs by peers for the coming rampage. Although he told the imaginary viewers not to blame his parents, Harris said, "I declare war on the human race. This is just a two-man war against *everyone* (italics mine).[25]

Such rage. Such venomous hatred. Such a warped view of self and the value of human life. And while I do not know what went on in the Harris and Klebold families, I do know that those two boys were not born with venom and hatred flowing through their veins. They were not then what *Time* magazine later called them—"The Monsters Next Door."[26]

WHAT CAN WE LEARN FROM KIDS WHO KILL?

What can we learn from all of this? First, *prevention is easier than repair.* As one former patient who came to talk about painful parental relationships said, "It's far easier to love and nurture a boy than mend a man." Every therapist I know would agree. It's far easier to rear a child who feels loved and worthy than try to repair a child full of rage who has no empathy or remorse or who possesses little or no conscience.

Since the attachment relationship between parent and child is in place by twelve to eighteen months of age, we need to value a child's earliest years and encourage mothers everywhere to surrender to mother love for a season and rear their babies themselves.

It's high time we stopped acting in this culture as if babies can experience the physical and emotional unavailability of their mothers without paying a high price. It's high time we stopped making on-site mothering a politically incorrect option. Babies' needs haven't changed simply because their mothers' lifestyles have changed. The data on how we're rearing many American kids are rolling in, and we need to acknowledge that our national experiment with absentee parenting during the past four decades hasn't worked. If things are going to get better in this country, we need to make new child-rearing choices.

I would also encourage those mothers at home who, along with their husbands, are making significant financial sacrifices daily to rear compassionate children to stop apologizing for their choice. Whenever I hear a mother say, "I am fortunate enough to be able to stay home," I want to tell her gently, "You're home—not because of good fortune—but because you and your husband made that choice. So stop apologizing for following your heart." We all make choices, and some of our choices help and some hurt—others and ourselves. But as I used to tell my patients, "If your choices are hurting you or others, you can always make new choices."

Speaking of new and positive choices, if a mother feels that she and her child do not have a close, secure attachment relationship, she can always choose to seek professional help.

If a mom is severely depressed and emotionally unavailable, she also needs to seek professional help. If she is too often absent, she needs to make new choices and spend more time at home.

If the family is dysfunctional and the marriage a disaster, then the couple must seek qualified intervention. The psychological research shows not only that boys are more emotionally vulnerable than girls from infancy onward, but they are also more disturbed by marital conflict.

We also know that discipline needs to be firm, but not harsh, and that it needs to be consistent. And if either parent has an anger problem, there are family origin issues that need to be confronted and resolved.

If you have an angry three- or four-year-old who is abusive to pets, attacks his siblings, or attacks you, get help. Get help while your child is very young because the problems you see now will not magically disappear.

When I questioned Michael Orlans about therapy for attachment-disordered kids, he said, "The younger they get treatment, the better." In fact, psychologists are able to predict with amazing accuracy which kindergartners will become troubled adolescents later on. Never ignore depression or rage or lying or stealing in young children, and don't just try to medicate the pain away. Get help and address its underlying causes.

What kind of help should you seek? Unfortunately, since attachment-disordered children cannot trust, traditional psychotherapy doesn't work for them. What does work is attachment therapy that attempts to turn rage into love by working on the source of the problem: the child's attachment relationship with his parents. This is a unique kind of therapy practiced by therapists who specialize in working with attachment-disordered children. Two clinics in Evergreen, Colorado, has successfully treated these children for years—The Attachment Center and Evergreen Psychotherapy Center founded by Dr. Terry Levy and Michael Orlans.

When I asked Michael Orlans how successful attachment therapy actually is, he responded, "Very successful." He continued, "It's amazing. I've had kids who were beyond hope. They had had ten therapists before they came to me. But corrective attachment therapy is a profound process. We redo what wasn't done in the first place, and it really works. These kids go on to become successful humans."

Corrective attachment therapy focuses on both the parents and the child. "We work as intensively with the parents as we work with the kids," said Orlans. "We teach them the proper way to manage difficult kids, and we help them resolve their own attachment issues." Families who enter attachment therapy are usually "traumatized"—angry and burned out. But as the parents and their child are better able to communicate and become more emotionally available to each other, healing begins to occur.

Attachment therapists also help the child create an attachment relationship with each parent, something that failed to happen in infancy. They do this by revisiting prior significant attachment and trauma experiences, such as separation, abandonment, abuse, neglect, multiple caregivers, and violence in the home.[27] As the child revisits these painful events and relives the emotions, he begins to heal. He can do this because the therapeutic relationship provides a safe place, possibly the first safe place he has ever known. He then learns to deal with his emotions, to develop a positive self-image, and to practice impulse control. All of this is done in the context of a unique "nurturing holding therapy" where several therapists and the parents physically hold the child or adolescent while he works through a painful past. And I've learned that often the parents experience holding therapy since they, prior to their child, have unresolved emotional pain. Amazingly, all of this is accomplished in a two-week intensive session.

What about Moms at Home?

What about all of you at home who are doing a good job of nurturing your sons and daughters? While this may have been an alarming chapter to read, you also can take action to protect your children and even help attachment-disordered children.

What action can you take? You can go to your child's school to see what the administration is doing to keep your child safe and to identify severely attachment-disordered children. While I have said it's not always easy to identify these kids, many schools need to try. School personnel need to become educated about emotional development gone awry. You can become an activist who challenges teachers and school administrators to take action to help troubled kids and their families.

You can also go to your church and ask your minister or priest what he is willing to do to heal fractured families. Will he teach about a child's real needs for parental time, love, and attention? Will he speak out about a baby's need for abundant time with his mother? And if he won't, then ask him why not, and give him a copy of this chapter.

You may also consider homeschooling your child, if that will give you peace of mind. It's a wonderful part of mothering, with a long and lovely history. A number of famous men—Abraham Lincoln, John and Charles Wesley, John Ruskin, Thomas Edison, the French poet Lamartine—were educated at home by their mothers. This is certainly an option if you feel that your child is unprotected at school and the administration is unresponsive.

One thing is certain; it's going to get worse in America before it gets better.

It's Going to Get Worse Before It Gets Better

Even as I was working on this chapter, the morning news broke the tragic story of a six-year-old boy who killed a six-year-old girl. When we look down the road to 2005, we see that as a nation, we will continue to experience the consequences of our choices in child rearing.

What can we expect? For one thing, we can expect more girls to become violent. Heretofore, school shooters have been lost boys, but unattached girls are violent, too. Michael Orlans told me of a facility for lost girls in Denver where the girls are so violent and destructive that the authorities are having to build a larger facility just to house and contain these wild females. Recently, I read about an African-American adolescent girl who killed a mother of two in Washington, D.C., over a minor traffic disagreement. The stocky teenager banged the mother's head on the pavement until she died.

I know this has been a sobering chapter, but it is time for our nation to wake up and understand that we cannot neglect our children except at great peril. We are already in the midst of the unraveling of our society. We must speak up and become champions of the nation's children. Change will only occur when we begin to value our children's earliest years and encourage mothers everywhere to give their hearts and their time to their children.

Who knows if we have not even been created for such a time as this? In the book of Esther in the Old Testament, Mordecai the Jew goes to the Persian queen, Esther, to tell her that her people are about to be exterminated. It is a time of personal and racial peril. Mordecai asks Esther to go to her husband, King Xerxes, to tell him of the plot against her people, even if it costs her her life. He says:

> "For if you remain silent at this time, relief and deliverance for the Jews will arise from another place, but you and your father's family will perish. And who knows but that you have come to royal position for such a time as this?" (Esther 4:14, NIV)

Like Esther, we live in a time of national crisis as far as our children are concerned. And we, like Esther, cannot afford to remain silent. But as we act and as we speak out, we will have the sense that God is using us and that we are alive in this era for such a time as this.

PART TWO

Chapter Eight

CEOs IN THE SUBURBS

*The amount of contact parents have with
their children has dropped 40 percent
during the last quarter-century.*

WILLIAM R. MATTOX, JR.

A t one time, Sarah Edwards was a harried working mother. According to Sarah, "Juggling a successful career and motherhood meant being dead tired most of the time and not being able to do either job with the dedication I wanted."[1]

One day, however, Sarah went to see two consultants she had worked with as a government administrator. Both were successfully operating home-based businesses. When Sarah left them, she told herself, *This is for me.*[2]

It took Sarah several years before she was finally able to work at home. Only after training to became a psychotherapist did she finally start a private practice at home as a clinician. Sarah says, "Working at home was like having flowers delivered to me every day."[3] Not only did Sarah become a healthier, happier woman, but she also became a more relaxed mother.

Sarah's husband, Paul, soon joined her at home, starting his own business as a political consultant. Today these husband-wife entrepreneurs are contributing editors and columnists for

Home Office Computing magazine and cohosts of the weekly *Home Office* show on the Business Radio Network, as well as the Los Angeles radio show, *Here's to Your Success*. Sarah and Paul Edwards have also written a book titled *Working from Home*, which is a must read for anyone desiring to start a home-based business.

THE MOVEMENT TOWARD HOME

Sarah and Paul Edwards are part of the "electronic cottage" movement Alvin Toffler forecast in his book, *The Third Wave*. Futurist Toffler predicted that increasing numbers of men and women would tire of long and expensive commuting and elect to work from home. According to Toffler, when the cost of installing and operating home telecommunications falls below the cost of commuting, a great upsurge in the number of home-based workers will occur. Toffler rightly noted that many men and women already worked from home, among them lawyers, designers, secretaries, therapists, architects, music teachers, salesmen, and insurance agents.[4]

According to *World* magazine, in the '90s the number of teleworkers increased fivefold to twenty million. One survey found that nearly half of the human resources executives polled said that telecommunications would be the biggest workplace trend in the new millennium.[5]

Why is America moving toward a "home-centered society"? Toffler said that the nuclear family is in trouble, and he predicted that people would shift their workplace from city to home as a way of strengthening the family. According to Toffler, "Work at home suggests a deepening of face-to-face and emotional relationships in both the home and neighborhood."[6]

Aware of this, more and more women are leaving the marketplace to work at home. These are the new CEOs of the suburbs. According to the U.S. Census Bureau, some 2.9 million women own their own businesses.[7] Of these, slightly more than half are home based. Who works at home? While many of these small entrepreneurs have only a high school education, roughly two-thirds have taken business courses or attended seminars to increase their knowledge. Most started their businesses with little or no capital, borrowing from banks or families or using savings accounts for start-up cash.

WHY WORK AT HOME?

Why are greater numbers of women electing to work at home? According to Marion Behr and Wendy Lazar, authors of *Women Working at Home,* the reasons are obvious: proximity to children, the desire to avoid commuting, the need for additional income, flexibility, and the low cost of operating a home-based business.[8] Possibly the greatest reward of working at home is that "home is where the kids are." What mother hasn't felt anguish when she has had to drop off an ill or unhappy child at day care?

Listen to one mother's unhappiness as she struggles with her own absence from her children's lives: "I have a B.S. degree in home and family services and work for the juvenile court. I see what happens to so many kids who do not get the attention they need. I have always been opposed to working outside the home, but feel trapped because I have not been able to come up with a workable alternative."

This mother of two preschoolers is afraid of what the future holds if she doesn't come home to nurture her children, but she has no idea of how to translate her skills and education into a marketable at-home career. What, she asks, is she to do?

How well I remember those feelings. Moving to Seattle after two years in London, I needed money to supplement the monthly child support. So I determined to find the perfect part-time job that would mesh with my education and skills while allowing me to be home halfdays. I found nothing that interested me. At the height of my frustration, when I had begun to wonder if I would have to work full time, a friend called. Jim Leach was then the director of the Washington State Criminal Justice Education and Training Center.

"Have you ever written a newsletter or quarterly journal?" asked Jim, after hearing that I still hadn't found a job.

"No," I said. "But I did teach college kids to write, so I know I could produce the articles."

"What about working with a printer?" he asked. "Do you know anything about layout?"

"No," I said hesitantly. "But I'm sure I could learn."

Within a few days I had agreed to produce a quarterly journal for the Criminal Justice Education and Training Center, applied for a business license, ordered business cards and stationary, and decided on an hourly fee. My editorial consulting firm was launched.

I worked at the Criminal Justice Center for a few hours each week, obtaining my assignments and conferring with Jim. Then I scheduled interviews with lawyers and judges or worked at home writing articles. This schedule worked well. The hours spent at the center or in interviews gave me essential adult contact, and the hours at home provided the necessary solitude for creative work.

Best of all, I could be with Holly and Kristen before and after school. I dropped them off at their schools each morning and picked them up each afternoon. Though Kris spent a couple of hours each day at the local day-care center after morning kindergarten, I picked her up at 2:00 P.M., and we had the rest of the afternoon together—time for shopping, outings, friends, and activities. My children have many happy memories of those years I worked at home. Both say those were the happiest years of their childhood.

The mother who works from home has the opportunity to spend quality afternoons with her children. Cherie Fuller, an accomplished writer, left her job as a teacher to pursue her writing at home. Says the author of *When Mothers Pray,* "I've never regretted that decision. With my new flexibility, I can watch Chris's 3:30 basketball games, pick up Alison from school, and be home when one of them is sick. I do have trying times when deadlines stack up like piles of laundry and it's my day to volunteer at school. But overall, I'm delighted with my arrangement."[9]

Lest one think that working at home is a second-rate way to go, here are some famous companies that got their start at home: Apple Computer, Baskin-Robbins Ice Cream, Domino's Pizza, Ford Motor Company, Hallmark Cards, Mrs. Fields' Cookies, Nike, Reader's Digest, and Hewlett-Packard, to name a few.[10]

One woman who started her business in her basement flat and lived to see her shops open in such cities as Milan, New York, Tokyo, London, and Melbourne was the late Laura Ashley. A mother at home, Laura began by printing designs on fabric, which were later made into towels and sold in London shops. Although the business started in 1953 and grew slowly, Laura Ashley's papers and fabrics are now highly prized by women throughout the world.[11] So a woman has no idea how far her talents will take her when she begins to turn her gifts into profit from home.

WHERE TO BEGIN?

You may be thinking, "I'm convinced, but where do I begin? How do I translate my skills into profit?" Though an in-depth response is beyond this chapter's scope, I hope to provide you with a plan for proceeding.

First, ask yourself the following:

- What do I love doing? What would make me want to get up in the morning?
- What do others identify as my skills and talents?
- What are my hidden talents?
- Do I have the personality characteristics needed for working at home?

For the moment, disregard that censorious voice that says, "Oh, you can't do that," or "You'd never make any money at that." If you're like me, your inner censor can kill creativity, so you must quietly and firmly turn it off. As a high school English teacher preparing students to write essays, I often said, "When you're anxious or your mind is blank, just write down everything that comes to mind. Do some brainstorming. Then group the ideas together logically."

Once you sit down with pen and paper and write down what comes to mind, you will begin to get in touch with inner desires as well as perceptions about your abilities. A friend told me that as she approached forty, she felt a need to dream a new dream. So she sat on the beach one day and asked herself, *What do I really want to do with my life?* As she watched the breaking waves, she realized she desired to become an accountant working from home. Since she hadn't finished college, she knew she'd have to go back to school to achieve her goal. With her two children in school all day, this woman determined to complete her education and acquire the essential credentials so she could start her own home-based business.

Next, think about your skills and talents that your friends praise and actually utilize. Can any of these be parlayed into a new career at home? Jane Dull began her business in interior decoration when her friends started asking her to help them organize and decorate their homes. "I always loved interior design," says Jane, "but my father wanted me to become a teacher instead." Yet even as she prepared to become a teacher, Jane took all of her college electives in interior design.

About a year ago a friend asked Jane to help her choose "everything" for a new home. Jane says, "I did it just for fun, but then another friend hired me to redo her house. I loved it. It was a ball, and I got paid for it."

This was the impetus Jane needed to start her own home-based business in interior design. Her activities span the gamut of creating plans to sewing fabric for cornices. And Jane works as her schedule permits. She uses little child care, consulting on evenings or weekends when her husband can look after the kids. As a mother of five children ranging in age from four to seventeen, Jane likes her job's flexibility. Even when she spends time with her family (her first priority) rather than pursuing clients, Jane finds that "every time we need the money, something falls in my lap."

POSSIBILITIES FOR A HOME-BASED BUSINESS

Accounting service	Bartering service
Advertising agency	Bed-and-breakfast
Aerobics classes	Cake decorating
Answering service	Calligraphy
Architectural designer	Career counseling
Art instruction	Catering
Babysitting referral service	Cleaning services
Balloon decoration	Color consulting

Computer programming or tutoring
Dancing instruction
Data processing service
Desktop publishing services
Editorial services
Fashion consultant
Financial consulting
Gift-buying service
Gourmet-cooking school
Graphic designer
Interior design services
Job placement and referral service
Landscape designer
Literary agent
Management consultant
Marketing consultant
Music instruction
Needlepoint instruction
Personnel consultant
Pet-sitting for unusual animals
Photography
Public relations service
Quilting
Resume-writing service
Shopping services
Singing-telegram service
Tax preparation
Technical writer
Toy making
Tutoring
Wardrobe consulting
Word processing or secretarial services
Writing newsletters and trade publications

(Taken from *Working from Home* by Sarah and Paul Edwards)

After assessing your skills and interests, it is time for a moment of truth. Do you have the personality characteristics needed for successful home working? Are you motivated? Can you plan your time and execute a project, meeting deadlines? Do you enjoy working alone?

Susan managed a large office with thirty employees before her baby, Carlin, was born. Now she works in public relations from home and loves it. "My former job was so stressful," says Susan. "Now I find myself relishing the freedom to set my own schedule and spend time with my baby."

On the other hand, Marietta, who enjoys the social contacts that work outside the home provides, found working at home lonely. For a time she tried working at home for her former boss, but decided she would rather go to the office for two days each week. "When I am at work, I work and socialize," says Marietta, "and when I'm home, I throttle back to live a relaxed lifestyle, caring for my daughter, meeting friends for lunch." Obviously, home-based businesses are not for everyone.

As Sarah and Paul Edwards put it, "Working at home means more control over your schedule and your environment than ever before. You are in charge, and there is no boss standing over your shoulder. There is no time clock to punch, no bell to tell you when to start and when to stop. There is no procedures manual for working at home—it's up to you. It can be a dream come true or a nightmare, depending on what you do. It's 100 percent up to you."[12]

People who flourish working at home are those who can create their own structure, who can set and achieve goals, and who are highly motivated to succeed.[13]

Next, find out all you can about your area of interest and about how to turn your interests into profit. As you read books and magazine articles about working at home, you will form a plan you feel comfortable with. Read local library notice boards for listings of seminars and workshops for beginning entrepreneurs. One mother who heads a successful home-based advertising agency says that she learned valuable information about self-management and marketing from seminars she attended.

If your library is limited, search bookstores for books such as *Homemade Money* by Barbara Brabec and *Working at Home* by Lindsay O'Connor. The following recent publications deal with working at home: Lynie Ardent's *The Work at Home Sourcebook,* Norman Schreibei's *Your Home Office,* and *Start,*

Run and Profit from Your Own Home-Based Business by Gregory and Patricia Kishel. These books contain chapters on establishing a home office and pricing and marketing your skills, services, or products. An excellent reference book is a must for the beginning entrepreneur.

Begin networking. Canvass friends and family acquaintances to find other mothers working at home in your area of interest or expertise. Have these women over for lunch or take them out for dessert and coffee. I have learned an enormous amount from talking to such women on the phone—women who meet deadlines, care for their children, and are willing to share their expertise with me. Whenever I've started a new venture, I've searched for a role model, someone who is already doing successfully what I want to do. Often this role model will give me access to her network.

Women in the workplace know the value of networking, and women who work out of their homes should too. Networking not only provides emotional support, but also saves valuable time. In my area, contacts with other writers have helped me learn about literary agents, writers' conferences, advances, editors, and marketing articles. I recently put a friend in touch with the editor of a national magazine I had worked for. She, in turn, gave me contacts at a national newspaper and a summer writers' conference.

Writer Georganne Fiumara, who has published in national magazines such as *Family Circle,* recognized the value of networking. She founded the Mothers' Home Business Network and publishes a New York-based quarterly publication by that name to help women network nationally.

Now create a work space or set up an office and learn about legal matters—from securing a business license to finding out about your city's or county's zoning ordinances. According to

Cherie Fuller, the U.S. Small Business Administration has local chapters that provide such information, as well as a free business start-up kit and counseling services.[14] Since eighteen states have laws governing work from home, Sarah and Paul Edwards suggest seeking legal assistance in establishing a small business.[15] These are essential matters that need to be settled before you send out a press release or tell your community that you are in business.

Realize that the hardest task you may have is self-management. Writer Ann Hibbard, who has two school-age children, plays tennis regularly, and is heavily involved in her church, says one "has to be an extremely disciplined person to write at home."

Hibbard, who wrote *Family Celebrations* and *True Friends,* admits she "goes in and out of discipline. Sometimes I'm totally disciplined and sometimes I fritter my time away."

Any mother who works from her home has to create a schedule that works for her. Some women find this easy; others find it impossible. If a woman is to succeed working at home, she not only has to create a workable schedule, but she also needs to maintain it. But what if children get sick or stay home on snow days? Sometimes this means working late nights, early mornings, or weekends to meet deadlines. Those I've interviewed who are happiest working at home are those who have the greatest flexibility in their schedules. In most cases, however, these mothers were earning less than those who have carved out more regular hours and have rigid deadlines to meet (and who hire child care when needed).

THE PAYOFF

Finally, what are the rewards of working at home? Most mothers who have successfully launched home-based businesses feel that they have the best of both worlds. They can be mothers first, adapting their work to their children's needs, but be entrepreneurs as well. "It's good to be home with my son," says Lisa Greenfield. "I feel I know more about his needs than anyone else. I couldn't have left him to go to work when he was small."

While Lisa can spend valuable hours with her small son, she also has the good feelings gained from managing a successful advertising agency, working for such clients as the American Red Cross and *Best Weddings*. Before her son was born, Lisa worked as the art director for an ad agency and supervised five designers. When she decided to leave her job, she took her skills and contacts with her. In working for projects for both Fortune 500 companies and small businesses, Lisa subcontracts some of her work to other designers and marketers.

Writer Nancy Pearcey loves working at home because of the intellectual stimulation it provides. Becoming pregnant when she was a seminary student, Nancy, who has published in *The Human Life Review* and *The World and I,* began her writing career producing science readers for elementary school-children. Nancy has now worked at home for thirteen years, and until recently earned a third of the family income. Now writing her first book, Nancy says her work satisfies an intellectual hunger, since in writing she is not just taking in but is also giving out—a rich experience.

Working at home allows a woman to be available to her children most hours and to provide additional family income. It also gives her life a depth and richness it might otherwise lack. This is not to say working at home doesn't have its crazy moments or humorous asides. One mother was in her basement office talking to a client when her two-year-old started screaming from the top of the basement stairs. The mother began stammering as she struggled to focus on her client's needs and block out the toddler's persistent shrieks. Supposedly in the care of his older sister, the toddler continuously banged the door, yelling *"Mommeee."* Finally, the client could stand it no longer and asked, "Do you have your office in a day-care center?"

This is only one problem the home-based entrepreneur faces. Another is to monitor the hours her children are in the care of others while mom works at home. If a woman is staying home to be accessible to her children and then spends most of her children's waking hours in her office (or finds that her emotional well is empty), she needs to question what she is doing. It is not enough simply to be present in the home if a sitter is providing most of the child care or the parent is emotionally inaccessible.

To provide "good enough mothering," a woman needs to manage her time, herself, and her moods. Moreover, she needs to take the longer view of her life and understand that she is only home for a season.

The following chapters are designed to help mothers with these critical issues in their lives so they are better able to meet the needs of their children.

Chapter Nine

HOME FOR A SEASON

I grow lives. Sometimes as a writer;
always as a mother. And I grow my own.
SHERRY VON OHLSEN

How are women different from men? While popular writers such as psychologist John Gray have written extensively about gender differences, to date, psychologists have failed to conceptualize a theory of normal female development. When they have done developmental studies, they have studied men and then extrapolated from the results to women.[1]

The late psychoanalyst Erik Erikson, who theorized about the eight psychosocial stages of development, wrote about men but had little to say about women's development. When he did speak of women, it was to say that a woman's identity could only be found after she chose a mate. In Erikson's model, while men forge an identity in adolescence and then seek heterosexual intimacy in young adulthood, women seek intimacy and in so doing, find their identity. So women's identities are embedded in their relationships.[2] The implication is that men know who they are before women do.

In *Finding Herself*, Ruth Josselson says that the "most important task facing women today is the formation of identity, for it

187

is in the realm of identity that a woman bases her sense of herself as well as her vision for the structure of her life."[3] What does Josselson mean by *identity*? This term includes a woman's choices, principles, and the priorities she establishes for her life—a stable sense of self.

In 1971 Josselson began a study of women's development of identity. Initially, she conducted interviews with sixty college seniors; twelve years later, she again interviewed thirty-four of these same women.

She found that while separation-individuation is a key theme for men in establishing an identity, women are more concerned about staying connected to the key players in their lives. For one thing, women never completely separate from their mothers. The relationship a daughter has with her mother is intense and lifelong. Josselson says, "Separation between mothers and their daughters then is only partial; at some level they always remain bound up with each other as though neither ever quite sees herself as a fully separate person."[4]

Josselson found that identity for the women in her study was not tied to political or occupational issues, but rather to social and religious realities. Also, she found that daughters internalize the core values and priorities of their mothers and either accept them or fight against them.

According to Josselson, "the internal presence of mother, her wishes and her approving smile, hovers just at the corner of consciousness, an ever-present other to whom a woman is continually responding."[5] Josselson believes that every woman must somehow integrate something of her mother's values and priorities into her own life or risk identity diffusion. To totally reject mother is to never quite know who one is. Says Josselson: "Some aspect of mother must be mixed in the identity in order to bind it, to make it cohere.[6]

Recently, Kristin told me a story that illustrates the strength of the mother-daughter bond. She was at the grocery store and overheard an African-American woman talking to the butcher. The woman said, "My mama has just pinched my last nerve, but I still call her every day."

The butcher grinned. "Well, you've only got one mama!"

And so the research shows. In Josselson's study, 85 percent of the women were close to their mothers ten years after graduating from college, and 50 percent said their mothers were either their closest or second closest connection. (Forty-eight percent remained close to their fathers, and only two women said dad was either the closest or second closest person in their world.) Josselson suggested that many would find this data surprising since the post-feminist woman is supposed to have left her mother "in the dust."

I remember the discomfort and anxiety I felt in the seventies when I read in popular magazines that daughters reject their mothers as role models if mom stays home. At the time my children were in high school struggling to separate from me, and some days they were quite rejecting. I wondered if they had any idea of the financial sacrifices Don and I were making so that I could be home and available to them.

In the intervening years, I have found this cultural message to be false. Each of my daughters has identified with me to some extent. Holly, who shares my love of literature and writing, was an English major and published short stories while in college. And Kristen, a psychology major, is planning to someday pursue her doctorate in psychology. Both daughters have become colleagues and friends. Holly has edited my books, Kristen and I discuss developmental research, and I have published books with both daughters. So I was not, as a mother at home developing her gifts, rejected as a role model.

Josselson's findings support this. She found that even when the women in her study worked, they still identified with their traditional mother's commitment to nurturance and family.

Identity and Confusion

Basically, the women in Josselson's study anchored their lives and identities in relationships. Many were disillusioned by less-than-satisfying careers. For these women in their early thirties, even those who were employed, identity was based on connections rather than career. Josselson found that this was true in her clinical practice as well. She has treated highly successful professionals for up to two years in intensive psychotherapy and found that they talk about their relationships rather than their work.

"Work success," says Josselson, "does not compensate for unfulfilled needs for human relatedness."[7]

Harvard psychologist Carol Gilligan, who found that achieving women do not describe themselves by their work but rather by their relationships, supports Josselson's perceptions. "If anything," says Gilligan, "they regard their professional activities as jeopardizing their own sense of themselves, and the conflict they encounter between achievement and care leaves them divided in judgment or feeling betrayed."[8]

This was underscored for me recently when I received a letter from a woman who is a corporate executive. Childless at forty, she writes:

> My life today is the "glamorous" life that is pushed on many American women. I work for a large firm, have an impressive title, and share responsibility for a staff of a hundred people at the vice presidential level. I am grateful for all the opportunities that have been given

me, but I am also aware there is little real glamour in my work, and *I have missed much that mothers have experienced.*

MAKING THE MOST OF SUMMER

With this in mind, how can a mother at home maximize those frustrating but sweet years of child rearing—the summer of her life? What positive steps can she take to create a life that nourishes both herself and her family? How can she find the emotional support she needs to keep sane some days?

God has given each of us gifts to develop and a life to enjoy. It is not important whether our gifts are major or minor. What matters is how diligent we are in cultivating what we have been given.

We need to discover and value our gifts—whatever they are.

I met an admiral's wife at a party years ago, and I asked her what she enjoyed doing. She replied, "Silly little things— needlepoint and gardening." I felt sad that this gracious, southern woman denigrated the activities that obviously gave her pleasure. Not all of us have highly visible gifts that the culture applauds, but we can enrich our world nonetheless.

Dare to Pursue Your Interests

One of the little-acknowledged secrets of life is that a woman's gifts can flourish during her years at home. Whether she is a potter, karate champ, aerobics fanatic, gardener, neighborhood psychologist, budding politician, or artist, the mother at home has the opportunity to expand her horizons, take a talent, and run with it. As a corporate executive has said, "Any man who works forty or sixty plus hours per week and commutes has little time, after functioning as husband and father, to pursue his own interests." The woman at home has that privilege. Granted, she has little time available when her kids are small and constantly demanding, but once they are in school, she will find she has hours each day to think her own thoughts and begin to dream her own dreams again. And as she uses the time well, capitalizing on the opportunities that come her way, she will develop abilities and interests she never imagined possible.

Eleanor Carr feels she grew as a person using her gifts during her years at home. When her sons, Peter and Jim, were in nursery school, Eleanor taught at the school for Wee Learners nine hours per week to earn her sons' tuition. "This helped me meet new people," says Eleanor, "and it helped me value mothering more highly." As her sons grew, Eleanor became involved in their activities, serving as a den mother for their Cub Scout groups. Eventually she took upholstery classes, and during those years when she and her husband frequented flea markets, she reupholstered her secondhand items like a professional.

When her daughter Julie was eleven, Eleanor traded her hat as a den mother for that of a Girl Scout leader, discovering she had considerable gifts as an organizer and administrator. It took some thought to plan all those weekend cookouts for Julie's hungry troop. It wasn't long after her stint in Girl Scouts that Eleanor became an elder in her church, cofounder and executive director of Home by Choice, Inc., a national network for mothers at home, and chaired a Washington, D.C., fundraiser for the homeless.

Eleanor discovered what abundant psychological research has supported: Self-esteem increases when we help others. As other adults praised her for her competence and dependability, she became more extroverted and confident.

In time Eleanor grew concerned about poverty and homelessness. So when her children were teenagers, it was a natural next step for her to work at Bethany Women's Shelter in Washington, D.C. There, Eleanor, an upper-middle-class, suburban woman, sometimes cooked for homeless women. Years later she became interim director of Bethany House and served on their Board of Directors.

Eleanor has a heart for homeless women. This wife and mother who jokes about perpetually charbroiling her family's food has not only cooked for Bethany House, but has on occasion bathed homeless women. "I realized these women are just like me," says Eleanor. "Although many are mentally ill, they have families. Some, at one time, had careers. All have their hurts. Most people view the homeless with fear, but that's because they don't realize the homeless are just like us in many respects."

In Eleanor's work with the homeless, she has also ventured into the drug underworld. A deeply religious woman, she on occasion went into crack houses looking for the young woman who for years called her for help, sometimes in the middle of the night. "It felt strange," says Eleanor, "going into a dark basement room with a D.C. police car sitting outside. But I wasn't afraid. I felt God was with me."

Eleanor believes her years of volunteering have greatly enriched her life. "You start out doing one little thing," she says, "and over time you realize how much more you have to offer. Besides that, people are appreciative of what you give."

Jane Dull is another mother at home who used her energies and talents well. Jane admits she has been a "neat nick" since adolescence. While most parents fail to get their teenagers to keep their rooms clean, Jane used to shake her chenille scatter rugs and walk *around* them so she wouldn't leave any visible footprints.

Having five active children, however, has cured Jane of that compulsive behavior. Nevertheless, this woman, who lives by the rule, "Don't put anything away until it's done right," also divides large jobs into small segments and organizes her home one area at a time. She uses masking tape to label her pantry shelves, dumps a drawer each day that gets organized by nightfall, and is currently using her organizational skills to help other women get the clutter out of their homes.

Schedule Time to Develop Your Gift

It matters not whether we live in chaos or order, because our homes reflect something of our personalities. For very little money, Sherry, once a prowler of flea markets and garage sales, has assembled a Ralph Lauren look. She has curtains made from Laura Ashley sheets, flea market baskets brimming with towels or magazines, and green and red plaid pillows on the white sofa that flanks her stone fireplace. Though she and Carl struggled financially in the early years of their marriage, theirs is one of the loveliest and most original homes I've ever visited. This is, in part, because Sherry is an original. A self-educated woman who later graduated from college, Sherry has been developing her considerable gifts at home for years.

Married to Carl, a warm, fun-loving man, Sherry is the mother of two daughters, Erin, thirteen, and Lindsay, eight. Ever since I met Sherry years ago, she has wanted to be available to her family, but also to develop her gifts, particularly her writing. It was hard when her girls were young, and Sherry used to say that some years she only wrote forty-five minutes a day. "That's why it took me five years to write my first novel."

When Lindsay started school, Sherry began to write with

a vengeance. She now publishes articles regularly in such publications as the *Christian Science Monitor* and *Bride* magazine. Her last assignment was in Saudi Arabia for *The World and I* magazine—interviewing U.S. troops. Sherry chooses to experience everything she writes about, including soaring and acupuncture, to name a few. She has even been swaddled in mud wraps in her search for the perfect scoop.

How does she find the time? Sherry is a disciplined woman. Her house is tidy when she sits down to write at 8:30 A.M. She takes an hour off at noon for exercise, and then it's back to work until her girls come home, and she resumes her role as mother. Each summer Sherry takes a week at a writers' conference to polish her craft. This past year she was asked to be a writing workshop leader and was paid for her expertise.

Sherry says her writing has given her life at home a sense of focus and direction. When she's with her family, she's wholeheartedly present; when she's writing, she is concentrating on her craft. Both give her life richness, depth, and texture.

Because we mothers at home have tasks that are repetitive and sometimes boring and frustrating, we need time each week to develop our gifts. If we paint, we need to find a few hours to set up the easel and uncap the watercolors. If our passion is for gardening, let us plant, hoe, and prune whenever we can. A garden can be a work of art. I tramped around the organic garden of a *Mother Earth News* writer last May and was delighted by what I saw. A wire rabbit run outlined the perimeter. This garden contained mounds of flower areas as well as lettuce, peas, and spinach. Created by a mother who worked with a baby on her back, this garden has been televised on the local evening news!

So make home the studio where you unfurl your canvases, unsheathe your garden shears, or boot up your word processor.

Find a room or a corner of a room that is completely yours, a plot of ground for your garden, or an organization to recognize your talents. And lose yourself in creativity a few hours each week. If you do this diligently, you will be surprised where your gifts take you—and how they restore your emotional energy.

Home As a Place to Create Memories

Next, a mother needs to think of herself as a scientist and her home as a memory laboratory.

Psychologists have discovered that we have different types of memory. Each of us has a short-term memory where we store information from a few seconds to a minute. We also have a long-term memory that holds information indefinitely.[9] While the evidence suggests that we forget what we take into short-term memory unless the information is passed into the long-term memory, psychologists believe that what goes into long-term memory probably stays there throughout life. If we can't remember our childhoods, this in no way means these memories have disappeared. It merely means retrieval cues have changed or that we repressed painful memories.

When I was teaching summer school at Georgetown University, my students and I watched a film in which Canadian neurosurgeon Wilder Penfield touched different sections of a woman's brain with a microelectrode. Part of the skull had been removed, and the patient's brain lay exposed. Since the brain has no pain receptors, this procedure did not hurt the patient, who was fully awake. As the doctor touched different areas of the brain, he asked the patient what she felt, and she responded that she was experiencing sensations in different areas of her body. At one point, she began to hear music, and she hummed a theme from a concert she had attended as a child.

Penfield's research suggests that memories from our early life are recorded in the brain. While we may have forgotten sights, sounds, and intense personal experiences, nonetheless they are permanently recorded on our magnificent brain. We may hear a song or smell a particular odor, and an event will come rushing back.

The famous French writer Marcel Proust dipped a little cake, a madeleine, into a cup of tea, and suddenly he remembered his childhood in Combray. The sight and smell of the tea and the shape of the madeleine released a flood of involuntary memories which he recorded in his classic *Remembrance of Things Past.*

What are the implications of this for the mother at home? I believe this should encourage a woman to consciously work at creating warm, happy memories for her children—memories with which they can warm themselves by the fire of remembered joy. This is not to say that we will never create unhappy or painful memories for our children. No one can raise a pain-free child. But we can attempt to celebrate life and consciously use the moments of the day to produce rich, warm memories.

My earliest memory dates from somewhere between the ages of two and five, the years I lived with my grandparents. I remember being terrified of thunderstorms. When a loud electrical storm raged at the end of a hot, muggy summer day, I would clap my hands over my ears and squeeze my eyes tight.

One day my grandfather, who came in from the pasture smelling of earth and sweat, saw me and scooped me up in his arms. He carried me to the front porch so we could watch the storm together. I can still feel the warm spray of rain on my face, still see the branches tossing wildly in the wind. "Listen to that thunder roll," said Granddaddy, obviously enjoying the moment. "You don't need to be afraid if you're not out there in the storm." That day I felt safe and secure as I watched the raging storm, held in my granddaddy's arms, and I have enjoyed summer storms ever since.

Whatever sense of security I have is due to times such as those I experienced at my grandparents' farm. Drawing on this storehouse of happy memories, I have consciously tried to create nourishing memories for my children. I have been a companion to them the way my granddaddy was to me, often piling them in the car on summer days for outings. I have talked to them just as my grandparents did to me.

Granddaddy, who dropped out of school in the eighth grade, was quite a storyteller. He regaled me for hours with tales of his courtship of Granny. Additionally, Granny, as adept as any social worker, was the first people detective I ever knew. "Now tell me how you feel," she would say about the significant events in my life. People tell me I am a prober *par excellence,* which simply means I was a good pupil.

Seize the Moment

During our years at home with our children, some events will be more intense than others. People tend to remember moments of emotional intensity, whether positive or negative. That's why some occasions in life seem to say "this moment is memorable." Seize it. Holidays and birthdays are such times. Recently we had a single friend to dinner on her birthday because she said her family never celebrated her birthday growing up. Consequently, she had not planned to do anything special on her birthday.

At our house, birthdays are always special events. The

birthday person dictates the activities, which include a party, or at least a family dinner, with favorite foods and cake. Also, gift requests are honored, and at the family meal we tell the birthday person what he or she means to each of us. I have a small stack of cards that were given to me by friends and family, and in the event of a fire, I'd rush to grab this treasured packet.

"A Place to Be"

Another way to create rich memories for ourselves and our children is to share our homes and lives with others.

A home can be a place of refuge for those who just need to be with a family for a while, as well as for those in emotional pain. One family who ministers beautifully from their home is the Hamiltons. Will and Susie met in London twenty years ago when Will was practicing medicine and Susie was a worker for L'Abri Fellowship.

Now living in Fairview, North Carolina, Susie and Will have five children, ranging in age from ten to twenty-five. Over the years Susie, a Wellesley graduate, taught all her children art and piano, and both she and Will have been deeply involved in the life of their church, which used to meet in the renovated garage behind Will's office. Susie also helped with her father's campaigns for the U.S. Congress. And for years she has supervised the harvest and sale of apples from twenty-five acres on her parents' nearby farm. In addition, almost since their wedding, Susie and Will have taken in those who show up on their doorstep.

One mountain girl, Rita, came to Will and Susie after her father thrust her out of their trailer home. Rita slept beside a cow the first night just to keep warm. A minister brought her to Susie's the next day and asked Susie to take her in. During the five years Rita lived with the Hamiltons, she helped Susie with household chores, babysat, and attended vocational school until she could support herself. During Rita's stay, I noticed Susie had a peculiar sign attached to the side of her kitchen wood box: "Don't spit in the wood box."

"What's that for?" I asked Susie, who flipped her blond ponytail and gave an embarrassed smile.

"Oh, Rita dips snuff. We would reach in for logs and get this brown stuff all over our hands. I finally figured out what it was."

In addition to Rita, who has become part of the Hamilton family, Susie and Will have had young people from all over the world stay with them.

Are there advantages to having a perpetual influx of people? Susie, who feels that having an open home flows from her faith in God, believes that her children's lives have been enriched by the many cosmopolitan visitors. She also admits that she and Will need the labor their guests provide. "We don't hire people to help us, so those who come have to help out," says Susie. "The boy from Covenant College is helping us with our plumbing, and we once had a Swiss hairdresser who gave everybody haircuts." Since Susie and Will have pigs, chickens, and ponies to feed as well as gardens to plant, they need the help that their visitors provide.

Susie, who now has a worldwide network of friends, is quick to say that it is relatively easy for her to have people live with them since they have the "big house," the parental farm, just up the road. Susie's parents have a thousand-acre working farm that readily absorbs human labor. Also, as part of an open church community, Susie and Will can "plug people into" their laid-back church. She speaks truth when she says, "We take care of our loneliness when we reach out to other people."

While most of us will not choose to take people into our homes for months or years, we can learn from the Hamiltons. They provide role models for the rest of us, who live more insular lives in suburbia. They teach us that as we give another "a place to be," we are enlarging the boundaries of our own spiritual and emotional lives. And we are teaching our children to have open hearts and, later, open homes.

Susie's married daughter, Annie, has a young woman sharing the log house where she, baby, Sydney Rose, and husband, Isaiah, live. Just as her mother before her, she has opened her home to others.

There's another payoff for the kind of generosity the Hamiltons have exhibited. This summer twelve of them (family and friends) will stay in two rent-free houses in Brittany for two weeks. Why rent free? Susie and Will housed a French student for a year. In exchange, his parents and grandmother are giving the Hamiltons free housing. So what we send into the lives of others comes back into our own.

As women, we are only home for a season. Since our time at home is short, let's make the most of the summer. Then armed with positive memories, we can embrace more fully the world beyond our doorstep. We can dance into a winter of rich reward, rather than shuffle into a season of regret.

But what about those of you who were unnurtured as children and who feel isolated and alone?

You may struggle with depression or have a hard time organizing your day and reaching out to other women. What do you do if you feel overwhelmed by your life?

Chapter Ten

WOMEN AND DEPRESSION

*I really do believe that I enjoy hardly
anything on earth while it is present:
always looking back, or frettingly peering
into the dim beyond.*

EDWARD LEAR

Maxine, thirty-three, leans forward, delicately balances her coffee cup, and says softly, "I've never been deeply depressed, but I do have my low hours and days. Sometimes, especially in the winter when I have been locked in the house all day with the kids, I feel very low. Then when Tom comes home, I look at him and say, 'Is this all there is to life?'"

Stacey, thirty-five, a mother of three small children, is battling more than a few hours or days of depression. She has been depressed for several months now, ever since her last child, a colicky, demanding daughter was born. The child of alcoholic parents, Stacey senses that her early life is somehow related to her present vulnerability but she doesn't quite know how. Meanwhile, she struggles with a mounting desire to leave her husband and kids. "I've thought of leaving Charlie before," she says, "but lately I've wanted to run away from the kids also."

Selena, twenty-nine, and Mike are the parents of one-year-old Cecily. A computer expert at a northern Virginia corporation, Selena likes her job but is often exhausted by the multiple demands of her life. She feels that she is supposed to manage child, job, marriage, and home effortlessly, but she finds her life becoming increasingly joyless. Mike tells her she is short-tempered most of the time. Standing in front of the refrigerator on sleepless nights, Selena wonders what is wrong with her life. "I love Mike; I love my job. But I feel stretched all the time. Life isn't fun anymore."

WHO GETS DEPRESSED?

Most women struggle with either mild or moderate depression at some time in their lives, whether they are employed at home or in the workplace. Obviously, not all experience the same degree of depression. Some get the blues occasionally and feel depressed for several hours or a few days. Others experience full-blown clinical depression and know they are lost in the pit of despair. Sometimes the mother at home believes that if she were only back at work, she would be free of the blues. She feels guilty because although she is home, she is not emotionally available for her children. To be effective at home, women need to understand depression: what it is, who gets it, and how to overcome it.

To be human is to be vulnerable to depression. What man or woman alive would say he or she has not, on occasion, felt depressed? To admit this is to join good company, as anyone knows who has read the psalms of David, the lamentations of Job, or the laments of Shakespeare's Timon of Athens. Clinicians consider it normal to experience transient feelings of sadness and disappointment from time to time—what some of us call "the blues." What is not normative, and what concerns mental health professionals, is depression that lingers on, permeating the whole cloth of life. When depression is "unduly persistent and pervasive," when it hangs on for several weeks or months, it is considered pathological.[1]

While the majority of Americans will suffer from serious depression at some time in life, women, more than men, fall prey to it. In 1980 Myrna Weissman at Yale, along with her colleague Gerald Kierman, found from extensive study that depression is much more common among women than men. This finding persisted whether researchers studied hospitalized patients, outpatients, or participants in community surveys. Women outnumbered the men almost two to one.[2]

Why is this so? Weissman suggests that in women, clinical depression is often in synchrony with the reproductive cycle. We get depressed around the time of menstruation and during postpartum. She also believes that women have a disadvantaged societal position and may suffer from chronically low self-esteem because of feelings of dependency or their "legal and economic helplessness."[3]

While I agree that we women are tied to our hormones, I believe we are more vulnerable to depression because we are by nature more relational. As women, we value our relationships highly. Any woman who has ever been involved intimately with a husband or child or a close female friend is a prime target for depression. Demographers have found that mothers, whether married, separated, widowed, or divorced, are particularly depression prone.[4]

In her book, *Unfinished Business: Women and Depression,* Maggie Scarf writes that even as babies, females smile more often, are more responsive to the cries of other babies, and pay greater attention to photographs of human faces than do male babies, who at three months still cannot discriminate between photos.[5] We women are not only more sensitive to human faces, but also to touch, taste, and pain. Moreover, we are acutely sensitive to the loss of our significant relationships.

WOMEN AND DEPRESSION

Scarf interviewed Marcia Guttentag, head of the Harvard Project on Women and Mental Health, about a review she did of popular literature. Guttentag found that material geared for a male audience contained themes of adventure, mastery, and triumph, while material directed at women was oriented almost exclusively toward loss. Women were advised about how to handle the loss of lovers, spouses, children, parents, friends—the rupture of their lives' most significant relationships.[6] To care about relationships is to be vulnerable to devastation if they end.

When my first husband left me, I sank into a profound and terrifying depression for the first time in my twenty-eight years. I couldn't sleep. Some nights it was 3:00 A.M. before I drifted off into a troubled slumber. In addition, I had difficulty swallowing. All that I could consume was milk, so I rapidly lost ten pounds. I felt desolate and lethargic, as if some part of my body had been dismembered. It was all I could do to get up in the morning, dress and feed my children, and confront the day. The depression lingered on.

I felt undone by the events in my life. I alternated between rage and sadness over the death of my marriage. Mostly, I grieved. My divorce revived all the anguish of my earlier losses.

I felt I needed to be with other people for my sanity—I could not bear lonely days and empty nights. My family lived hundreds of miles away, and since I had just moved to Connecticut, I had few friends. So I took a job teaching English at a local high school.

For nine months I worked, battled despair, and tried to be a good mother with what energy I had left. Employment helped but did not erase my depression. (Depression has a life of its own; employment is not necessarily a cure.)

In time, the depression lifted. When the three of us moved to London, I stumbled onto a powerful antidote to depression: friendships with other women. I developed close friendships with several other mothers at home, and in so doing I found the emotional nurture I needed to heal.

Women need other women, cradle to grave. I have written extensively about women's relationships in my book, *In the Company of Women*. The truth is that we wither in isolation; we blossom with nourishing friendships. We need our female friends in the good times of life, and we especially need them when we are grappling with the loss of a spouse, parent, or friend.

Lynn is struggling just now with the loss of friendships. She and her husband, Noah, a minister, have just moved to a new community for Noah's career advancement. Lynn, who happily agreed to the move, has been surprised at how depressed she has become. "Moving means I have to start all over again," she says. "In Statesville I had friends and a definite role in the church. Here I have nothing important to do. I have no one to call for coffee. No one to invite over for lunch. I know I have to reach out and, believe me, I'm trying. But it's still hard."

Unfortunately, the American family moves once every five years on average. So lots of women experience powerful feelings of dislocation and transient feelings of depression as they struggle to redefine themselves, make new friends, and find new outlets for creativity. When we lose an important friendship, have trouble in our marriages, or experience isolation with small children, we are likely to feel depressed. I once said to a patient, "Show me a woman who has been at home alone with small children for a week, and I'll show you someone who is depressed."

WOMEN AND DEPRESSION

In sum, women are more likely to get depressed than men, and losses exacerbate depression. This is true because we look to our relationships to help define us and to maintain a sense of positive self-esteem. When we lose someone we love, move, or lose good friends, we mourn for a time. When we have a rousing fight with our husband, he may go off to work and forget the animosities while we are depressed all day!

Vulnerability Factors

It is important to note that some women are more vulnerable to depression than others. Researchers George W. Brown and Tirril Harris, studying some five hundred women living in London, found that women are vulnerable to depression when they have a lack of intimacy with a husband or lover, have three or more children in the home, or have lost a mother to death prior to age eleven. Nearly half of the depressed women in this study had experienced early maternal death, compared to 17 percent of the nondepressed women in the study. Loss of mother after age eleven or loss of father at any age was unrelated to depression.[7]

Brown and Harris speculate that a mother's death before her daughter is eleven produces an enduring change in the daughter's personality, a change that will generate greater dependency and a decreased sense of self-esteem. The loss of her mother gives a girl a lasting sense of insecurity and feelings of incompetence—the feeling that she cannot control the "good things" of her life. The authors of this study argue that before a child is eleven, the mother is in charge of the child's world. So mother's death equals loss of control, something from which the girl has a hard time recovering. As a result, she finds later losses intensely threatening.

Brown and Harris found that early maternal loss was also

associated with lack of intimacy with a partner. While the researchers believe a confiding relationship with a partner can act as a protective buffer against depression, the depressed mothers in their study lacked such a relationship. It is my conviction that children learn how to speak their innermost thoughts at their mother's knee. If a mother dies—or is emotionally inaccessible for any other reason—her daughter may never have learned to speak the language of the heart.

A woman can learn how to have a confiding relationship from other women or from a sensitive, open, patient husband. If a woman has a combative or distant relationship with her mother but feels loved by her father, she is often uncomfortable with other women. She has learned male communication skills (rationality, get-to-the-bottom-line argumentation), but she lacks the ability to confide in other women. She does not speak, or listen to, the language of intimate feelings. This woman may simply conclude that she doesn't like other women, or that they don't like her. Also, her difficulties with other women may reinforce the negative ideas she holds about womankind—ideas she acquired from her relationship with her mother.

Women and men are fortunate, indeed, if they are taught to speak their feelings, both positive and negative, by a warm, sensitive, accepting mother. This makes men better husbands and women better mothers.

Some of you may say, "My mother and father are still alive. I have experienced no great losses. So why do I struggle with depression?" Our early experiences in our families also have a lot to do with our later vulnerability to depression. Those who come from families short on nurture, guidance, or emotional support are prone to depression later on, while those who grow up in sociable, warm, emotionally close, and compassionate families seem to be inoculated against serious depression.

Moreover, loneliness in adolescence and adulthood springs from the same soil as depression. One study found that adolescents who remembered their parents as "emotionally distant, untrustworthy, and hostile" were lonely, while those who remembered their parents as "warm, close, and helpful" were not.[8]

In addition, parental rejection in childhood has been linked to later depression. Psychologists Monroe Leftkowitz and Edward Tesiny studied children when they were eight years old and again when they were nineteen.[9] They found that maternal rejection was significantly correlated with depression in daughters and that father rejection was even more powerfully linked with a daughter's later depression. These researchers suggest that when a daughter fails to measure up to parental expectations—when parents are harshly critical, or when they withhold affirmation—she may grow up feeling helpless. These feelings of helplessness later get translated into adolescent and adult depression.

Today Evelyn, the mother of two small sons, looks like a vulnerable child. Her eyes are sad as she informs me of her boys' latest shenanigans and finally warms to the reason she called and scheduled an appointment. She wants to talk about her mother. Evelyn is sorting out her insecurities and wondering why she is so frantic about winning her mother's love. In the past she has thought, "If only Mike met my needs, then I would love myself more."

As a result of our work together, Evelyn is beginning to understand that an ebb in marital romance is not her most besetting problem. Granted, Mike has his difficulties communicating from the heart (he had his own painful early life), but

Evelyn's low self-esteem has deeper roots. "I love my mother," she says, "but I'm beginning to see that she has had little love to give me in return. Recently I went to see her. She picked up my boys and hugged them, but when I went up to her and put my arms around her, she stiffened. That hurt. Because my mom has rejected me, I keep expecting others to also reject me. I'm afraid of losing important relationships, and that makes me feel vulnerable. I keep trying to fill up the emptiness inside."

DEPRESSION LEADS TO BLACK-AND-WHITE THINKING

Depression is feeling inside, *I am unloved; no one will ever truly love me. Nothing will ever be worthwhile.* These feelings are persuasive and powerful. When one is in perpetual darkness, one's will is paralyzed; bleak feelings cloud the emotional landscape. I spoke to a woman who recently emerged from a deep depression that had lasted for several months. She feels better now, though the previous night she couldn't sleep. "I told myself I had accomplished nothing in my life, and I never would do anything significant in the future," says Ellen, an unmarried schoolteacher.

The woman who is prone to depression is harsh in her self-evaluations. Where do these perfectionistic thoughts come from? Psychiatrist Robert Leahy, in his book, *The Development of the Self,* says the individual who is at risk for later depression forms certain thought patterns early in life that spill over into adulthood.

For example, a woman who experienced parental death or divorce in childhood may think, "No matter what I do, it can all be taken away."[10]

This concept of thought patterns sounds very like John Bowlby's internal working models of attachment. Remember his assertion that we form these attitudes toward ourselves and others early in life? Bowlby also feels that once formed, our internal working models operate outside of our conscious awareness, and this makes them hard to change. But this is just what we must do to conquer depression. And conquer we can.

Overcoming Depression

Cognitive therapy is possibly the most effective form of psychotherapy for treating depression today. Created by psychiatrist Aaron Beck, one of the world's foremost authorities on mood disorders, cognitive therapy focuses on the way we think. According to one of his protégés, psychiatrist David Burns, Beck's thesis is simple: We *feel* the way we *think,* and when we are depressed, we think in illogical, self-defeating ways.[11]

In his book *Feeling Good: The New Mood Therapy,* Burns says that when depressives believe life has always been impoverished, they decide the future will be just as gloomy. "As you look at your past," says Burns, "you will remember all the bad things that have happened to you. As you try to imagine the future, you see only emptiness or unending problems and anguish. This bleak vision creates a sense of hopelessness. This feeling is absolutely illogical, but it seems so real that you are convinced your inadequacy will go on forever."[12]

Our negative thoughts are distorted, says Burns. A depressed person engages in all-or-nothing thinking ("because I failed this exam, I'm stupid"); overgeneralization ("no one will ever like me"); mental filter ("she would reject me if she really knew what I am like"); and labeling ("I'm a loser").

What do we do once we recognize that we engage in these cognitive distortions? Burns suggests that by writing our automatic thoughts down we can begin to counter the negative, illogical thoughts with rational responses. If a mother punishes her child unfairly and then regrets it afterward, instead of saying, "I'm a bad mother because I spanked Jimmy for something his sister did," she should say, "What I did is unfair, so I'll make amends to Jimmy and try to do better next time."

What about the mother at home who is struggling with the winter blues and a sick, cranky child? Suppose she goes to an office party with her husband only to have an aggressive career woman walk away upon learning the mother stays home. Instead of telling herself the next morning, "What I'm doing here at home isn't valuable," she might say, "So what if *one* unmarried woman spurns me! I know what I'm doing is important."

And the divorced mother who struggles with loss? It is too easy to say: "My husband rejected me; no other man will love me." It's far better to tell herself, "One man has rejected me. That's his loss. I can find love again."

Burns believes that as we become aware that our thoughts precede—and determine—our feelings, and as we learn to control our thoughts, we can banish depression. This is happy news for those of us who battle more than a few blue hours or days. This approach gives us the feelings we are not pawns in the universe or helpless victims because of our early life experience. Rather, we are people who can actively help ourselves.

And if we don't exert our wills? Then we can be lured into deeper darkness.

Perhaps no celebrated life illustrates the volitional aspect of depression better than that of poet and mother, Sylvia Plath. Plath committed suicide when she was thirty, just after the publication of her novel *Bell Jar* and shortly after separating from her husband, poet Ted Hughes, who was involved in an affair. In *Bitter Fame,* Anne Stevenson's biography of Plath, Stevenson chronicles Plath's deliberate descent into darkness.[13] Plath, who had attempted suicide at age twenty, lost her father to death when she was eleven. She wrote obsessively about death and was filled with rage at her father and God. *Ariel,* her last collection of poems, is the work of a gifted depressive who courted the guardians of the dark gates.

SCRAMBLING TO SAFETY

It was liberating when I finally discovered I did not have to give in to my tendency toward depression—making myself and others miserable. I was not chemically depressed; I had learned to think negatively about myself and my future from childhood on. Therefore, I could *choose* to help myself. I could *choose* to seek the company of others when I felt, as a writer, too isolated. I could also redefine myself and let go of the perfectionism that had dogged my steps. In addition, I could begin to deal with all those early losses. And I could choose to cry out to God to help me. He always heard and responded. Perhaps it is overly simplistic to say we choose to be depressed. We can, however, choose to get the help we need.

Karen admitted that at one level she wanted to remain depressed. "I deliberately gave in to it," she says. "It was as if I deserved to be depressed. I know that sounds schizophrenic—to cry out to God while sinking into despair, though I didn't see it at the time. But I can remember both kinds of thoughts."

We remain in the darkness at our own peril. If we allow the darkness to engulf us, we may not be able to combat the inertia that sets in. We must learn to catch ourselves at the beginning of our downhill slide. As we monitor our self-talk, we fight back. We can substitute rational, positive thoughts

HOME BY CHOICE

for negative ones. Also, we can engage in some self-care and nurture the woman inside who desperately needs some care-taking.

Although it's hard to care for ourselves properly if we weren't adequately cared for as children, nonetheless we must. We must reparent ourselves and do a better job of providing for our physical and emotional needs. I recently encouraged a mother of two small children to hire a sitter, have lunch with a friend, buy herself her favorite flowers, and then schedule a night away with her husband at their favorite bed-and-breakfast. This young friend had the winter blues and needed an immediate life. She told me later that she took my advice and had a great time with her friend and husband.

Programming Pleasure into Our Lives

We will begin to feel worthless and depressed if we consis-tently deprive ourselves of those good things that bring us pleasure. If this deprivation continues for a long period of time, we may become increasingly paralyzed. David Burns says that depressives suffer from "do nothingism." His answer is to have clients log daily activities and make lists of activities that yield fun and pleasure. He believes people feel better when they become productive and engage in activities that nourish the spirit.

I enjoy lunches out with other women. This is somewhere near the top of my "pleasurable activities list" (after quality time with my husband and daughters). When I feel, because of writing, that my solitude is leaving me prey to low feelings, I schedule time with good friends. I immediately feel better after scheduling the luncheon date on the phone!

What activities do you enjoy? If it's tennis, schedule a match next week. The physical activity as well as the social time will serve as a tonic. If you like to shop, golf, or drive in the country, call another mother, pack a picnic lunch, and pile the kids in the car for an excursion.

Maybe you enjoy art galleries or museums or reading poetry. If so, find the time, even a few hours a week, to do these things you enjoy. Sometimes what a woman needs is a room of her own, "a place to retreat to pursue activities that nourish the spirit and define the self." Said one young mother, "I'm going to engage a sitter a few hours each week so I can retreat to a room upstairs to read, write, and think my own thoughts."

Close female friendships, unless they're going awry, are nearly always a hedge against depression. Yet I have been surprised at how few women seek emotional support from their friends. Once after I had spoken about depression to a group of young mothers at a church, I asked how many saw a friend once a week. Out of twenty women, only one raised her hand. Several indicated they took the kids to McDonald's once a month with another mother. "I am lucky if I have a heart-to-heart talk with a good friend every six months," said one woman who had talked about her own private struggle with depression. As I left the group that day, I realized anew just how hard it is for some young mothers to take good care of themselves emotionally.

MOTHERS' SUPPORT GROUPS

That's why I later became involved in a national organization to help mothers at home create the emotional support they desperately need. In 1987 three other mothers and I formed Home by Choice, Inc., a national network to encourage mothers at home. Starting with just four women, Home by Choice soon had 3,500 constituents in all fifty states and several foreign countries. One of the things we four believed strongly was that mothers at home needed help in creating supportive networks. We concluded that a major thrust of Home by Choice would be to help mothers start and run support groups that would meet either weekly or biweekly to discuss topics of interest.

The focus of the HBC mothers' support groups, then, was to provide parenting information and education, as well as encouragement and emotional support. We learned that friendships develop and that women flourish as a result of finding other mothers who share their Judeo-Christian values in a nurturing group setting. Although the organization no longer exists, the principle still holds: Women need other women in every stage of life, and they need to meet with a few compatriots on a weekly basis.

Psychological research confirms that we women need emotional support throughout our lives, but especially when we have young children. Bowlby said that mothers of young children are most vulnerable and need all the help and support they can get.[14] This is especially true in contemporary America where the nuclear family is in dire straits, and many parents feel isolated and alone, even powerless at times. A way to combat this feeling of powerlessness (and the absence of extended family) is to encourage women to create meaningful networks.

Home by Choice was one of the earliest support groups to spring up around the country, an indication that mothers at home were hungry for some recognition of their needs. A number have told me that after only a brief period in an HBC support group, they felt much better about themselves as mothers and about their decision to stay home. Listen to one woman describe her experience.

Cheryl Crigger Morgan, a C.P.A., experienced culture shock when she and her husband moved to Washington, D.C., from her hometown in Charleston, West Virginia. Knowing no one, Cheryl and her three-year-old daughter spent a number of days alone after the move, until a neighbor invited her to an HBC support group.

Cheryl, who was four-and-a-half-months pregnant, was pleased to meet another mother whose due date was close to her own. "I was so excited to finally be with other women my age and have adult conversations that I spoke as rapidly as was humanly possible," says Cheryl. "Fortunately, no one seemed to notice."

According to Cheryl, the HBC support group helped make her transition to Washington, D.C., easier. Having worked "crazy hours" as a C.P.A. during most of her daughter's life, Cheryl was unprepared for the unstructured life at home. With the group's help, however, she was "able to feel good about leaving the workforce and approach life at home with greater confidence." Most important, Cheryl found close friendships within the group—women who celebrated the birth of her son, Grant, with her and her husband.

Had she remained alone at home, Cheryl might have become depressed. Instead, she found invaluable support and friendship. As a result, her self-esteem soared, and she has made the transition from the office to home in fine style.

Belonging to a support group where a mother can share her feelings honestly is a powerful boost for flagging self-esteem. One woman said, "I haven't thought about low self-esteem for about a year—the same period of time I've been in this group. I guess being with other moms who share my values has made me feel stronger."

Although the Home by Choice organization no longer

exists, any mother can start a Home by Choice group simply by inviting three or four other mothers to meet with her weekly. We suggested that each group have structure—that the women study a book or have speakers periodically and always start with a devotional and end with prayer for the real needs of the women present. A simple format, but it worked. We, the founders, felt that women craved talk time, so all meetings needed to allow time for in-depth sharing.

What to do with the kids? Some groups kept the children underfoot, while others hired a sitter to come to a home or a church. What was important was that the women met at the same time and the same place weekly. That way they could count on time with other women as the week cranked up, and they could, in time, become important to each other much as the little prince became important to the fox in Antoine de Saint-Exupéry's classic, *The Little Prince*.

I would like to recommend two organizations for mothers at home that provide publications and conferences for those committed to on-site mothering:

HEARTS AT HOME
900 W. College Avenue
Normal, IL. 61761
(309) 888–MOMS

MOTHERS AT HOME
8310A Old Courthouse Road
Vienna, Virginia 22182

Although neither organization sponsors support groups, Hearts at Home provides a forum for those mothers who believe strongly in what they do. The women in this organization view moms as professionals, and they provide a venue for sharing experiences and meeting other women at their regional conferences. I have had the pleasure of speaking twice for this organization, and these moms have the best-organized and the most nurturing conferences at which I have ever spoken. I loved being with them, both in Normal, Illinois, and this past year in Chicago. They also publish a magazine and devotional for their audience of some thirty-five thousand moms.

Mothers at Home publishes a quality magazine written by and for mothers called *Welcome Home*. The leaders of this organization are savvy, smart women who believe strongly in the value of mothering, and they carry their message to senate subcommittees on Capitol Hill as well as to the media. I have worked with these moms on occasion and have great admiration for them and believe in what this organization is about. Mothers at Home has been "a voice for mothers for seventeen years," and an effective one at that.

So contact these and other mothers' organizations or create a weekly Home by Choice support group. Not only will you feel better about yourself and your life, but your family will also prosper. You've heard the saying, "If Momma ain't happy, ain't nobody happy!" Well, it's true. And little makes Momma happier than time spent with other women in nourishing friendships.

For many women, this will be enough. Because they received sufficient parental love growing up, they struggle with only occasional blue hours or days. But what about the woman who suffers from heavy-duty depression—the woman who has what I call the *unnurtured self?* How can she find the love and healing she so desperately yearns for? Where does she go for relief from pain? And who can possibly understand her deepest hurts?

Chapter Eleven

HEALING THE WOUNDED SELF

Success is counted sweetest by those who ne'er succeed.
To comprehend a nectar requires the sorest need.

SALLY DICKENSON

Sophie sat on my chintz sofa, stroking our overweight calico cat, Muhammad, who reclined in her lap. Sophie, an émigré who left Moscow six years ago, began to tell her story in halting English.

"My mother went to work part time when I was a little girl, and then when I was four, my parents divorced, and my mother started to work full time. I was sent to a neighbor who lived nearby, but her children resented me. They said, 'Why don't you go to your own home?' and I would cry. Then when my mother came home at night, I was difficult, and she punished me."

Sophie hit her chest lightly with her fist. "I have always felt something was missing," she said. "Something here." And she hit her chest again.

I sat quietly, resisting the impulse to put my arms around this woman who looked so much like a distressed child. I sensed what Sophie needed was to "own" her pain and feel my comforting presence across the room. She continued, voicing an old, deep woe that seemed to emerge from her

221

HEALING THE WOUNDED SELF

most primitive, vulnerable self. Sophie said she had longed for her father's love, but because her mother had been so embittered, she refused to allow Sophie to even see him. Sophie cried quietly, her shoulders heaving.

Struggling to regain her composure, Sophie said, "Now when I try to play with my child—she's two—I can't. I want to, I really do, but somehow I just can't."

"I understand," I responded, knowing that this woman who had failed to experience sensitive, caring mothering would have a hard time giving to her child. As one child psychologist said, "To give a child good mothering, you need to have received it yourself." Sophie's mother had not been present, either physically or emotionally, for her daughter in early childhood. Moreover, she had been insensitive to Sophie's losses, so it was understandable that Sophie was having great difficulty responding to her small daughter.

In truth, Sophie needed to be mothered herself. Only as she finds nurture for her unnurtured self can she break out of that pattern of attachment insecurity her mother and father bequeathed to her. This chapter, then, is for those mothers who *wish to be home* for their children but who, because of their attachment histories, feel they are inadequate mothers.

OUR MOTHERS/OURSELVES

In 1977 Nancy Friday published *My Mother/Myself,* which became a national bestseller. In her book, Friday explored the complex relationship a daughter has with her mother. Speaking for herself and for many other women, Friday wrote: "All my life I had shown the world an independent person, a brave exterior that hid the frightened child within. This split in which I had lived had sapped my strength, leaving me divided against myself. The split had begun to heal when my writing forced me to recognize that my fears and angers were those a child felt toward a mother of long ago who was also a woman, like myself."[1]

Friday wrote about the conflicted and distant relationship she had with her mother, and her story helped millions of women to recognize their mothers as key players in their adult lives, not only influencing their capacity to parent but also their feelings about themselves as women.

In keeping with Bowlby's attachment theory, psychologist Seymour Epstein believes that a woman's level of self-esteem in adulthood is highly correlated with her mother's acceptance or rejection of her in childhood.[2] Those women who experienced responsive mothering in childhood tend to have high self-esteem in adulthood, while those women whose mothers were insensitive or rejecting in childhood struggle with low self-esteem and feelings of depression. To feel "love worthiness" as an adult, a woman needs to have experienced her mother's acceptance and love early in life.

This high self-esteem enables us to parent well. A study of twenty-eight mothers with their infants supports this theory. The researchers studied children who were one year old and found that those mothers who had securely attached children not only reported higher self-esteem, but also had positive memories of childhood relationships with their mothers, fathers, and peers. The women who had anxiously attached children reported less acceptance from their parents than did the mothers of the securely attached children.[3]

Another study found that mothers whose infants avoided them in the reunion episodes of the *Strange Situation* (see chapter 3) had memories of unresolved maternal rejection in childhood. However, those mothers in this study who were in touch with their feelings of rejection and anger toward their mothers had securely attached babies.[4]

HEALING THE WOUNDED SELF

IMPLICATIONS OF THE RESEARCH

What are the implications of this research? Attachment patterns get passed on cross-generationally. A daughter who has experienced maternal rejection may have difficulty creating a secure attachment relationship with her own child. Notice, however, that those mothers who were in touch with their feelings, who had "worked through" or were in the process of working through their feelings of maternal rejection, had securely attached children. The key, then, is to understand or to "own" the past and "work it through" to some new place of forgiveness and healing. I have spoken with enough women, however, to know that some find this extremely hard to do, and it is usually something women cannot do by themselves. Either they have denied painful memories, or they feel that to examine the parental relationship is tantamount to betrayal.

As a therapist, I once worked with a patient, a young woman, who said during her first visit that she had almost no memories of her dead mother. "This is curious," she continued, "because I was nearly thirteen when my mother died." A few moments later she acknowledged she had never felt close to her mother—a tip-off that she was blocking painful memories. This woman then indicated, not surprisingly, that she was having difficulty relating to her own adolescent daughter, and this was generating great pain for her.

I suggested that because she desired to be close to her own child, she had great motivation for looking at her past, particularly the relationship with her mother, to examine the lack of closeness and all that she had missed. "I know it will hurt," she said reflectively.

"Yes," I said, "but you are carrying pain now, and it's far better to process it and get rid of it. And I commend you for seeking help so that you don't send your daughter out into the world with a distant relationship with her mother."

How does a mother become aware of her unnurtured past, with all of its ramifications? There are many ways "home."

In *The Art of Psychotherapy* Anthony Storr writes: "In psychotherapy, many of the things which the patient discovers about himself are things that he may say he has known all along but has never clearly recognized.... Putting things into words, like writing an examination paper, clarifies both what one knows or what one does not know."[5] Storr indicates that as one verbalizes painful material, he can then begin to critically evaluate his emotions.

In addition, a therapist can help an individual trace connections that are not immediately obvious between events, symptoms, and personality characteristics. As the therapist does this, he is, in effect, attempting to change a person's internal working models. "Psychotherapy then becomes what has been called a 'corrective emotional experience,'" says Storr, "in which negative assumptions about other people are gradually modified by means of the repeated analysis of the patient's changing relationship with the therapist."[6] Basically, the therapist "reparents" the patient through the process of transference. By finding someone who values and understands him, the patient is then able to "generalize" that he will get better treatment from others than he initially received from his parents.[7]

Simply put, this means that as a wounded mother "owns" her pain, examines past events, better understands her own mother, and forgives, she can experience greater intimacy with others and be a better parent to her children. I have written extensively about how to make peace with our mothers in my book, *In the Company of Women*.

"Mothering Mom"

There are, however, other paths to inner healing than traditional psychotherapy.

Selma Fraiberg created one well-respected intervention model to help hurting, deprived mothers whose infants were failing to thrive. In the Fraiberg Intervention Model, a trained therapist visits the mother in her own home. Initially the visits focus on the needs of the baby, who is not developing as he should. Later as the therapist focuses on the mother's needs as well as the baby's, the mother is often able to talk about her own impoverished life. As she grieves over the inadequate mothering she received, she begins the process toward healing and becoming a better mother.[8]

Fraiberg writes of a little boy named Billy who was referred to the Infant Mental Health Program at the University of Michigan because he was starving. Five months old, Billy vomited every time he was fed and had gained no weight over a three-month period. Although he weighed eight pounds at birth, Billy weighed only fourteen pounds at five months; he was a "tense, morose, somber baby who looked 'like a little old man.'"[9]

The therapist visited the home and watched as Kathie, Billy's seventeen-year-old mother, placed the baby and bottle on the floor. Billy crept toward his bottle, grasping it hungrily, and Kathie said, "He likes it that way. He likes to have his bottle alone, on the floor."[10] Not only did Kathie withhold nourishment from Billy, but she also held him face down over the bathroom sink after he had taken his bottle to ensure that he would not vomit on her. Thus, Kathie was preventing her baby from gaining any weight and guaranteeing that he was always hungry.

The therapist understood that by nurturing Kathie, she

would eventually enable her to become a better mother. But at first the therapist concentrated on showing Kathie how to feed and burp Billy. Then she helped apathetic little Billy establish eye contact with his mother, since Billy often looked away from Kathie.

To bring this about, the therapist ingeniously asked Kathie if she ever told Billy any stories. When she said no, the therapist proceeded to tell both mother and child the story of the three bears, using voice inflections. Writes Fraiberg: "Billy and his mother *both* loved the story. Billy began to smile and make eye contact with the therapist and his mother, as together they watched him. Kathie herself so enjoyed this as both child and mother, that she herself began to tell Billy stories and, of course, Billy quickly began to respond."[11]

In time, the therapist encouraged Kathie to talk about her painful past. Kathie spoke "with great sadness" about her relationship with her mother. Apparently, she could never please her mother, who overtly rejected her. As she talked, Kathie cried and scolded the mother "who never heard her cries and needs."[12] During subsequent visits, as Kathie worked through her pain and voiced her unmet needs, she became more empathic and comforting toward her son. "When Kathie's own cries were heard by the therapist," writes Fraiberg, "she began to respond to her baby's cries."[13]

Kathie's story is a powerful example of the hope that exists for any mother who has failed to experience sufficient mothering in her own childhood. If an unnurtured mother can find a caring, empathic individual to nurture her, she may find a balm for her wounded soul.

But must this nurturer always be a trained clinician? That depends on how wounded the mother is.

A mother who is dealing with great inner devastation will

most likely need to work with a trained professional. I have helped numerous depressed mothers work toward a better relationship with their mothers and themselves. Always there was anger and grief and then a surrender of their right to good enough mothering before forgiveness and healing could come. But a woman may be lucky enough to find a nurturing, empathetic woman who will help her toward wholeness.

I am impressed that we humans are programmed toward mental health, and we will seek help and utilize it whenever we can find it. Surcease from pain and greater psychological growth may come from relationships with others, particularly older women who can act as mentors or surrogate mothers. If a caring person can become a secure base, someone to be counted on and trusted, then she can become a nurturer and, ultimately, a healer for a hurting younger mother.

Home Start, a London-based program launched more than ten years ago, utilizes "ordinary" mothers in the healing process. Isolated mothers who are at risk for child abuse are provided the opportunity for weekly visits, not from a mental health professional, but from the mother of a school-age child.[14] Bowlby called this process "mothering mom," indicating that the more support a hurting mom has, the better off she will be. He noted that in all the years the program has been operational, not one mother has gone on to physically abuse her baby. Instead, many have themselves become volunteers in the program.

Harvard's Karlen Lyons-Ruth and her colleagues investigated the effects of weekly home visits on a disadvantaged population. In this study of depressed mothers whose infants were at risk for lower mental and language development, mothers and babies were visited weekly in their homes by ordinary mothers, as well as by psychologists. The researchers found that the home-visited infants were further along in their development than the infants who were not visited.[15] Also the home-visited infants were *twice* as likely to be securely attached to their mothers.

The researchers focused on the mother's need for positive emotional support. They modeled different behavior with her baby, teaching the mother certain actions they wished her to emulate. Also, they were extremely supportive of the mother-child relationship and in keeping with the Fraiberg model, attempted to build the mother's self-esteem.

At an infant attachment conference I attended recently, the consensus of the experts was that mothers of infants are extremely responsive to intervention. Moreover, these experts said that it's not that difficult to put a mother "back on the parenting track" if her deep needs begin to be met and she receives parenting education and "well-informed" outside help in parenting her child.

So intervention is another method for helping the unnurtured mother and tutoring her in more effective parenting. But professionals are not the only ones who can give this kind of help. London's Home Start program and Lyons-Ruth's research both indicate that other, more experienced, mothers can nurture unnurtured moms as well.

A PERSONAL ASIDE

Over a decade ago I sat where Sophie sat, on the same chintz sofa, aware like her that something vital was missing. All the old issues I thought I had resolved years earlier came back to haunt me, and I was confused. *Why?* I wondered. Why did things I had worked through earlier in my thirties trouble me?

At age forty-two, just when I began working on my doctorate, I found myself confronting the painful issue of loss.

This was triggered, in part, by the fact that Holly and Kristen were readying to leave home for college, and they were in the throes of what psychologists call the separation-individuation process. My relationship with my daughters had meant the world to me, and it hurt terribly to think they would soon leave home. At bottom, I feared they would leave my life.

I did not know then what I have since learned—that if we release our children, they will come back as adult friends. All I felt during that time was apprehension and a sense of loss. As my dependency needs heightened, I even became afraid of losing Don's love. After all, I reasoned, Thomas had left years earlier. Would everyone go? As a result of my inner turmoil, Don and I went through a period of marital tension and strife as I clung to him. It didn't help that I was also caught in the throes of hormonal changes due to menopause.

I needed to talk to someone about my inner turmoil. The unhealed places were simply too pervasive to ignore. Feeling estranged from my husband, my children, and myself, I finally went into therapy with a clinical psychologist who zeroed in on my relationship with my mother. Relentlessly, he hammered away at my defenses: my fear of betraying her by examining our relationship, all my excuses for her behavior, my eternal hope that someday she would recover from the emotional illness that worsened during my adolescence and finally meet some of my emotional needs. Once Dr. Raban even shouted at me, "Give her up. Let her go." As a popular song says, I had a "fortress around my heart."

During this period, I prayed that God would heal me and help me let go of my mother. I could not handle the turmoil any longer. Psychiatry and psychology, as I understood them, were effective at diagnosing human ills, but could psychotherapy exorcise the soul? My psychologist had said that the best psychotherapy can do is help people control symptoms. "Therapy does not heal the soul," he said. Anthony Storr says that the psychotherapeutic cure "means to be able to modify and make use of one's psychopathology rather than getting rid of it."[16]

Yet I longed for more than symptom control or harnessing my psychopathology. I wanted to be free from psychological pain and live a happier, freer life. Thus, I prayed, "God, I don't understand this mother yearning or how to find healing and inner freedom, but I'm asking You to help me." And then I tried some honest manipulation. I added: "If You don't heal me, how can I ever tell anyone that You set us free?"

As I continued to work through painful issues in therapy and simultaneously asked God to make me whole, a wonderful thing happened. One day I noticed that the old yearning had simply disappeared. Inside, all was quiet. Unlike the maternally deprived writer Richard Rhodes, I no longer had "a hole in [my] world."

Not surprisingly, my marriage improved, and my relationship with my daughters changed for the better. Although I had been close to them, I could finally let them go. They, who had meant so much to their **"affect hungry"** mother, could leave home physically and psychologically. Moreover, I was soon able to change my relationship with my mother.

Within a year my mother arrived unexpectedly for a two-week visit and for the first time in my adult life, I felt peace in her presence. I was finally able to accept her as she is—not as I wished she would be. I realized that my mother could give physical, though not emotional, nurture. An industrious woman, she washed dishes after every meal, helped me with organizational correspondence, and ironed the mountain of clothes that permanently resides in the ironing basket. During

HEALING THE WOUNDED SELF

her stay we avoided all those topics she finds hard to handle, and not a sharp word was spoken. When mother finally left, I walked into the room where she had stayed and cried. Those two weeks of calm between us had been a great gift.

In the years since then, we have had many times together that have been enormously satisfying to me. These times have been gifts from God.

I have finally made peace with my mother. I have finally made peace with myself.

HEALING COMES THROUGH OUR CHILDREN

Another way we find healing is through the love of our children. As we care for them from infancy on, we are constantly challenged to seek greater wholeness for their sakes. They love us without reserve, believing we are gods and goddesses in the early years.

I shall always be grateful I have been a mother. As my daughters have trusted me since infancy, their love has remade me. Because I wanted greater wholeness for them than I ever experienced, I have struggled to stretch and grow to meet the challenges that good parenting requires. Oh, I've blown it many, many times, but today we are emotionally close and have honest communication. My children have been one of my life's greatest gifts, and now I have the pleasure of loving a grandchild and watching my daughters live as compassionate, responsible adults. How glad I am that I did my inner work so we three could have the close, positive relationships we enjoy today.

CHANGE IS POSSIBLE

From my own experience, I know that with the help of a compassionate therapist, one can travel down the road toward inner healing. Yet sometimes therapy alone isn't enough. Research shows that only about half of those who go into traditional psychotherapy find relief from their symptoms. When one is in pain, one wants better odds for recovery. Sometimes God has to settle our subterranean wars and set us free from the destructive patterns of the past—our cross-generational legacy.

A man who experienced this phenomenon is Roger Helle, a former Vietnam veteran. When Roger and his twin brother were four, their father, an abusive man, abandoned the family, and the brothers were placed in an orphanage. Helle's mother, an alcoholic, remarried years later and came to get her sons. But Helle found no relief from a pervasive sense of loneliness and worthlessness in his new home with a workaholic stepfather. Leaving home at eighteen, Helle enlisted in the Marines and headed for Vietnam. Caring little about himself, Helle says he "volunteered for every dangerous mission I could."[17] Later wounded by an exploding grenade, Helle lay dying in a hospital in Da Nang. As he lay there, unable to speak, Helle cried out in his spirit, "God, let me live, and I'll do anything You want."[18]

Helle lived, returned to the States, married, and forgot his promise. Only when he was unable to create marital intimacy and divorce was imminent did he remember that earlier event—the time God had been close and had restored his physical health. Asking God to save his marriage, Helle seemingly became aware for the first time that he had worth, not from his parents, but because of God's love.

That awareness began to produce personality change, and Helle and his wife were able to experience a richer, more intimate marriage. Today both are involved through Teen Challenge in helping young people who, because of feelings of

HEALING THE WOUNDED SELF

worthlessness, are drug users. Now himself the father of a son, Helle says that he looks at his son and says, "I love you, Joshua. I can't tell you how much you're worth."[19]

Though we bring our early experience into all our later intimate relationships—and change is difficult—it is *not* inevitable that we remain captives to our past. Nor is it inevitable that we pass on cross-generational patterns of attachment. Neglect, rejection, and abuse do not *invariably* breed the same conditions in subsequent generations. What is important is that people have "corrective emotional experiences" that change their internal working models.[20] That is, we need to have intense, emotional experiences that change our long-held concepts of ourselves and others. Personality change is difficult, but it is possible, particularly when old issues demand resolution.

It happened to me. Home became a place of healing once I stopped running, owned the pain, and confronted the past with all its rack and ruin. Home can be a place of healing for you, too, when the "former desolations" of the spirit are repaired.

Of course, it is the Holy Spirit who ultimately heals our brokenness. When we come to Him and ask that He go back, time out of sight, and heal the infant and young child, He begins His alchemy. And when Christ sets us free, we shall be free indeed.

But what about our husbands? Sometimes it is the husband who struggles with his past. How does a woman better understand and nurture the man in her life?

Chapter Twelve

THE MAN IN YOUR LIFE

*Our early lessons in love
and our developmental history shape
the expectations we bring into marriage.*

<small>JUDITH VIORST</small>

Once you become a mother, the man in your life assumes ever greater importance; no longer just husband, lover, friend, the man you love is now also the father of your child. Not only is he a more powerful figure, but the marital stakes are also higher: You perhaps wonder how your husband will respond to your greater dependency and vulnerability now that you have a baby to care for. Does he possess the emotional and psychological resources to be a good father? Will he support your compelling need to be a good mother?

The pressures in any marriage increase after the birth of the first child. No longer two relatively independent beings sharing a marital dream, now a man and woman must interface on a hundred fronts as they share a parenting dream. And the most significant blueprint each brings to the task of parenting is the one acquired during the earliest years of life.

In her book, *Necessary Losses,* poet Judith Viorst writes that we "bring into marriage the unconscious longings and the unfinished business of childhood, and prompted by the past,

235

we make demands in our marriage, unaware that we do."[1]

Viorst says the marital state is characterized by both love and hate. In marriage, men and women attempt to reclaim (or discover for the first time) mother's unconditional love; if they fail, they "hate" the mate for withholding what is needed. "We do not, of course, enter marriage with the conscious intention of marrying daddy—or mommy," says Viorst. "Our hidden agenda is also hidden from us,"[2] she adds. "But subterranean hopes make for seismic disturbances."[3]

As noted earlier in the discussion of my own research, the birth of a child is a time when a woman may rethink her own parenting history. It is also a time when she needs for her husband to be especially sensitive to her needs for emotional support as she is giving to her newborn around the clock. And it's a time when she needs to understand him and what drives him and his fathering.

THE WIFE'S NEEDS

I had a conversation recently with Beverly, a young mother who carried a carrot-haired seven-month-old daughter. "What do I do," she asked, "when my husband urges me to go back to work?"

"That's tough," I replied. "Did he have a full-time working mother?" When she slowly nodded her head yes, I added, "That means he doesn't see any need for you to be home with your baby, right?"

Seeing the connection, Beverly responded quickly, "That's true. My husband tells me he was raised by nannies, and he turned out all right, so why shouldn't his child also be raised by a baby-sitter?"

This young mother had raised a thorny issue I frequently encounter, especially when I speak at conferences. From conversations with women over the years, I know that Beverly is not alone. Numerous women have told me that they want to stay home, but their husbands demand that they work. Some say their husbands are afraid to be the sole provider and depend psychologically on that second income; others indicate that their husbands like to brag about the wife's job and fear marriage to a housewife. One justice department lawyer said, "My mother never worked. We have nothing to talk about anymore. That's why I want my wife to have a career."

But what if a woman's heart tells her that her children need her at home at the same time her husband pushes her to get a job? She will obviously experience great turmoil. She is hurt if her husband fails to understand her need to nurture her baby and their baby's need for exclusive maternal care.

If a husband makes such a demand, I believe he is probably unwittingly re-creating his own emotional pain.

Let me explain. If a man had a mother who was physically or emotionally absent for most of his childhood—if he was raised by baby-sitters or a succession of other caretakers—he will most likely not know what emotional closeness or intimacy feels like. So how can he possibly know what his child is missing? Also, he probably won't be in touch with his feelings (lots of men aren't). Perhaps in childhood, he simply walled off his anger and his yearning for closeness by repressing these unfulfilled emotions.

If I were to describe such a man, I would say he is efficient, aloof, possibly a workaholic. His wife might describe him as cold, distant, and incapable of intimacy. She probably yearns to be close to him but finds it hard, so she is excited about the possibility of establishing intimate connections with her new baby. The husband may even unconsciously feel jealous of the duo without fully understanding why.

Rob is an engineer who urged his wife, Annelise, to return to her job as a pediatric nurse shortly after the birth of their first child, David. Rob's mother worked with his father in their country store in Louisiana. Although both parents were nearby—the store was next to Rob's house—they worked long hours, and Rob's mother was preoccupied with housework when she wasn't doing the bookkeeping. Rob remembers lonely, solitary days as an only child.

He says with pride that he became independent at an early age. Out of touch with his feelings—with his emotional life—Rob doesn't understand that his infant son needs something a baby-sitter can't supply. Besides, he and Annelise use the money she earns for vacations, dinners out, and new clothes. A pediatric nurse who was close to her own mother, Annelise knows her baby needs her. Moreover, she is afraid David will become too attached to the sitter. She's frustrated, but she can't change Rob's mind, and her emotional pain is becoming more intense as time passes. The couple fight, but they can't seem to resolve their dilemma.

It's not only the husband who urges his wife to return to work who creates conflict. So too does the husband who reluctantly agrees to have his wife stay home. This man is also insensitive to his wife's need to nurture and be nurtured in return. Said a friend, "How can any woman feel good about what she is doing if her husband *grudgingly* assents to having her stay home with the kids?"

Ford, Meridith's husband, falls into this category. He is openly critical of the way his wife manages their home and cares for their children. "Meridith used to manage major accounts as a stockbroker," says Ford, "but now she is overwhelmed by a toddler and a baby. I came home the other day, and our son was in the living room playing with plastic bags!

HOME BY CHOICE

What could she have been thinking of?" Ford adds that he occasionally keeps the kids and has found that it's no big thing.

Caring for small children is a difficult task. It's sometimes a boring and lonely occupation. Small children make unremitting demands; they hurt themselves; they call; they act hungry. Any mother can feel overwhelmed if she is caring for a toddler and an infant simultaneously. When my own daughters were very young, I felt like a "giving machine." I even made up a little rhyme that I chanted when they clamored:

One mother, two hands,
Two children, making demands.

How many men are willing to handle what a mother of small children deals with regularly? Said one male psychologist, "You don't see men rushing home to change diapers and feed their babies." True. But whether he spends hours caretaking or not, every father has a vital role in providing emotional support for his wife. The research shows that a husband is every wife's primary support player when she has a baby. A woman's own mother came in second. For a mother to do effective mothering, she needs not only a harmonious marriage, but she also needs her husband to be emotionally supportive. Any woman who lives in a chaotic marriage without sufficient emotional support cannot possibly devote herself fully to mothering. Her baby's clamorous needs will be more than she can cope with. Every husband needs to understand his strategic role in fostering his wife's sense of well being.

Understanding Postfeminist Males

Just as a woman needs to be supported in her mothering, so too does a man need his fair share of understanding and support in marriage. According to writer Sam Allis, postfeminist males are "confused, angry and desperately seeking manhood."[4] Allis adds that men are speaking up in locker rooms across America about their rancor at being criticized for their inadequacies in the boardroom and bedroom. "They are airing their frustration," says Allis, "with the limited roles they face today, compared with the multiple options that women seem to have won."

American males are not only angry and confused, Allis says, but they are also exhausted from trying to live up to the performance standards they feel women impose. Modern men must be sensitive, but not wimps; they should exhibit "tempered macho" and be super successful in their careers.

It's tough, says Allis, to be a man today. The man in the new millennium not only faces the difficult challenge of forming a sense of identity in liberationist America, but he is also unlikely to find much love and acceptance from a woman in the process.

Father Daniel O'Connell, a Jesuit priest and chairman of the psychology department at Georgetown University, further explains the male quandary: "I am convinced that when a woman becomes an abrasive feminist, she competes with a man on his own turf. She encourages the very chauvinism she objects to because she is being chauvinistic herself. This makes it impossible for a man to show gentleness and reverence for women."

Father O'Connell, who has lived in freshmen dorms for much of his academic career, believes men today are needy. "They need to be instructed and informed," he says, "in an atmosphere that isn't threatening. That is precisely what the gentle woman provides. A gentle woman can teach a man to be gentle, respectful, and reverent of her womanhood as complementary to his own manhood."

It is important to understand the male psyche and see beneath the bravado, or even arrogance, to the vulnerable souls. Psychological research has found that males are more physically and psychologically vulnerable than females. Psychologist Dee Shepherd-Look writes that from conception, males are more susceptible than females to every type of "physical disease, developmental difficulty, and environmental assault."[5] Although 140 males are conceived for every 100 females, 35 of these male fetuses will die during gestation. Three-fourths of all babies stillborn before four months are males.

Additionally, males are more vulnerable to malnutrition, and they are more likely than females to have speech, learning, and behavior problems. They are also three to five times more likely to have reading problems. In the arena of emotional disorders, more males than females suffer from night terrors, hyperactivity, and autism.

Moreover, adolescent males have a higher incidence of schizophrenia, delinquency, academic underachievement, and suicide than females. Writes Shepherd-Look, "Until adulthood, it is difficult to find a pathological condition in which the incidence among females is higher than among males."[6]

Boys are also more likely than girls to suffer if mom returns to the workforce. We have already discussed the NICHD findings and the fact that if mother works thirty or more hours, sons are more likely to be insecurely attached than daughters. As for older boys, researcher Michael Lamb says that in studies of elementary school children, sons appear to suffer when mother works outside the home.[7] Effects, however, differ in lower-class and middle-class families. In lower-class families, sons have difficulty with their fathers when the mother works. Lamb believes that in these families maternal employment represents the father's failure to provide for the

241

family, and this creates tension. In middle-class families, sons of employed mothers do not do as well academically as sons of mothers at home.

Not only do sons lose out when moms work full time, but husbands also suffer. In *Juggling,* psychologist Faye Crosby says that husbands lose in four areas when their wives try to combine work and family life.

Crosby, who chairs the psychology department at Smith College, says that men in traditional marriages can count on their wives' help as they climb the corporate ladder. Wives direct family life, care for the kids, and feed and help clothe their husbands. This leaves men free to pursue careers. It is not surprising, says Crosby, that men in dual career families feel deprived when wives work outside their homes.

Also, men lose their role as sole provider when wives work full time. Men grieve, says Crosby, when this role is lost because being a good breadwinner is central to their self-concept. Men may also see the entry of women into the marketplace as an indication that they have somehow failed in the provider role. Some men, as a consequence, grow to dislike their jobs. When a woman assumes or shares the provider role, Crosby says, even the most liberated husband will feel a keen sense of loss.

Crosby also states that when wives earn paychecks, men lose authority at home. The balance of power shifts. Crosby, who has little sympathy for men on this front, says that men lose freedom and privilege in decision making, and some men find this frightening.

Finally, families—and husbands—lose intimacy when wives attempt to juggle home and career. Why? Because a woman simply can't respond to everybody's needs as they arise. This is possibly the greatest privation for the family when mom works full time in the marketplace.

Recently Sally and Chad experienced a loss in intimacy when she resumed her career full time as a therapist. While she enjoyed the work, Sally found the job emotionally draining. She warned everyone as she walked in the door at night, "Don't tell me any of your problems. I can't handle any more pain today."

After Sally cut back to part-time employment, she was surprised at the effect on Chad. Knowing that he has a particularly difficult job working on a defense program, she asked him what had changed at work. "Nothing," he responded. "You've changed. When you worked full time, you were often tired, crabby, or preoccupied, and I had to pick up the slack at home. Now when I come home, you're cheerful and ready to meet some of my needs, as well as the kids' needs. You're happier, and that affects me."

Intimacy. An empathic listener. That's a lot for a husband to give up for a paycheck. And when emotional intimacy disappears in a marriage, it isn't long before sexual intimacy evaporates as well. Crosby cites one study in which *80 percent* of the husbands felt their sex lives had dwindled because of their wives' working. The men and women in this study complained of fatigue, depression, anxiety, and preoccupation with work as interlopers in the connubial bed.

Faye Crosby, who appeared with two mothers-at-home and me on *The Jenny Jones Show,* believes that juggling various roles is good for women. But whether she knows it or not, she makes a strong case against juggling by citing in her book all the losses men (and their wives) incur when women try to combine family life with paid employment. She adds that men need to have emotionally and physically accessible wives to feel secure.

THE MAN IN YOUR LIFE

As I read *Juggling,* I was struck by the fact that grown men, as well as little children, need *someone* at home to function as a "secure base." The wife and mother, it seems, is the architect of intimacy for her husband as well as her children.

A friend of mine, who worked as a BBC cameraman and traveled the world, once told me that when he came home from a trip and Katie wasn't home, it was like the house was cold and dark—he needed her to be *there,* happy that he was *home.*

The point of this brief examination of male vulnerability is to assert that sons and husbands need the women in their lives to nurture them, appreciate them, and express interest in their lives. Both little boys and high-powered male executives suffer from female neglect.

Ralph, a corporate manager, believes that all men need sensitive women in their lives. "A sensitive woman," says Ralph, "can get quickly to the heart of the matter. We men dance around personal issues. We're competitive and don't probe the way women do." Women have traditionally pushed for intimacy in their marriages because all our lives we have focused on relationships and our human connections. Men speak the language of the rational mind with an emphasis on separateness, whereas we speak from the heart, our perceptions grounded in connectedness.

While men and women speak different languages, each assumes that the other speaks the same.[9]

Shortly after they were married, Bruce and Marissa discovered that he spoke "Swahili," and she spoke "Urdu." Marissa didn't really understand Bruce in the heat of an argument, and while he said he understood her, she knew he didn't. It was only after seeing the movie *Beaches* that Bruce emerged enlightened from the darkened theater. Having watched the two female protagonists communicate with considerable heat, Bruce said, "There's no way a man can speak on such a wide range of personal subjects with that kind of emotional intensity."

Nurturing Our Husbands

So how do we nurture our husbands? First, we need to look beneath the exterior and see the little boy inside. It is easy to feel that a man with a chest size of forty-two inches is invincible. Though men possess greater physical strength than women, they do not possess our emotional strength. This may be difficult to grasp, particularly if a woman had a distant relationship with a detached father or no relationship at all.

Because I grew up without a father or a brother, I have had great difficulty understanding what men are like. As I've mentioned, I was close to my granddaddy, but I didn't live with him on a daily basis after early childhood. So when I approached men in my twenties, they were something of a mystery to me. My husband Don has worked hard to demythologize the adult male by showing me his soft, vulnerable side. Remember, he says, inside every man still lurks a little boy. "Men are tender plants," he adds, smiling. Recently, on a trip to Iowa for his college reunion, I became freshly acquainted with this little boy in my husband.

As we stood in front of the unpretentious white frame house still standing on Main Street in Hamilton, Illinois, Don told me about the happiness he had experienced there during the first seven years of his life. "This is the ditch where I fell and cut my knee," he said, standing near a culvert in front of the white house. "The cut was deep enough that my knee required a splint. My friends then pulled me around town in a red wagon for three days." His tone of voice had just a touch of pride. Under the spell of his memories, my husband's face softened and the years fell away. With obvious emotion, Don spoke of one adventure after another that transpired in his safe, contained world of childhood. And I understood, as never before, the meaning these early friendships had in my husband's life.

After his early years, Don's parents moved frequently, and Don found it harder to make and keep friends. He had friends, he told me, but the relationships weren't as deep or as meaningful as his earliest carefree friendships in small-town Hamilton. Don's high school experience in Chicago was particularly lonely since he had to take a streetcar to school and his buddies lived in another neighborhood across town. The situation was exacerbated because Don's parents, though they loved him, were not particularly interested in having his friends visit their home.

On that trip I understood more clearly why my husband loved his small college in Dubuque, Iowa. There, just as in Hamilton, he was encircled by friends. There he found soul mates. As student body president, he was king of the road again, just as he had been when he had cruised the sidewalks in his little red wagon.

When we attended his class reunion, his fellow alumni responded to Don as they remembered him thirty-five years ago, and I saw my husband in a new way. Before my eyes, this gray-haired lawyer became, once again, fraternity brother, friend, "prez."

I realized anew that it strengthens a marriage and is nurturing to a man for a wife to try to understand who he was as a child and how he has changed over time. To peer inside at the child our husbands once were, with all their fears, longings, and rich experiences, is to get in touch with their soft side. This was brought home to me at Don's reunion when I spoke to a professor's wife about her sons. When I asked if she missed having daughters, she replied, "Oh, no. My boys, who are eight and ten, love to play sports and go hunting with their father, but they also enjoy talking to me about their feelings."

If we understand this, we gain a more complete understanding of the man we live with, who exudes confidence at work and at home. My husband is an optimistic, competent man who, by his own admission, awakens every morning with high energy and a cheerful outlook on life. But the longer we live together, the more facets I see of this man who shares his hurts, longings, hopes, and desires. And after twenty-five years, it seems we have only just begun.

FATHER HUNGER

In understanding our husbands, we also need to examine, along with them, their early relationships with their parents, particularly their fathers. I have talked to a number of men who suffer from "father hunger." This is the term coined by James Herzog, assistant professor of psychiatry at Harvard, to describe young children who experienced prolonged separations from their fathers.[10] In my experience as a psychotherapist, I found that many men suffer from father hunger, not only because their dads were absent, but also because they were passive and uninvolved.

Gene, a thirty-two-year-old physician, is the son of an IBM manager, a silent, religious man who was home most evenings and weekends. An active member of his church, this man dutifully paid his bills, cared for his wife and their sons, but seldom connected with his sons emotionally. "I don't remember that he ever hugged me or played ball with me," says Gene reflectively. "He absolutely never told me about his feelings. I have distinct memories of my father standing alone, staring out the window. At times, he seemed like a ghost to me. He's dead now, and I have a yearning for what never was."

Rich, at fifty-five, had a similar experience with his father, now a retired businessman. His father has never told him that he loves him. "We just started to shake hands a few years ago," says Rich. "The stress of managing a small-town newspaper engulfed him. You hear about other people taking family vacations; well, we never did. We never sat down to talk." Rich does remember that once in high school he asked his dad to advise him about a problem. "Only that once did we drop our guard," says Rich. Rich says he believes that his father is committed to him and loves him but that he simply cannot express his feelings. A man who still longs for his father's touch, Rich says that for him to hug his dad now would be like "diving off a high diving board."

Our Husbands/Their Fathers

Writer Michel Marriott addresses this same issue in his article, "Father Hunger."[11] Fathered by a harsh and unaffectionate man, Michel says he cannot relate intimately with his father and struggles to do so with his son. He fears that his relationship with his son just may not "hold."[12]

Former professional football player Bill Glass, who works with prisoners, says if a man is denied his father's affirmation or blessing, he will search for it all his life.[13] The absence of a father's acceptance and unconditional love can, according to Glass, cause a man to become an overachiever or a convict. "I have never met an inmate who loves his dad," says Glass, who has worked in six hundred prisons over the last twenty years. "They'll make excuses for their moms, but they hate their dads' guts. There's something that makes a man mean when he doesn't get along with his father. It makes him dangerous.

You better not turn your back on him."

Glass feels strongly that all fathers need to confer a blessing (approval) on their children, but especially their sons, through touch and verbal affirmation. He has no patience with fathers who expect their children to know intuitively that they love them. "A blessing is not a blessing until you say it," says Glass, who regularly tells his sons that he loves them and that they are "fantastic." Glass's sons are both 6'6" and weigh in at 285 and 275 pounds. Recently, Glass grabbed his elder son and told him he loved him. "Tears welled up in his eyes," says Glass. "They always do." Glass believes that we never outgrow our need for our father's blessing.

Finally, Glass feels that not only should fathers touch and verbally affirm their sons, but they must also never withdraw their unconditional love. He notes that when parents of runaway kids are contacted, two out of three say they don't want their children to come home. No wonder the kids run from that kind of rejection.

Glass believes children need, ultimately, to be affirmed by both parents, though he admits that most people he has encountered have never experienced this.

So what can your husband do if he has been denied his father's blessing? Glass suggests that if his father is alive, a man should go to him and ask for it. And if the father is dead? "Then a man needs to go to his dad's grave and forgive him. Otherwise," says Glass, "the son will become bitter." On a more positive note, Glass suggests that a man consider finding a father substitute who will confer the blessing.

So what is a woman to do who finds herself and her children affected by her husband's father hunger? She can be empathetic, realizing that her husband struggles with low self-esteem, inner pain, and perhaps some unconscious despair.

She can try to teach her husband about intimacy. But he may resist this. She can work on her own problems with closeness. She can pray.

<h2 style="text-align:center">MELANIE AND JOHN:
A MARRIAGE THAT CHANGED FOR THE BETTER</h2>

John grew up in a middle-class family in the South with a father who indicated repeatedly that his son, an underachiever and poor athlete, failed to measure up to his expectations. A busy bank executive, John's father also served on the local school board and the community zoning committee. He was seldom home. Lonely, John's mother threw herself heavily into volunteerism, and John spent more time with his housekeeper than with either parent.

John's past affected his marriage and effectively blocked emotional intimacy with his wife and his sons—Ron, twelve, and Timmy, nine. As a result of her lonely marriage, Melanie says that for about three years she thought of leaving John. "My husband shared his deepest feelings with me when we were dating, but after we were married, the wall came up. He seldom told me how he felt, and he didn't spend much time with our sons. He certainly never shared his feelings. He told the boys he'd play ball with them or take them fishing, but he never did."

Not only was John a workaholic like his father, but when he was home, he was often negative with his sons, particularly Timmy, who had dyslexia. "I was especially worried about Timmy when his teacher called and said that he'd been hitting the younger boys," says Melanie.

While Melanie was considering divorce, she clung to the hope that she and John could get help and grow closer emotionally. A Christian, she was uncomfortable with divorce, but felt trapped in her marriage. When she was honest with herself, she had to admit that both she and John were responsible for the sterility of their marriage. One day, feeling desperate, she confided in several friends who met with her to pray.

As they prayed together and Melanie became more open with her friends, her anger at John surfaced. One day she confronted her husband. "I was shocked at the intensity of my rage," says Melanie, "but I had bottled up my anger way too long." Surprised at the depth of his wife's feelings, John withdrew, spending even more time away from home.

During this time when Melanie was becoming more honest about her emotional pain, a series of crises occurred, increasing the marital pressure. John's father died; John lost a lot of money in the stock market; and Timmy, while riding his bike home from soccer practice, was struck by a car. For several days he hovered between life and death.

John, who never cried, sobbed when he saw his son's broken body in the intensive care unit of the hospital. As Timmy floated in and out of consciousness, Melanie, beside herself with fear and grief, watched her husband fall apart before her eyes. "He kept saying, 'Now I won't be able to take Timmy on that fishing trip I promised him.' It was all that I could do to keep myself from screaming that he never did any of the things he promised the boys."

During that time, Melanie and John began to receive love from different sources. Church members visited, and their pastor met them at the hospital. When he put his hand on John's shoulder to comfort him, John broke down and wept. "During the days after Timmy's accident, John's defenses started to crumble," says Melanie. "I guess it was the combination of his father's death and the near loss of our son."

Melanie and John spent long hours together, driving to and

from the hospital and caring for Timmy at home as he recovered from the accident. One night John played basketball with Ron. He started to linger with his wife over coffee, struggling to share his feelings—his anger, grief, and regret over his relationship with his father and his sorrow over his lack of involvement in his sons' lives. Because she had turned to her friends and to God earlier, Melanie was able to reach past her anger and pain and feel love for her husband.

John also attended a retreat at their church, and during that weekend he had a deeply spiritual religious experience. "I had not wanted to go," says John, "but as I listened to men talk about God as Father, I realized that I hated my father. At the same time, I yearned to be close to him. I also knew that I had to forgive him to ever be free. As I struggled to forgive him, I slowly started to feel that God loved me."

After that weekend, John and Melanie continued to work on their marriage. They found a therapist, and in time, John saw the connection between his father's rejection and his lack of involvement with his sons. Also, he and Melanie learned to speak from their hearts. And Melanie, who had once considered leaving her husband, now says, "John is changing. He wants to be close to the boys and me. He is meeting my emotional needs."

John told Melanie recently, "I can't believe we've been married fifteen years. Our marriage gets better all the time." Melanie smiles, grateful that God intervened and started to heal her husband's heart, something she could never have done.

It's when we get to the end of ourselves and throw ourselves upon God's mercy that wonderful things begin to happen—and what we have yearned for, but despaired of ever attaining, become ours.

Chapter Thirteen

WORLD ENOUGH AND TIME

*A woman's whole life
is a history of the affections.*
WASHINGTON IRVING

C ontrary to the prevailing cultural attitude, it is not inevitable that the mother at home fall hopelessly behind her careerist counterparts in the race for the good life. I realize what I have just said contradicts the media portrayal of the mother at home.

I remember a television program several years ago in which Sally Jessy Raphael forecast a bleak future for any mother who sacrifices career for family. Sally said that if a woman stays home until age forty, no corporation would hire her. No one challenged Sally Jessy Raphael that day. One sensed that she had touched a nerve since the audience and guests failed to respond. Many women fear that they will lose irretrievable ground in the job market if they stay home. They will be either unemployable or have to take mediocre jobs in their forties.

MOLLY'S DILEMMA

How does this fear affect the professional woman who is at home? I have before me a letter I received recently from a mother who is a physician in Colorado. She says that because she had her first child prior to the end of her internship, she has never practiced medicine full time. Now she has four children, and the youngest is twenty months old. This mother has chosen to stay home and has even been homeschooling her older children. But while she admits that her roles as "wife, mother, teacher, homemaker, bookkeeper for her husband's medical practice" completely fill her time, she is not happy.

Molly is torn. While she doesn't have time to work even part time (maybe later), she worries that she is losing ground in her profession and might never catch up. "I feel a constant burden about this," Molly writes in a letter she composed at midnight, when the house was finally quiet.

Molly, like many other women, is caught on the horns of a dilemma. Home by choice because she believes her children need her, she is still anxious and afraid. What is she to do?

When I responded to Molly's letter, I told her that I understood how she felt. I had those feelings myself when my children were in elementary school and junior high. Sometimes I asked Don, "What should I do?" He always suggested I continue doing what I felt was best for our family—pursue my at-home writing career and be available to the girls. "But become wholehearted about your life," my husband ended each conversation, "or you will miss the best that this season of your life has to offer."

CAREER AND KIDS

An article in *Ms.* by Edith Fierst says that many of today's successful women took years off to rear their children. Fierst writes of women, among them Sandra Day O'Connor, Supreme Court justice, and Patricia Wald, chief judge of the U.S. Court of Appeals, who spent between five and fifteen years out of the labor force. These women obviously didn't suffer in the workforce because of years spent at home with their kids.

Some of the women Fierst interviewed even felt they returned to the workforce too soon. Wald, who was considered for U.S. Attorney General, stayed home for ten years and only worked part time when she finally went back to work. Yet when she was asked if she would do the same thing all over again, she said she would have, "stayed home longer for the benefit of the youngest child and not have pushed myself so hard."

The fifty women Fierst interviewed, who were in such careers as medicine, psychology, government, science, and teaching, did not regret the years they devoted to nurturing their young children. Said one, "As I get older, my children and family life become more important. Raising children is hard—and I'm glad I didn't miss it."

While most of the women in Fierst's study felt that part-time employment was ideal for mothers (it kept their self-esteem high and enabled them to maintain contacts), even those mothers who stayed home full time fared well when returning to the workforce. One, a lawyer who spent ten years at home full time, became a vice president of an Illinois firm. Another mother who stayed home for twenty-one years became an editor for an environmental protection publication. The women felt "their relatively advanced age was a help in finding a good job, because they had the advantage of experience with life, if not paid work."[1]

In a conversation, Edith Fierst told me that she believed one of the greatest discouragements to mothers of young children is the fear that staying home a few years will "do them in" professionally. "Despite the general pessimism," said Fierst, "I think they can catch up."

Perhaps it will comfort Molly and others like her to know many women pursue satisfying careers once they return to the workforce. Granted, Molly may have to take a year or so to "catch up" professionally, but she will find she can draw on her earlier medical training plus the experience she's acquired at home as a mother. Molly can, in fact, have several careers in her lifetime.

LIFE AFTER FORTY

We women have always had it better than men. While men struggle with careers in their twenties and thirties, only to turn toward relationships in their forties and fifties, we women, because of our biological clock, establish our marital and family connections during our twenties and thirties. Then in our forties and fifties, when men are turning homeward, we begin to focus on productive ventures outside our homes. Unlike the single-minded male who discovers the value of relationships in midlife, a woman can have multiple careers throughout her lifetime if she so desires, and she will have had the boon of establishing nourishing, deep connections early on.

Besides, as we mature and grow, our needs and desires change. As one friend who gave up a partnership in a law firm to stay home with her three sons said, "If I ever go back to practicing law, I'll change my specialty. I'd no longer be a tax attorney, but I'd go into family law." We women do not have to live cookie-cutter lives.

So Sally Jessy Raphael is wrong. Any woman who takes time off for her family is not washed up and ready to be sent to pasture at age forty. Many women who take several years off reenter the workforce successfully. Of course, not all women wish to go back to work once their kids leave home. Some

HOME BY CHOICE

enjoy the fruits of their labors and spend their time rediscovering husbands, taking vacations, picking up new interests. My friend Joanna, who raised five children, now enjoys spending time at her lakeside cottage, both with family and alone. Sitting on the dock, Joanna says, "I deserve this."

What possibilities exist for women who take years out of the workforce to rear their children? How can they find meaningful careers or embark on new paths that don't conflict with family demands?

DREAM A NEW DREAM

This is the time to dream a new dream. The tyranny of the biological clock is past. The dream of intimacy and family has been realized. If her marriage is in good shape and her children are reasonably whole, a woman brings to her late thirties and forties tremendous drive and energy. No longer having to spend so much time and energy balancing the demands of her multiple roles, a woman "of a certain age" can simplify her life and pursue the things she's passionately interested in. She is, as one forty-year-old woman said, ready to look beyond her home and "save the world."

In my own life, I focused my energies on further education. I had wanted to get my Ph.D. in my twenties but felt sidetracked once I had children. At the time I couldn't ignore their incessant needs to work on a doctorate. When Holly was born, I was finishing my masters in English at the University of Buffalo. One day I went in to talk to one of my professors, and we were soon discussing my academic future. When he found out I had just had a baby, he leaned forward, planted his elbows on his desk, and said firmly, "What you should do now is push *hard.* Finish your Ph.D. while your child is young, and then you *can* have a career in academia."

He had obviously never been a nursing mother! Even as I listened, I was aware of my engorged breasts and was calculating just how much time I had left before Holly's next feeding. Weeks later, when I sat for the comprehensive exam that separated the doctoral sheep from the masters goats, I was among the first to leave. How could I concentrate on *Huckleberry Finn* and the novel's place in American literature when my breasts ached and were starting to leak? Instead, I rushed home to breast-feed my screaming baby.

Enrolling at Georgetown at forty-two, I felt free at last to slip into fourth gear and, as my family says, "chew up the earth." Even though my daughters were teenagers, I was able to become single-minded in a way I had never been before. This was reflected in my academic performance: I became a far better student than I had ever been in my early twenties. When the day came to defend my doctoral dissertation before the psychology faculty, I was anxious but exhilarated. I had finally achieved a long-deferred dream.

Other women take different routes in dreaming a new dream.

I have been fortunate enough to get to know Phyllis Schlafly, a nationally syndicated columnist who is also founder and president of Eagle Forum, a national organization that takes credit for defeating the Equal Rights Amendment. Since Eagle Forum's inception some twenty years ago, Phyllis has marshaled other politically active women to lobby in their local and state governments for traditional values.

The organization has been, and continues to be, a powerful voice in conservative politics on such issues as abortion, sex education in the schools, values clarification, child care, and parental leave. As president of Eagle Forum, Phyllis was invited to the White House during the Reagan and Bush administrations, and she regularly confers with other movers and shakers in government.

According to her biographer, Carol Felsenthal, who wrote *The Sweetheart of the Silent Majority,* Phyllis was valedictorian of her high school graduating class and the recipient of a Phi Beta Kappa key at college. She also worked full time while putting herself through college and graduate school. After she graduated from Washington University in St. Louis, Phyllis attended Radcliffe, where she obtained a masters degree in government.

Years later she brought this same formidable intellect and reservoir of energy to the task of mothering—teaching her six children to read before they entered school in second grade. The six Schlafly children reflect the accomplishments of both parents (Fred Schlafly graduated from Harvard Law School): Two are lawyers, one is a physician, one holds a Ph.D. in mathematics, another has a college degree in electrical engineering, and the youngest, Anne, runs her own catering business.

Phyllis founded Eagle Forum in 1975 when she was fifty-one. And when she was criticized for testifying before the Senate without a law degree, Phyllis enrolled in law school at St. Louis University in her fifties. She graduated in the top half of her class, "with a rank of twenty-seven."[2]

Phyllis Schlafly has had a real impact on American society, and she is a superlative example of someone who adheres to traditional values and fights for what she believes. She worked from home, raised her children, and then moved into a wider arena. She has been a national spokesperson for years, and her organization exceeds some eighty thousand committed members.

Another woman who had a far-reaching impact after

midlife was Mother Teresa of Calcutta. Mother Teresa cannot properly be called a mother at all—she never married or bore children—yet the past century hardly witnessed a more nurturing figure than this woman who, until she died on her feet, ministered to the poor and dying. Mother Teresa was a schoolteacher until her late thirties. Then she received her second call: "The call within a call…to minister to the poorest of the poor."[3] Leaving the Foret convent of Calcutta, she took to the streets.

According to Malcolm Muggeridge, Mother Teresa "stepped out with a few rupees in her pocket; made her way to the poorest, most wretched quarter of the city; found a lodging there; gathered together a few abandoned children—there were plenty to chose from—and began her ministry of love."[4]

It is ironic that in an age when charity, nurture, and volunteerism are devalued and children are viewed as impediments to the fulfilled life, a woman received the Nobel Peace Prize for nurturing the young and caring for the poor, the helpless, and the dying. What many women have always done in their nuclear and extended families, Mother Teresa did for the family of humankind. And she lived an enormously productive life in response to a second call that came when she was ready to dream a new dream.

Let's Talk, America

One of my favorite talk show hosts is Janet Parshall of Salem Broadcasting's *Janet Parshall's America*. As a friend and frequent guest on her show, I have watched Janet's meteoric rise on the national scene since the midnineties and have come to admire and respect her greatly. An award-winning broadcaster, the national spokesperson for the Family Research

HOME BY CHOICE

Council, and a frequent guest on national television talk shows, Janet is not only extremely bright and articulate, but she also has a faith in God that is inspiring and informs every aspect of her life.

How did she come to have such a stellar career? Did she park her four children at the baby-sitter's year after year while she worked her way up in broadcasting? Hardly. Janet, who married her high school sweetheart, Craig, twenty-nine years ago, told me: "You don't get a degree in this. There's no Harvard grad school degree in broadcasting. This career flowed out of my life as a mother. My babies pulled me into it."

Janet said she made her decision to be a mother at home when "the feminist movement was literally screaming that a woman's fulfillment could only be found in a career." But because she had become a Christian at age six, Janet was able to "listen to the Lord's still small voice" and devote herself to caring for her four children, who were born in rapid succession. Janet had her first baby, Sarah, when her husband Craig was in law school. "Most people think that we didn't have to make any sacrifices, because my husband was a lawyer," said Janet in her fast-forward, talk-show host voice. "Well, we did, and I learned dozens of creative ways to serve Spam."

Janet's first two children, Sarah and Rebecca, were born only sixteen months apart, and Samuel and Joseph came soon after. Having had four children in six years, Janet had her hands full. "I'd sometimes go into a closet, shut the door, and say, 'Lord, I'm wondering if this is what I'm going to be doing for a long time.' But God kept impressing upon me that this was a season of my life, albeit a very precious season."

Janet got into broadcasting by a circuitous route which she believes only God could have engineered. It happened this way. One day when her children were in first through sixth grades, one came home from school and told her mother about sitting in a Magic Circle and having the teacher ask: "Do any of you bite your nails or wet your bed? And if your parents divorced, which one would you want to live with?"

As president of the PTA in the state of Wisconsin, Janet was incensed by this experience. "I knew those teachers were not licensed psychotherapists and that they had torn down a veil of privacy so they could affix a label on my child. Craig also has serious concerns about First Amendment violations, so we asked to meet with the school board." Janet continued, "We sat across from fifteen school administrators and a long line of tables, and within minutes I felt I had been marginalized and labeled an extremist."

Because she would not be silenced, Janet began speaking out about her child's experience, and shortly thereafter she was called by the manager of a local radio station and asked if she would like to have her own talk show. "The show was on from noon till one, the kids were in school, my job wouldn't hurt my family, and I could take the summers off."

"I was learning that God had this in mind all along and that He was grooming me for the job I have now," Janet said. She worked as a broadcaster for two years and also became a volunteer for Concerned Women for America. Then in 1993 she received a call from Beverly La Haye asking her to come to Washington, D.C., to be groomed for the future presidency of CWA. The Parshalls believed that when God called one spouse, He would soon call the other, and within weeks Craig had also received a job offer to come east and work for the Rutherford Institute. At CWA Janet had lots of opportunities to meet with the press, and she cohosted *Beverly La Haye Live* daily.

"It was my relationship with my babies that led me here,"

said Janet, sitting in her office at the WAVA studio in Rosslyn, Virginia. "I had to live profamily before I could speak profamily. Sure, during those years at home I had boring, repetitive tasks, but you know, Paul had his three years in Arabia and Moses his forty years of tending sheep in the desert. I'm sure they had boring, repetitive tasks too. But God was molding, refining, and shaping my life when my children were small. And I praise God that I didn't lose those years. They were priceless."

Janet, whose brothers work as investors on the Chicago Board of Trade, believes that all those years of on-site mothering are about investment. "Just as my brothers invest in futures, Craig and I invested in our children's futures. We have a strong sense of family; our kids are close; and they are open with us. We didn't have to try to develop that after they had reached eighteen. Closeness and open communication are things you build into your kids when they begin to take their first steps."

When I asked Janet what she would want to say to mothers struggling at home in an achievement-oriented culture, she responded without hesitation. "I would tell them to seek first the kingdom of God and His righteousness, and He will give them a sure hope and future." She added, "The real question is, do you love Him enough to trust Him? Like I had a clue sitting in my closet that this is where I'd be once my kids were grown. If I hadn't looked well to the ways of my household, I wouldn't be here now. A mother needs to recognize her passion and understand that it can come right out of her children."

At the end of the interview, Janet said that "in two shakes of a lamb's tail" she would go back to those early years of watching her children unfold before her eyes. "Those were intimate years of watching them discover first-time experiences, like watching each one kneel beside his bed and accept the Lord Jesus Christ as Savior." When Janet said this, her voice became husky, and then she grew quiet.

"That touches you deeply, doesn't it?" I asked.

"Yes," said this woman who is seldom without words. "Those experiences were precious. Precious."

Women Writers and Midlife Success

While Janet Parshall is experiencing heady success in her mid-forties, it is not unusual for female writers to also achieve success in midlife and beyond. Although Madeleine L'Engle had published four novels in her twenties and continued to write during her thirties, major critical acclaim as a writer came to her only in her forties with the publication of her award-winning *A Wrinkle in Time*. Margaret Craven, a writer who has struggled with blindness, published her first novel, *I Heard the Owl Call My Name,* at the age of sixty-nine.

Another writer/mother began writing the novel that would rock a nation when she was forty-one. Bearing seven children in fourteen years, Harriet Beecher Stowe had little time for writing during the early years of her children's lives. And when she started her famous book, her family was not only broke, but Stowe's inner resources were also depleted. Less than a year before she sat down to write *Uncle Tom's Cabin,* her young son Charlie had died. Stowe would later say about this experience: "It was at his dying bed and at his grave that I learned what a poor slave mother may feel when her child is taken away from her."[5] According to Russel Nye, the themes of mother love and separation run throughout Stowe's famous novel.[6]

This wife and mother wrote "swiftly and at white heat" in the early 1850s out of the recollections of her early life. In the process she created a "moral weapon" used in the war against slavery. Not only was Stowe's book the first American novel to sell more than a million copies, but Charles Summer also credited Stowe with Lincoln's election as president, and President Lincoln is purported to have remarked when he met Stowe, "So this is the little lady who wrote the book that started this great war."[7]

Although Stowe made her major contribution to literature in her forties, another woman who achieved international fame did not even begin the career that would make her famous until she was in her late seventies.

Walking on the Shoulders of Men

Born in 1860, Anna Mary Robertson worked on her parents' farm and left home at twelve to become a "hired girl," cooking and cleaning for other families for the next fifteen years.[8] After Anna married in 1887, she had ten children, five of whom died. Eventually she and her husband settled on a farm in New York State near Albany. Only after her husband died did Anna begin to "keep busy and to pass the time away" by painting.

Anna Mary Robertson, better known as Grandma Moses, was discovered by art collector Louis Caldor in 1938, when he saw her paintings hanging in a drugstore near Hoosier Falls, New York. Soon Grandma Moses was an international figure in the arts whose paintings were shown in New York, Washington, D.C., and Europe. She was interviewed by newscaster Edward R. Murrow and visited President Truman at the White House. Moreover, she made the cover of *Time* when she celebrated her one-hundredth birthday. This woman, called one of the greatest folk artists of all time, painted scenes she remembered from her youth: wash day, a hurricane at home, Christmas at home, Hoosier Falls in the winter.

Obviously unimpressed with herself, Grandma Moses said of her gift: "If I didn't start painting, I would have raised chickens."[9]

When Anna Mary was a child, her father told her that he dreamed he was in a large hall and people were clapping their hands and shouting. Then he saw Anna Mary walking on the shoulders of men. Grandma Moses thought of this dream years later when she became famous and received mail from around the world. She did, at the end of her life, "walk on the shoulders of men." She was loved and venerated by ordinary people, as well as the rich and powerful.

Poet Archibald MacLeish wrote of Grandma Moses in 1948: "It is a great virtue in any artist to be what he is, whatever it is that has made him so, whether place or time or bad luck or good or a sound heart or no heart at all. Because Grandma Moses is what she is so sharply and so briskly and so simply…she is a true painter to be approached with honor and respect."[10]

To be truly oneself is to be an original. Only as we become ourselves are we in a position to give to others truly—to share our gifts, to shower little acts of love and mercy on those who need it, to speak with a voice that needs to he heard, to find our true path. But we must remember that Grandma Moses did not set out to be what she was—to find herself. Rather, she set out at age twelve *to live a life*. And she lived a life replete with family, husband, children, and homey experiences long before immortalizing them in her paintings.

We do not become ourselves overnight. We do it year by year, building act upon act, word upon word. We do it as we act responsibly toward our children and husbands, as we live our days honestly. Only by listening to our hearts and living principled lives can we hope to be productive individuals until death.

A friend who's sixty-six said in a reflective moment, "I don't want to sit around as I grow older. I want to live a useful life until I die." This is the Judeo-Christian concept of aging—that we serve God and others and "die on our feet."

But what if we listen to the siren's call and sacrifice our family relationships for career—or anything else, for that matter? Then we may move into old age with crippling regret.

One woman realized too late that she had neglected her only child while she poured her considerable energies into her career. "I kept him up all night before he left for Tulane," Sally said, "telling him how sorry I was that I had been absent for much of his life. Even when I was home, I was so preoccupied, so driven." Her son patiently listened to his mother's soliloquy of regret as he packed his bags that last night at home, but his life as a dependent child in the house on Hamden Road was over. What could he possibly say to his mother that would change the past?

As women, we ignore our human connections at real peril. Nor can we ignore our intelligence and gifts except at great personal cost. We can have it all—but not all at once. Our lives have their seasons, and I, approaching sixty, believe the season of raising my children has been the loveliest and most tender so far. So let's live each day fully so we won't look back over the terrain of our lives with emotional pain because we were inaccessible to our families while our children were at home. Instead, let us count our blessings as we watch our children grow up, leave home, marry, and start their own families.

In the winter of her life, Grandma Moses wrote, "I look back on my life like a good day's work; it was done and I feel satisfied with it. I was happy and contented…and life is what we make it, always has been, always will be."[11]

One could say the same, dear reader, about your life as a mother.

THE LEGACY

*His living has given so much more
than his dying could ever take away.*

JACK OWEN, SPEAKING ABOUT HIS FATHER

Christmas, 1999. Welcome to Lancaster, Pennsylvania. People bury their frozen chins deeper into their coats as they file into the Willow Street fire hall. Well over a hundred people have assembled for Christmas dinner, and the surrounding streets are jammed with cars, many bearing out-of-state plates. Though they come from such far-flung places as Texas, Florida, and California, these people share a common bond: They are the descendants or in-laws of one couple, Harvey and Martha Owen.

"At first we were together every year because our parents wanted it that way," says Mary Owen Clark, who is in her nineties. "Now we do it as a sort of tribute to them and because we enjoy it."[1]

What sort of couple inspired such familial pride and loyalty? Harvey and Martha were an unusual duo. Martha was seventeen when she married her twenty-one-year-old former schoolteacher in West Jefferson, North Carolina, in 1901. Settling in Lancaster, Harvey traded schoolteaching for small business ownership, first buying a dairy and later a grocery store. Harvey and Martha loved children and had twelve of their own. Though their family was large, the children remember happy childhoods and lots of individual attention.

"We all felt we were special," says Stella Owen Morrison. "When we grew up and talked about our parents, we were surprised to discover that each felt like the best-loved child." Maybe this was because Martha would dodge the question, "Who do you love the best?" by saying: "The one who's sick until he's well; the one who's gone until he's back among the rest."

However, the parents' love was probably best communicated by their actions. Harvey polished twelve pairs of shoes nightly and, as befits a former schoolteacher, tutored his and the neighbors' children. Martha loved for her children to bring their friends home for dinner. "We never thought about the work or inconvenience this caused her," says Stella, "because at our house there was always room for one more." To keep her family close, Martha instigated the yearly Christmas dinner which was held in the family home until the 1940s. When the family outgrew the home, the Owens moved their celebration first to a school, then to the fire hall.

Though the family had little money, the children didn't realize it as they grew up. "Daddy would always find a nickel for you if you needed it," remembers Stella. What they did have, the Owens shared with others. Harvey and Martha welcomed five cousins who came to live with them to attend school in Lancaster. And when Martha got the first washing machine in the neighborhood, she invited her relatives to use it. Even in old age, Harvey and Martha made quilts together each year, one for each of their children and several for the local hospital.

In addition to possessing a generous spirit, Harvey and

Martha were firm, but not harsh, disciplinarians. The parents' open hands could occasionally come down on their children's posteriors. When Stella, at age two, threw a bowl of oatmeal at her father, she was spanked. Worth was put under the dining room table when he hit a younger child. Most often, though, Harvey just talked to the offending child.

"He was not a pacifist, but he hated brutality," remembered son Jack. Says Mary, "Our parents disciplined us with feeling and care. They didn't fly into a rage and bawl you out." Once Stella broke the midnight curfew. The next day as she was standing in the kitchen rolling biscuits, her father came in and said kindly, "You were out a little late. I don't think I'd stay out that late again." She didn't.

In addition to modeling gentleness and self-control, Harvey and Martha showed their children how to have a happy marriage. Both Mae and Stella remember that their parents had a cooperative, loving union. Additionally, neither countermanded the other. "When mother made suggestions," says Mary, "Daddy didn't argue."

"But she made good suggestions," counters Stella. Once Harvey was about to prune raspberry bushes with his son-in-law Frank, and Martha asked him to wait to allow the children to pick the remaining berries. "Without missing a beat," says Mary, "Daddy turned to Frank and said, 'Let's go trim the grapevines instead.'"

While they had a harmonious marriage, Harvey and Martha were not perfect. In fact, there was one thing they never agreed on. Martha was a Baptist, while Harvey was Methodist. Although they worshiped in different churches, this was never a point of contention. At home they presented a united front. Harvey read the Bible aloud each evening, and the family sang hymns together.

To ensure that each child did not get lost in the pack, the family had a pattern that fostered strong attachments. Whenever a new baby was born, Mae, the oldest, took the dethroned sibling into her own bed and cuddled him. And when a child was sick, not only did Martha care for the child, but Harvey also brought his son or daughter favors from the store he owned.

Both Harvey and Martha come from strong, highly functional families. Stella remembers that though her grandmother died when her mother was four, an aunt quickly moved in to nurture the motherless children. Later, Martha's father remarried, and the stepmother got on so well with the stepchildren that Stella says she was a teenager before she knew her grandmother was actually her stepgrandmother. Martha and her stepmother were close, and Martha remained close to her aunt, the surrogate mother, as well. Harvey also came from a close, intact family. In fact, he and Martha chose to live with Harvey's parents when they were first married. Recalls Mary, "It was like a picnic to be with them."

Psychologists Jay Belsky and Emily Pensky note that happy marriages beget happy marriages.[2] This has been part of the rich legacy Harvey and Martha have passed on to their children. Among their twelve children only one divorced. In an era of easy divorce, five couples have stayed together for more than fifty years. Mary says that she and her husband Frank, who celebrated their sixty-fifth anniversary before he died, tried to emulate her parents, whose marriage lasted nearly three-quarters of a century.

In addition to creating their own strong families, Harvey and Martha's children have contributed much to American society. Sixteen members of this family have served their country in the armed forces. Additionally, the Owen children and their descendants have been pastors, teachers, nurses, missionaries, secretaries, salesmen, beauticians, carpenters, chefs, bank executives, research personnel, artists, and horse trainers, among others.

Today the 189 descendants are scattered throughout twenty-one states, the District of Columbia, Australia, and Ecuador.

Even the third generation has benefited from the lives of this unique couple. Mary's daughter, Sidney Clark, captured something of the richness of her family's legacy when she wrote "On the Death of My Grandfather" when Harvey died.

> White-haired patriarch.
> He tended grape arbors
> and knew his books,
> told summer secrets
> and laughed with her.
> Long winter nights
> He built dream houses
> with windows going everywhere
> and we could reach and climb
> to find the limits of our minds
> in the closeness of a time.
> He knitted wool-like love
> and spread the blanket
> over all he knew
> or hung it from a cloud
> to block a sometime shadow
> on the sun.
> Now friends throw flowers
> to the sky
> and we,
> sharing each other, hold fast his legacy.

The legacy. As parents, we invariably give our children a legacy of memories—a *sense of home or a deep, abiding feeling of homelessness*. It is only as we consider our children's well-being a high priority—and are willing to make the essential sacrifices—that we will give them a rich legacy of memories to treasure throughout their lives. In the process, we will not only strengthen society, but we will affect future generations as well.

I have lived long enough to see the effects of my mothering on a new generation. As I watch Kristen mother Austin, I see that she passes on to him something of the love and nurture I gave to her. This warms my heart and gives my life something of its meaning and purpose. And as I deal with a life-threatening illness, I look at my life and ponder regrets. Do I have regrets? Sure, I have some. But I have no regrets for the hours, days, and years that I have loved my children dearly. They have been my joy. They have been my life's most important work.

As the French Noble laureate Francoi Mauriac said, "We are molded and remolded by those who have loved us, and though the love may pass, we are nevertheless their work, for good or ill."

Postscript

LETTERS FROM THE HEART

The most important person on earth is a mother. She cannot claim the honor of having built Notre Dame cathedral. She need not. She has built something more magnificent than any cathedral—a dwelling for an immortal soul, the tiny perfection of her baby's body.... The angels have not been blessed with such a grace. They cannot share in God's creative miracle to bring new saints to heaven. Only a human mother can.

CARDINAL JOSEPH MINDSZENTY

Since the publication of *Home by Choice* in 1991, I have received hundreds of responses from individuals around the country. Most of the respondents have been mothers. I have been heartened by what they have said. Most agree that children need sophisticated one-on-one nurture. Most feel that children in America today are suffering as a result of too little parental time.

As I responded to call-ins across the country during my book tour, I heard from formerly employed mothers, both married and single, who had recently come home. Sometimes they came home because their kids were floundering. Other times they came home because they realized that time to influence and enjoy their kids' lives was running out. A midwestern radio producer who had "always worked" had quit her job two months earlier because her teenagers would soon leave home. She told me, "I realized I had thousands of things to say to them, and I had only two years left to say them." When asked what she had done since her return home, this mother replied, "Oh, we've mostly talked. And I've finally had time to go with my younger son to buy baseball cards."

In addition to hearing from employed mothers coming home, I have heard from women who speak about the enormous satisfaction they experience as mothers at home. They are not defensive; most have strong convictions and feel good about their decision to put the needs of their families before career success.

On various talk shows, a few angry employed mothers called in to accuse me of attempting to make working mothers feel guilty. I understand their anger. I did, after all, feel compelled to work during my daughters' infancies. And I felt guilty then. How do I respond to these callers? I usually suggest that survey data indicate that the majority of working parents feel guilty about spending too little time with their children and that most want to spend more time at home. Guilt, then, is endemic to dual career families. I point out that if a mother feels she is giving her child sufficient time and attention and her child is flourishing, no one can make her feel guilty. After that statement, there is usually silence on the other end of the line.

Because I feel you would like to hear from mothers across America, I've included some representative letters. I call them "letters from the heart." I hope you will read them and feel connected to that vast network of mothers at home across America, a courageous battalion of women who know they need all the emotional support they can get.

I applaud all of you.

Dear Dr. Hunter:

Your book was hard to find, but well worth the hunt. It's excellent. Having ordered it with only the title to go on, I was dubious about its contents. I figured it would be another emotional diatribe, full of vignettes and sad stories. Instead, I was surprised to read about the psychological research being conducted on the subject, along with a comprehensive look at a mother's life.

I am thirty years old. I have been married for five years and have a three-year-old and a one-year-old daughter. Before meeting my husband at the University of Pennsylvania (he was working there; I was a graduate student), I had struggled for ten years with a severe case of depression and bulimia. Through a short, but intense, session of EST training and a supportive group of friends, I learned to break my old thought patterns of defeatism and powerlessness inherited from my bullying father and an unsupportive mother. I then was able to end my self-destructive habits, finish my schooling, and enter into a satisfying, intimate relationship with a man.

When our first daughter was born, I went back to work full time after six weeks of maternity leave. I was full of fatigue and anger. Out of my twelve closest girlfriends, only one had children. My mother, who lived sixty miles away, didn't even bother to come down and help me with anything (even though this was her first grandchild in over twenty years). Although my husband was very supportive (he stayed home with the baby whenever she was sick and took her to the pediatrician for her medical check-ups), I felt alone, scared, and without a clue about how to be a mother.

There must be a God. Four months after my daughter was born, we moved to Washington so that my husband could look for a job. We lived with my best friend and her husband for ten months until Steve found full-time work. During that period my friend, who is a junior high guidance counselor, took me under her wing and showed me how to be a loving, caring parent. She also parented me, healing many old feelings of abandonment caused by my own mother. I soon began to enjoy being a mother and cried at the thought of having to leave the baby and go to work. (I had been working on a market research publication from home during that period, but it did not sell well.)

At the same time, I found a support group for mothers. I made friends with other stay-at-home moms, learning how they coped with life, where to find special baby items, and which physicians to go to, etc. I even started exchanging baby-sitting duties with another mom so that our children could play with each other and we could each have one afternoon a week to ourselves.

Finally, I confronted my own parents with my anger and hurt. After years of feeling abandoned, I could no longer carry around my emotional baggage. (Here's an example of my parents' behavior: When I was sixteen years old, I had a bad bicycle accident and was in a coma for two days. My parents were on a vacation at the time and decided that they would come home only if I were dying. I was in the hospital a total of five days, went home with a skull fracture and depression, and took care of myself for a couple of weeks.) I needed to get rid of that old hurt in order to have room to love my own daughter and husband. I wrote them a long letter and later confronted them in person. I have not forgiven them, and there is no happy ending. But I finally stood up for myself and now feel capable of getting on with my life.

As for having to go back to work, our finances dictated that I do so. Just as I was looking for full-time work again, I

HOME BY CHOICE

discovered I was pregnant with our second child. We thought about it long and hard and decided to stay in debt to allow me to stay at home with the children. My husband has had to do the most sacrificing, since there is no spare money for his "toys" or even new clothes. But I've never been happier in my life, and I can't fathom the thought of leaving my children now. I have come to see that young children are little more than balls of emotion, and the most important thing a parent can do is to let them know they are loved and the world is a safe place to be. People continually remark about how independent and confident our oldest daughter is. When I compare her to children who have been in day care, I can see the difference. I am truly blessed, for I have an extremely supportive spouse, a network of friends who are also mothers, and two bright, adorable children. My old friends from Pennsylvania still can't believe I am content staying at home doing "nothing" but being a wife and mother.

Sincerely,

Claire

Dear Dr. Hunter:

I am writing in regard to your book, *Home by Choice*. For five years, I had the job of my dreams, assistant professor at a small eastern college. In 1985, I received a Ph.D. and was thrilled to have this job so quickly. Then, one and a half years ago, Lily was born. I had five months of leave and was eager to return to work. Even though I was only on campus Tuesdays and Thursdays and my mother watched Lily, I was uncomfortable with the situation. When the semester ended, I resigned my perfect full-time position and am now at home (with the second child due in June).

My education provided me with a very distorted and biased view of the day-care situation. All of the literature I read was very positive about the effects on children. After having Lily, my heart and mind told me this was not right. I decided that my new concern, or perhaps soapbox, would be the child-care issue. I planned on doing a literature review when I was able. (I believed this would take several years with small children.) Then I found you've done the review for me! Thank you for providing me with such a strong foundation from which to work. The discussion of Piaget's concept of object permanence as it relates to absent mothers was wonderful. I also found the familial biographies of the feminists quite interesting.

Thank you for the efforts that you have made to have this fine book published. I'd like to become a part-time professional at home in the near future. Once again, thank you and great success with your book.

Sincerely,
Eleanor

Dear Dr. Hunter:

I am outraged by your position. I think it is a slap in the face to every woman who works outside the home and has children.

I am one of those mothers who has managed to raise a family and have a career. My children have always been in day care and after-school care, and I find them well adjusted.

The children I have encountered that have mothers who have stayed home with them are usually stubborn, self-centered, and unruly. These children pick on other children, cry, and are selfish.

I feel that you owe mothers who choose to work and those who have to work an apology—especially the single mother. You have laid a guilt trip on some mothers. I am very glad I chose to work. I can offer my children much more, and I don't have to sacrifice. Try explaining to a four-year-old, "You can't have that doll that Susie has because we are making sacrifices so I can stay home with you." Hogwash. The child could care less. She wants the doll.

Thousands of mothers stay home with their children—most of these are on welfare. We see how that has affected our young people. They are really well adjusted. Yeah, right!

This is not a Cinderella world. Unless your husband makes a very high salary, the mother who stays home will become frustrated if she is denied the essentials of a normal lifestyle—causing her children to become frustrated as well.

I would suggest you take a better look at our society as a whole. I am sure that after you do this you will change your mind about the "homeward bound mother."

Sincerely,

Jan

Dear Dr. Hunter:

I am a thirty-four-year-old whose mother worked. The three of us kids took care of ourselves, came home from school to a cold, dark house, and got ourselves ready for school and out to the bus with no one to help us. I am just now, through counseling, learning to grieve for a lost childhood.

When I was ready to get pregnant, I quit my flourishing career. I suppose I went overboard, but I have never regretted my choice. When Billy was born, we spent long hours rocking, gazing at each other, taking walks, and playing. Seven months later, I was pregnant again with my second and last child. The two boys and I have not done anything out of the ordinary, but we've talked and read books, baked bread, played games, taken naps, and laid on blankets under the clouds.

They are now six and seven and are self-confident, popular, ahead of their classmates academically, well mannered, and responsible. I am so pleased with how they are doing. Over the past seven years, there have been days of boredom, runny noses, exasperation, exhaustion, and messy, sticky floors. There were times when I would have loved to go to an office and *rest*. But I didn't, because I was committed to my idea of what a mother is, and now I can "dance into a winter of rich reward, rather than shuffle into a season of regret." (I love that!)

Sincerely,

Faye

Dr. Hunter:

My story is an unusual one, or maybe not, in this day and age.

For three and a half years, I have been separated from an alcoholic, abusive husband of twenty years. We had four children together (ages nineteen, sixteen, fifteen and twelve). I am forty-two. A few years ago, I got involved with a man and got pregnant. I now have a one-and-a-half-year-old daughter who is a joy to us all.

Since December 1991 we have lived in New Mexico. I am on assistance, and my children and I are in a program for homeless families. I am currently homeschooling my fifteen- and sixteen-year-old sons and am still nursing my baby.

What I'm getting at is this: I'm under a lot of pressure to

HOME BY CHOICE

get off assistance, get a job, and put my kids in school and my baby in day care. I truly believe that my children need a mother at home, and I would rather be on assistance to be home with my children. Am I wrong to feel this way?

My kids have been through so much. Everything from the past has taken its toll. I feel like my being out of the home would pull the bottom off the box.

I do odd jobs for extra money and am also the volunteer warehouse manager for local homeless families. My nineteen-year-old is on his own and is in college studying to be a counselor. No drugs, no alcohol, or smoking in our family. I am also learning secretarial skills through a correspondence course.

You see, I don't plan to be on assistance forever!

Laura

Dear Dr. Hunter:

Reference to Dr. Scarr's statement about today's child being resilient made me shudder. Of course, today's children are more resilient! What choice do they have?

I was resilient when I was orphaned at age nine because of an auto accident that claimed both my parents. As an only child, I moved into a two-income family and acquired three siblings. Resiliency was a survival choice. In my new family, physical needs were met well, but the emotional and spiritual nourishment I had been so accustomed to were seldom primary.

I thank God for my mom who cherished staying home with me and relished teaching me the precious values I cling to today. During the loneliest days of my life I was equipped to be resilient only because of the things I absorbed by daily being by her side on a farm in a tiny house. Had she chosen a career and those material comforts which would have seemed so important to me, God only knows how truly resilient I would be today. At thirty-eight, I write this letter as a tribute to the greatest lady I have ever known—my mom.

Sincerely,

Diane

Dear Dr. Hunter:

I was raised in a house with two workaholics; my brother, sister, and I were constantly shoved off on sitters. Our parents even took their vacations without us, so sometimes we would be with sitters two or three weeks at a time. My memories of my dad include his being at work, being out of town, remodeling our house, or secluding himself with a bad headache.

As an adult looking back, I can see that we children were "sitting ducks" to be sexually abused—and we were—all three of us to one degree or another. I was the pleaser, so my abuse lasted the longest—seventeen years. I was afraid I would hurt the abuser's feelings if I told him to leave me alone.

Early in my childhood, I remember thinking that if I ever had children I would never raise them the way I was raised. After the suicide of my mother, I have been working through the emotional pain and feel much better.

I have three wonderful sons who are four, five, and nine. I have realized that staying home has to be a commitment—a strong commitment! Motherhood has been my toughest but most rewarding role.

For us, it has also been a commitment of lifestyle for me to stay at home since my husband Alan's take-home pay is only $1,600, which in the Minneapolis area does not go too far. Due to our limited income, I have become much more resourceful than I would have been otherwise. During Christmas for the past several years I have baked cookies for a caterer (16,000 this past year). I occasionally do some catering jobs myself, and I have learned to decorate cakes. All of these abilities would have remained dormant had there not been a financial need and the commitment to stay home with the boys.

Sincerely,
Amy

Dear Dr. Hunter:

This morning I completed reading your book *Home by Choice,* and I felt compelled to write and share my opinions and thoughts with you.

I am twenty-seven and have been happily married for four years. I am the mother of a precious one-year-old boy. I was raised in a family of seven children (I'm the youngest) on a farm in South Dakota. We all worked hard and played hard, and I have many happy memories of growing up. After reading your book, I wrote my mom and thanked her for her presence, emotionally and physically, when my siblings and I were growing up. Some of my sweetest memories are of coming home from school and smelling her freshly baked bread. She did this regularly and would bake a special cinnamon loaf for us kids to eat (warm) as soon as we got home from school.

My husband, David, and I both dearly love children, and when expecting Todd we were very excited, but torn. We both wanted me to stay home with our baby but didn't see how we could possibly manage. In the end, I decided I would find a part-time job after the baby was born.

My coworkers were absolutely aghast that I would consider giving up my career; they even promised a handsome promotion if I would decide to return to my position. I really tried to explain that my career would now be my baby, but to no avail.

After Todd was born, I was pleasantly surprised at how strong and quickly the bond grew between us. How could I leave him with someone else? No one would love him like I would. I searched for something I could do at home. I take care of a little girl part time and set up appointments by phone for two financial planners. I also have a local paper route. Soon I'll begin a home business weaving rugs and place mats and drop the other jobs.

I want you to know that, yes, there are young women like me who are coming home and who intend to stay home with their children.

Sincerely,
Gina

Dear Dr. Hunter:

I just finished reading your book, *Home by Choice,* and wanted to write you and tell you how much I enjoyed it. I am a twenty-eight-year-old mother of three, going on four, who stays at home and would have it no other way. I am tired of hearing things such as "What's a smart girl like you doing at home?" or "I could never just sit at home all day, I'd be too bored." Bored? They've got to be kidding! As you pointed out in your book so well, I am a teacher, psychologist, cook, maintenance person, chauffeur, financial organizer and planner, housekeeper, and child-care provider.

I stay at home not because I have nothing better to do,

but because my husband and I feel it is best for our family—not just our children, but my husband as well. I may be busy, but I am available to them most of the time. Reading books, for example, is not something we squeeze in ten minutes before bedtime. It is a wonderful part of every afternoon. Ours are stable, self-confident children who are learning Bible stories and lessons right along with me. I don't mean to sound like I'm bragging. Our kids are certainly not perfect (nor am I, of course!), but I have always felt they have benefited tremendously from my being here most of the time.

I graduated magna cum laude from a prominent woman's college with a degree in English. I had a good job in public relations with a nationally known agency when I quit to stay at home with my newborn son.

That was four and a half years ago, and I have never regretted this decision.

I am the oldest of thirteen children (twelve biological and one adopted) and have been fortunate enough to have been raised by an excellent mother who stayed at home and made us, her children, a priority in her life. She taught us to read before we started kindergarten. She was almost always available to us. From the time I met my husband and we knew we wanted to get married, I wanted to stay home with my children and provide them with the kind of childhood I had. Fortunately, my husband agreed with me, and we are able to swing it financially. We have made some financial sacrifices. It's not always easy to pay the bills. We need a larger house for our growing brood but can't afford to move yet. But that's okay. We're happy.

Warm Regards,

Kathy

Dear Dr. Hunter:

I am a mother of four boys and two girls and a grand-mother of five. I stayed home and applied my knowledge from my degree in home economics education. I am not sorry! Three children are happily married. The three mothers of my grandchildren are college-educated and are happy to stay at home raising their children.

The other three children are happy, well adjusted, and successful. All have been the envy of the neighborhood and school. All have excelled in their chosen area. We have lived on one income. Although it has not been easy, it has been good for us, and the entire family is very innovative, competitive, and caring. Our highest income was $24,000, which did not come until three years ago, so I know it can be done. Our last is a college freshman.

Thanks for listening,

Betty

Dear Dr. Brenda Hunter:

I heard your interview yesterday with Dr. Dobson on *Focus on the Family.* I can't tell you how much it touched my heart.

I am a stay-at-home mom, and although I know without any doubt that I'm doing the right thing for my son, I'm under constant criticism from friends, family, and even other Christians. I've ordered your book, *Home by Choice,* and am so excited to begin reading it. I look forward to the affirmation that what I've chosen to do is good and okay. I know that you've been under tremendous pressure from the media because I, too, feel it, but on a much smaller scale. However, please know that you've renewed my confidence in my decision to raise my son myself and give him the irreplaceable gift of a *secure home in an insecure world.* May God bless you and give you strength as you minister to women such as myself and touch the hearts of women who are still working but would come home if they could.

Sincerely,

Janice

Dear Dr. Hunter:

Some months ago I was browsing through a local bookstore when I happened to spot your book, *Home by Choice.* The title intrigued me, as I had been under a lot of stress while trying to combine my return to full-time teaching with the responsibilities of new motherhood. My relationship with my husband was at an all-time low, and while I enjoyed my job, I never stopped feeling frantic, like I was running as fast as I could in a race that I was never destined to finish, much less win.

I bought your book that day, returned home, and read it all in one sitting. I didn't buy into it all at once, though. I let it languish on the coffee table for weeks, collecting dust. I was too busy and too tired to clean. You see, your message was a bitter pill for me to swallow. My mother did (and does) work full time; my friends work full time; the whole world, or so it seems, works full time. I was raised never doubting that I, too, would take my rightful place in the lineup of successful career women. I had, after all, been to college for five years. To languish at home would be a waste of a good education, right? My baby daughter would be well cared for by an excellent sitter and would never lack for anything, right? So, I kept going to work.

Well, sometimes God speaks in a thunderclap, and sometimes He speaks in a small, still voice. Looking back at that crazy time now, I have to laugh at the media's declaration that a little "quality time" spent with children could make up for daily maternal absence. I was supposed to work all day, pick up my baby after a forty-five minute commute home, cook dinner, do laundry, feed the dog, grade papers, talk to my husband, make sure baths were taken and teeth brushed, and STILL have time and energy left over to spend quality time with my baby daughter! Get real, *Working Mother* magazine! I don't know too many one-year-olds who feel like a rousing game of patty-cake or reading *Good Night Moon* at eleven-thirty at night.

And so, God spoke to me. He spoke to me through your book, through my husband's surprising agreement that I come home, and through my now eighteen-month-old daughter. I guess the clincher came over Easter vacation when I was able to spend a week at home. I dropped my usually shy daughter off at the sitter's while I shopped for a few hours. Upon my return, the baby-sitter remarked, "Courtney smiled a lot more than usual today. She cheered up over Christmas vacation, too. She always seems happier when you're home with her." Dr. Hunter, thank you for giving me the freedom to be "home by choice." Although we will struggle financially, I feel confident in my decision. *My daughter's smiles are worth far more than any paycheck.*

Warmly,

Michele

Notes

Author's Note

1. "Judge Leaves a Crumbling Society," *Wisconsin State Journal*, 15 November 1992.

Introduction: The Inner Home

1. John Cloud, "What Can the Schools Do?" *Newsweek*, 3 May 1999, 38.

2. Allen H. Platt, "The Importance of Home," *Time*, 28 January 1991, 9.

3. Anthony Storr, *Churchill's Black Dog, Kafka's Mice, and Other Phenomena of the Human Mind* (New York: Ballantine Books, 1988), 18–9.

4. Anthony Storr, *Solitude* (New York: Ballantine Books, 1988), 112.

5. Vivien Noakes, *Edward Lear* (London: Fontan, 1985), 14.

6. Ibid., 107.

7. Storr, *Solitude,* 113.

8. Joyce Maynard, "Home Stretch," *Elle*, October 1990, 202–6.

9. Nikhil Drogun, "Top PepsiCo Executive Picks Family Over Job," *Wall Street Journal*, 24 September l997, B1.

Chapter 1: Homeward Bound

1. John Bowlby, *Attachment,* vol.1 of *Attachment and Loss,* 2d ed. (New York: Basic Books, 1982), 177.

2. Ibid., xiii.

3. Sigmund Freud, *Outline of Psychoanalysis*, SE 23 (London: Hogarth Press, 1940), 188.

4. B. Egeland and E. A. Farber, "Infant-Mother Attachment: Factors Related to Development and Change Over Time," *Child Development* 55 (1984): 753–71.

5. Alan Sroufe and Everett Walters, "Attachment as an Organizational Construct," *Child Development* 48 (1977): 1186.

6. Ibid.

7. John Bowlby, *Separation: Anxiety and Anger,* vol. 2 of *Attachment*

and Loss (New York: Basic Books, 1973), 204.

8. Armand Nicholi, "The Fractured Family: Following It into the Future," *Christianity Today,* 25 May 1979, 11.

9. Ibid.

10. Selma Fraiberg, "Ghosts in the Nursery," in *Selected Writings of Selma Fraiberg,* ed. Louis Fraiberg (Columbus, Ohio: Ohio State University Press, 1987), 102.

11. Ibid., 135.

12. B. J. Cobler and H. V. Grunebaum, *Mothers, Grandmothers and Daughters* (New York: Wiley, 1981).

CHAPTER 2: FORGING ATTACHMENTS

1. Evelyn B. Thoman and Sue Browder, *Born Dancing* (New York: Harper and Row, 1987), 5.

2. Ibid.

3. Ibid., 127–9.

4. John Bowlby, *Attachment,* vol. 1 of *Attachment and Loss* (New York: Basic Books, 1969), 199–202.

5. John Bowlby, address given to the American Psychiatric Association (APA) in Washington, D.C., 1986.

6. Michael E. Lamb, "The Development of Mother-Infant and Father-Infant Attachment in the Second Year of Life," *Developmental Psychology* 13 (1977): 637–48.

7. John Bowlby, *A Secure Base* (New York: Basic Books, 1988), 11.

8. Michael E. Lamb, "The Development of Parent-Infant Attachments in the First Two Years of Life," in *The Father-Infant Relationship,* ed. F. A. Pederson (New York: Praeger, 1980), 35.

9. Bowlby, *A Secure Base,* 10.

10. Ibid.

11. Ibid., 11.

12. Ibid.

13. John Bowlby, *Separation: Anxiety and Anger,* vol. 2 of *Attachment and Loss* (New York: Basic Books, 1973), 204.

14. Ibid. 204–5.

15. John Bowlby, *Loss: Sadness and Depression,* vol. 3 of *Attachment and Loss* (New York: Basic Books, 1980), 55.

16. Ibid., 231.

17. Bowlby, *Separation*, 208.

18. Bowlby, *A Secure Base*, 28.

19. Bowlby, address given at APA convention, 1986.

20. Bowlby, *A Secure Base*, 11.

21. Fritz Goossens and M. H. von Ijzendoorn, "Quality of Infants' Attachments to Professional Caregivers: Relation to Infant-Parent Attachment and Day Care Characteristics," *Child Development* 61 (1990): 832–7.

22. Graeme Russell, "Shared Caregiving Families: An Australian Study," in *Nontraditional Families: Parenting and Child Development*, ed. M. E. Lamb (Hillsdale, N.J.: Lawrence Erlbaum Associates, 1982), 139–64.

23. Graeme Russell, "Primary Care Giving and the Role Sharing Fathers," in *The Father's Role*, ed. M. E. Lamb, (New York: Wiley & Sons, 1986), 31.

CHAPTER 3: MOTHER CARE OR OTHER CARE?

1. Sandra Scarr, *Mother Care/Other Care* (New York: Warner Books, 1984), 77.

2. Ibid., 231–2.

3. Ibid., 232.

4. Jay Belsky, "Risks Remain," *Zero to Three*, Special Reprint, 22.

5. John Bowlby, address given to the American Psychiatric Association convention, Washington, D.C., May 1986.

6. Robert Karen, "Becoming Attached," *Atlantic Monthly*, February 1990, 47.

7. Mary Ainsworth et al., *Patterns of Attachment* (Hillsdale, N.J.: Lawrence Erlbaum Associates, 1978), viii.

8. Ibid., 55–63.

9. Mary Ainsworth, "Patterns of Infant-Mother Attachments: Antecedents and Effects of Development," *Bulletin of New York Academy of Medicine* 61 (November 1985): 776.

10. Karen, "Becoming Attached," 50.

11. Ainsworth et al., *Patterns of Attachment*, 59.

12. Ainsworth, "Infant-Mother Attachments," 777.

13. Karen, "Becoming Attached," 50.

14. Mary Main, "Avoidance of the Attachment Figure in Infancy:

Descriptions and Interpretations," *Behavioral Development: The Bielegeld Interdisciplinary Project* (New York: Cambridge University Press, 1981), 31–59.

15. Erik Larson, "When You Have to Say Goodbye," *Parents,* March 1990, 104.

16. William Damon, *Social and Personality Development* (New York: W. W. Norton & Co., 1983), 35.

17. Ibid., 34.

18. Larson, "When You Have to Say Goodbye," 104.

19. Judith Viorst, *Necessary Losses* (New York: Simon and Schuster, 1986), 31.

20. John Bowlby, vol. 1 of *Attachment and Loss,* 184.

21. Timothy Green, *The Restless Spirit* (New York: Simon and Schuster, 1986), 31.

22. L. M. Casper, "Who's Minding Our Preschoolers?" *Current Population Reports,* no. 53 (Washington, D.C.: U.S. Census Bureau, 1996), 70.

23. Ibid.

24. Belsky, "Risks Remain," 22.

25. Robert Karen, *Becoming Attached* (New York: Warner Books, 1994), 337.

26. Ibid.

27. Pamela Schwartz, "Length of Day Care Attendance and Attachment Behavior in Eighteen-Month-Old Infants," *Child Development* 54 (1983): 1073–8.

28. D. Wille and J. Jacobsen, "The Influence of Maternal Employment, Attachment Patterns, Extra-Familial Child Care and Previous Experiences with Peers or Early Peer Interaction," (Paper presented at the International Conference in Infant Studies, New York, 1984.)

29. P. Barglow, B. E. Vaugh, and N. Molitor, "Effects of Maternal Absence Due to Employment on the Quality of Infant-Mother Attachment in a Low-Risk Sample," *Child Development* 58 (1987): 945–54.

30. P. L. Chase-Lansdale and M. T. Owen, "Maternal Employment in a Family Context: Effects on Infant-Mother and Infant-Father Attachments," *Child Development* 58 (1987): 1505–12.

31. J. Belsky and M. Rovine, "Nonmaternal Care in the First Year of Life and the Security of the Infant-Parent Attachment," *Child*

Development 59 (1987): 157–67.

32.   J. C. Schwarz, R. G. Strickland, and G. Krolick, "Infant Day Care: Behavioral Effects at Preschool Age," *Developmental Psychology* 10 (1974): 502–6.

33.   Ron Haskins, "Public School Aggression among Children with Varying Day Care Experience," *Child Development* 56 (1985): 700.

34.   Carolee Howes, "Can the Age of Entry into Child Care and the Quality of Child Care Predict Adjustment in Kindergarten?" *Developmental Psychology* 26 (1990): 292–303.

35.   Jay Belsky, Infant Attachment Research Seminar, Washington, D.C., 4–5 February 1991.

36.   Early Child Care Research Network, "Infant Child Care and Attachment Security: Results of the NICHD Study of Early Child Care," Symposium, International Conference on Infant Studies, Providence, R.I., 20 April 1996.

37.   Early Child Care Research Network, "Results of the NICHD Study of Early Child Care," presented at the meeting of the Society for Research in Child Development, 4 April 1997.

38.   Early Child Care Research Network, "Child Care and Mother-Child Interaction in the First Three Years of Life," *Developmental Psychology*, 35, no. 6 (November 1999): 1399–1413.

39.   Susan Seliger, "The Key to Intelligence," *Working Woman*, May 1997, 39.

40.   P. Forman, "Day Care Diseases," *Family Policy*, a publication of the Family Research Council, Washington, D.C., May/June 1989, 14.

41.   Wendy Dreskin, "Day Care: A Child's View," in *Who Will Rock the Cradle*, ed. Phyllis Schlafly (Washington, D.C.: Eagle Forum Education and Defense Fund, 1989), 127.

42.   Ibid., 130.

43.   Selma Fraiberg, *Every Child's Birthright: In Defense of Mothering* (New York: Bantam Books, 1977), 34.

44.   Ibid., 98.

45.   Ibid., 102.

46.   "Child Support for Custodial Mothers and Fathers: 1991," U.S. Department of Commerce, Bureau of the Census, Series P-60-187, August 1995.

47.   Ibid.

NOTES

1. Barbara Kantrowitz and Pat Wingert, "How Well Do You Know Your Kid?" *Newsweek*, 10 May 1999, 39.

2. Ibid., 38–9

3. Joseph Zanga, "Letter from the President," *American Academy of Pediatric News,* January 1998, 7.

4. Ibid.

5. Richard Louv, *Childhood's Future* (Boston: Houghton Mifflin, 1990), 18.

6. Ibid., 17.

7. Ibid., 19.

8. Catherine O'Neill, "School's Out, Mom's Out, So's Dad," *Washington Post,* 21 October 1986, 13.

9. Armand Nicholi, "The Nontherapeutic Use of Psychoactive Drugs," *New England Journal of Medicine* 308 (April 1983): 925–33.

10. Ibid., 931f.

11. Ibid.

12. Jean L. Richardson et al., "Substance Use among Eighth Grade Students Who Take Care of Themselves after School," *Pediatrics* 84 (1989): 556–65.

13. Ann C. Crouter, S. M. MacDermid, S. M. McHale, and M. Perry-Jenkins, "Parental Monitoring and Perceptions of Children's School Performance and Conduct in Dual and Single Earner Families," *Developmental Psychology* 26 (1990): 649–57.

14. Michael Ryan, "Now They're at Harvard," *Parade,* 17 July 1988, 20.

15. Ibid.

16. Kevin B. MacDonald, *Social and Personality Adjustment* (New York: Plenum Press, 1988), 166.

17. Ibid., 163.

18. Norman Kiell, *The Universal Experience of Adolescence* (New York: International Universities Press, 1964), 12.

19. Erik Erikson, *Childhood and Society* (New York: W. W. Norton, 1964), 262.

20. E. James Anthony, lecture given at the Department of Psychiatry, Georgetown University Hospital, Fall 1987.

21. Elyse Tanouye, "Antidepressant Makers Study Kids' Market,"

Wall Street Journal, 4 April 1997, B1.

22. R. L. Simon and P. I. Murphy, "Sex Differences in the Causes of Adolescent Suicide and Ideation," *Journal of Adolescence* 14 (1985): 423–34.

23. Kantrowitz and Wingert, "How Well Do You Know Your Kid?" 40.

24. Larry Brain, lecture given at the Department of Psychiatry, Georgetown University Hospital, Fall 1987.

25. J. M. Mishne, *Clinical Work with Adolescents* (New York: The Free Press, 1986), 207.

26. Ibid., 208–9.

27. Ibid., 210.

CHAPTER 5: FALL FROM GRACE

1. Betty Friedan, *The Feminine Mystique* (New York: Dell, 1963), 21, 27.

2. Michael E. Lamb, "Maternal Employment and Child Development: A Review," in *Non-Traditional Families: Parenting and Child Development,* ed. M. E. Lamb (Hillsdale, N.J.: Lawrence Erlbaum Associates, 1982), 46, 48.

3. Ibid.

4. Anne Roiphe, *Fruitful* (New York: Houghton Mifflin Company, 1996), 13.

5. Ibid., 20–1.

6. Lynn M. Casper, "Who's Minding the Preschoolers?" U.S. Census Bureau, Current Population Reports (Washington, D.C.: U.S. Government Printing Office), 70–6.

7. Ibid.

8. Lynn M. Casper, Mary Hawkins, and Martin O'Connell, "Who's Minding the Kids?" (Washington, D.C.: U.S. Government Printing Office, 1994), 70-6

9. U.S. Census Bureau, Current Population Survey, March 1997.

10. Claudia Wallis, "Women in the Nineties," *Time,* 4 December 1989.

11. Alecia Swasy, "Stay-at-Home Moms Are Fashionable Again in Many Communities," *Wall Street Journal,* 6 May 1997.

12. Kirstin Gromlsey and R. H. Melson, "Fulltime Moms Earn Respect, Poll Says," *Washington Post,* 22 March 1998.

CHAPTER 6: WHY DO SOME WOMEN REJECT MOTHERHOOD?

1. Rhona Rapoport and Robert Rapoport, *Dual Career Families* (Baltimore: Penguin, 1971), 282.

2. Laurel Oliver, "The Relationships of Parental Attitudes and Parent Identification to Career and Homemaking Orientation in College Women," *Journal of Vocational Behavior* 1 (1975): 1–12.

3. Margaret Hennig and Anne Jardin, *The Managerial Woman* (New York: Simon and Schuster, 1976), 130–2.

4. Ibid., 125.

5. Ibid., 123.

6. Ibid., 129.

7. M. J. Gerson, "The Lure of Motherhood," *Psychology of Women Quarterly* 5: 207–18.

8. Ibid., 217.

9. B. E. Lott, "Who Wants the Children? Some Relationships among Attitudes toward Children, Parents and the Liberation of Women," *American Psychologist* 28 (1973): 573–82.

10. Marcia Cohen, *The Sisterhood* (New York: Fawcett-Columbine, 1988), 61.

11. Ibid., 58.

12. Ibid., 59.

13. Ibid., 69.

14. Ibid., 29.

15. Ibid., 31.

16. Ibid.

17. Ibid., 37.

18. Ibid., 38.

19. Germaine Greer, *Daddy, We Hardly Knew You* (New York: Knopf, 1990), 23.

20. Ibid., 38.

21. Cohen, *The Sisterhood*, 45.

22. Ibid., 50.

23. John Bowlby, *The Making and Breaking of Affectional Bonds* (London: Tavistock, 1979), 139.

24. Cohen, *The Sisterhood*, 50.

25. Deborah Fallows, *A Mother's Work* (Boston: Houghton Mifflin, 1985), 206.

26.   Greer, *Daddy, We Hardly Knew You*, 311.

CHAPTER 7: WHY KIDS KILL

1.   "Jury Hears Teen Killer's Words in Sentence Phase," *Washington Times*, 3 November 1999, A5.

2.   John Cloud, "Just a Routine School Shooting," *Time*, 31 May 1999, 36–7.

3.   Debbie Howlett, "Boy, 6, Fatally Shoots Classmate," *USA Today*, 1 March 2000, 3A.

4.   "Hearing Before the Subcommittee on Children and Families of the Committee on Labor and Human Resources," (Washington D.C.: United States Senate, U.S. Government Printing Office, 18 July 1996), 1.

5.   Ibid., 2.

6.   Ibid.

7.   Ibid., 7.

8.   Ibid., 2.

9.   Ramit Plushnick-Masti, "A Family's Shame," *Washington Post*, 5 November 1999, Metro.

10.   Cloud, "School Shooting," 36–7.

11.   Ibid.

12.   Terry M. Levy and Michael Orlans, *Attachment, Trauma, and Healing* (Washington, D.C.: CWLA Press, 1998), 3.

13.   Ibid.

14.   Ibid, 47.

15.   Curt R. Bartol, *Criminal Behavior: A Psychosocial Approach* (Englewood Cliffs; N.J.: Prentice Hall, 1991), 65.

16.   Levy and Orlans, *Attachment, Trauma, and Healing*, 65.

17.   Ibid.

18.   Ibid.

19.   Ibid., 93.

20.   James P. McGee and Caren R. DeBernando, "The Classroom Avenger," *The Forensic Examiner*, May/June 1999, 18.

21.   Terry M. Levy and Michael Orlans, "Kids Who Kill," *The Forensic Examiner*, March/April 1999, 20.

22.   Cloud, "School Shooting," 36–7.

23.   McGee and DeBernardo, "Classroom Anger," 17.

24.   Ibid.

25. Patrick O'Driscoll, "Release of Tapes Infuriates Families," *USA Today*, 4 December 1999, 3A.

26. *Time,* 3, May 1999, cover text.

27. Levy and Orlans, *Attachment, Trauma, and Healing,* 127.

CHAPTER 8: CEOS IN THE SUBURBS

1. Paul and Sarah Edwards, *Working from Home* (Los Angeles: Jeremy P. Tarches, Inc., 1990), 1.

2. Ibid.

3. Ibid., 2.

4. Alvin Toffler, *The Third Wave* (New York: William Morrow, 1980).

5. Candi Cushman and Lynn Vincent, "OSHA at the Door," *World,* 5 February 2000-, 24.

6. Toffler, *The Third Wave,* 192.

7. "1982 Characteristics of Business Owners," U.S. Census Bureau, August 1987.

8. Marion Behr and Wendy Lazar, *Women Working at Home* (New Jersey: W. H. Press, 1981), 11.

9. Cherie Fuller, "Ways for Moms to Make Money at Home" *Focus on the Family,* January 1991, 2.

10. Edwards, *Working from Home,* 41.

11. "Selling Romance, British Style," *Time,* 21 December 1981, 66.

12. Edwards, *Working from Home,* 27.

13. Ibid., 38.

14. Fuller, "Make Money at Home," 3.

15. Edwards, *Working from Home,* 198.

CHAPTER 9: HOME FOR A SEASON

1. Ruth Josselson, *Finding Herself* (San Francisco: Jossey-Bass, 1987), 26.

2. Carol Gilligan, *In a Different Voice* (Cambridge, Mass.: Harvard University Press, 1982), 12.

3. Josselson, *Finding Herself,* 3.

4. Ibid., 170.

5. Ibid., 173.

6. Ibid.

7. Ibid., 185.

8. Gilligan, *In a Different Voice*, 159.

9. Henry Gleitman, *Basic Psychology* (New York: W.W. Norton, 1987), 183.

CHAPTER 10: WOMEN AND DEPRESSION

1. Myrna M. Weissman, "Depression," in *Women and Psychotherapy*, ed. A. M. Brodsky and R. T. Hare-Mustin (New York: Guilford Press, 1980), 980.

2. Ibid., 98–9.

3. Ibid., 101–2.

4. P. D. McLean, "Behavioral Treatment of Depression," in *Behavior Modification*, ed. W. E. Craighead, A. E. Kazdin, and M. J. Mahoney (Boston: Houghton Mifflin, 1981), 223–41.

5. Maggie Scarf, *Unfinished Business: Pressure Points in the Lives of Women* (Garden City, N.Y.: Doubleday, 1980), 566–7.

6. Ibid., 4–5.

7. G. W. Brown and T. Harris, *Social Origins of Depression* (New York: The Free Press, 1978), 179.

8. Jay Belsky and Emily Pensky, "Developmental History, Personality and Family Relationships: Toward an Emergent Family System," in *Relationships within Families: Mutual Influences*, ed. R. Hinde and J. Stevenson-Hinde (Oxford, England: Oxford University Press, 1988), 203.

9. M. Lefkotitz and E. P. Tesiny, "Rejection and Depression: Prospective and Contemporaneous Analyses," *Developmental Psychology* 20 (1984): 776–85.

10. Robert Leahy, "The Costs of Development: Clinical Implications," in *The Development of the Self* (New York: Academic Press, 1985), 267–94.

11. David Burns, *Feeling Good: The New Mood Therapy* (New York: Morrow, 1980), 12.

12. Ibid.

13. Anne Stevenson, *Bitter Fame: A Life of Sylvia Plath* (New York: Viking, 1989), 265.

14. John Bowlby, lecture given at American Psychiatric Association Convention, Washington, D.C., May 1986.

1. Nancy Friday, *My Mother/Myself* (New York: Dell Publishing, 1977), x.

2. Margaret Ricks, "The Social Transformation of Parental Behavior: Attachment across Generations," in *Growing Points of Attachment Theory and Research: Monographs of the Society for Research in Child Development,* ed. Inge Bretherton and Everett Waters, vol. 50, nos. 1–2 (1985): 221.

3. Ibid., 220–1.

4. Ibid., 220.

5. Anthony Storr, *The Art of Psychotherapy* (New York: Routledge, 1990), 25.

6. Ibid., 73

7. Ibid.

8. *Selected Writings of Selma Fraiberg,* ed. Louis Fraiberg (Columbus, Ohio: The State University Press, 1987), viii–ix.

9. Ibid., 139.

10. Ibid., 143.

11. Ibid., 149–50.

12. Ibid.,161.

13. Ibid., 162.

14. John Bowlby, talk given to physicians at the American Psychiatric Association convention, Washington, D.C., May 1986.

15. Karlen Lyons-Ruth et al., "Infants at Social Risk: Maternal Depression and Family Support Services as Mediators of Infant Development and Security of Attachment," *Child Development* 61 (1990): 85–98.

16. Storr, *Art of Psychotherapy,* 157.

17. Roger Helle, "Getting to Be Somebody," *Guideposts,* April 1987, 3.

18. Ibid., 4.

19. Ibid., 5.

20. Jay Belsky and Emily Pensky, "Developmental History, Personality and Family Relationships: Toward Our Emergent Family System," in *Relationships Within Families: Mutual Influences,* R. Hinde and J. Stevenson-Hinde (Oxford, England: Oxford University Press, 1988), 209.

CHAPTER 12: THE MAN IN YOUR LIFE

1. Judith Viorst, *Necessary Losses* (New York: Simon and Schuster, 1986), 192.

2. Ibid.

3. Ibid.

4. Sam Allis, "What Do Men Really Want?" *Time*, Fall 1990, 80.

5. D. L. Shepherd-Look, "Sex Differentiation and the Development of Sex Roles," in *Handbook of Child Development*, ed. B. B. Wolman (Englewood Cliffs, NJ.: Prentice-Hall, 1982), 408.

6. Ibid., 408.

7. Michael E. Lamb, "Maternal Employment and Child Development: A Review," in *Non-Traditional Families: Parenting and Child Development*, ed. M. E. Lamb (Hillsdale, NJ.: Lawrence Erlbaum Associates, 1982), 57–8.

8. Faye Crosby, *Juggling* (New York: The Free Press, 1991), 163.

9. Carol Gilligan, *In a Different Voice* (Cambridge, Mass.: Harvard University Press, 1982), 173.

10. Michel Marriot, "Father Hunger," *Essence*, November 1990, 74.

11. Ibid.

12. Ibid., 116.

13. Bill Glass, speech given to Prison Fellowship staff in Reston, VA, Fall 1990.

CHAPTER 13: WORLD ENOUGH AND TIME

1. Edith Fierst, "Careers and Kids," *Ms.* May 1988, 62–4.

2. Carol Felsenthal, *The Sweetheart of the Silent Majority* (Chicago: Regnery Gateway, 1981), 117.

3. Malcolm Muggeridge, *Something Beautiful for God* (Garden City, N.Y.: Image Books, 1977), 5.

4. Ibid., 17.

5. Harriet Beecher Stowe, *Uncle Tom's Cabin* (New York: Simon and Schuster, 1963), ix.

6. Ibid., xiii.

7. Ibid.

8. "Biographical Sketch," in *Grandma Moses* (Washington, D.C.: National Gallery of Art, 1979), 14.

9. Ibid., 15.

NOTES

10. Ibid., 9.
11. Ibid., 15.

THE LEGACY

1. "Owen Clan Gathers, Celebrates in a Big Way," *Sunday News,* Lancaster, Pa., 16 December 1990, E-3.

2. Jay Belsky and Emily Pensky, "Developmental History, Personality and Family Relationships: Toward an Emergent Family System," in *Relationships within Families: Mutual Influences,* ed. R. Hinde and J. Stevenson-Hinde (Oxford, England: Oxford University Press, 1988), 198.

In the Company of Women

Deepening Our Relationship with the Important Women in Our Lives

by Brenda Hunter, Ph.D.

ISBN 0-88070-839-5

This influential book teaches women how to build and nurture
vital, deep relationships with other women. Covers such topics
as developing lifelong friends, becoming a nurturing mother,
handling conflict, and more!

Printed in the United States
by Baker & Taylor Publisher Services